SUCH MAD FUN

SUCH MAD FUN

Ambition and

Glamour

in

Hollywood's Golden Age

ROBIN R. CUTLER

VIEW
TREE
PRESS
2016

Library of Congress Control Number: 2016906375
View Tree Press

Library of Congress Cataloging-in-Publication Data
Cutler, Robin R.
Such Mad Fun: Ambition and Glamour in Hollywood's Golden Age
Includes bibliographical references and index.
Hall, Jane E. [Mrs. Robert Cutler] 1915-1987. 2. Motion picture writers-
    United States-Biography. 3. Popular Culture-United States-New York,
    N.Y.-Virginia 4.Fiction writers-United States-1925-1945.
Cover and Book design by Elliott Beard
Printed in the United States of America
ISBN-13: 978-0997482300
ISBN-10: 0997482303

Cover illustration: "Beauties," pastel by Bradshaw Crandell. In the author's
collection. Featured on the cover of *Cosmopolitan,* October 1939. Photograph
by Kim Hall.

For additional images:
https://robinrcutler.com/such-mad-fun/salome-hollywood-gallery/

To Liz, Carlyn, Alex, and Will
Jane Hall's granddaughters and great-grandsons

"Inconstant Earth"

The world may laugh at genius' flame,
And scoff at high ambition.
But woe betide the foolish one
Whose life is void of mission.

—Jane Hall, age fifteen, published in the
Los Angeles Times, May 11, 1930

"Everything you are and do from fifteen to eighteen is what
you are and will do through life."

—F. Scott Fitzgerald, letter to his
daughter, Scottie, September 19, 1938

CONTENTS

Mrs. Robert Frye Cutler, Oil on Canvas,
Bradshaw Crandell, circa 1955.

PROLOGUE

All the Things You Were

I PICKED UP THE BOOK CAREFULLY, WARY OF THE MOLD ON ITS faded cover. Rodents had gnawed through the corners and the edges of its pages. On this oppressive June day when the humidity intensified all sweet and sour odors, the book smelled terrible. It was headed for the landfill, but the playful inscription to Jane Hall and the bold signature on the front endpaper caught my attention: *F. Scott ("Pretty Boy") Fitzgerald Metro-Goldwyn-Mayer* 1938.

My mother was twenty-three when Fitzgerald brought her this copy of *Tender Is the Night*. She'd been an art student and aspiring author on its publication date in 1934. Three years later, the snappy dialogue in her short stories caught the interest of celebrated Hollywood agent H. N. ("Swanie") Swanson; within a few months she was hard at work at MGM's studios in Culver City, California. Before long, Jane Elizabeth Hall and F. Scott Fitzgerald were colleagues in adjoining offices at Hollywood's most successful studio.

I carefully tore out the page with the inscription and filed it with other papers that seemed to be worth keeping. It was 1987, and Jane, as I will call her in this book, had died on April 18, the Saturday before Easter. I had tried to telephone her on that brilliant April morning to let her know when we would arrive at Poplar Springs. After the fourth attempt I began to panic; she always answered the phone. But she was there, lying peacefully on her double bed, her hands clasped on her

1

chest, surrounded by books, papers, half-empty boxes of Milk-Bone dog biscuits, a small television on the bureau that was always on, and eleven anxious German shepherds trying to wake her up. Her loaded .38 revolver—a gift from the local sheriff because she was so alone in that sprawling stone manor house out in the Fauquier County countryside— was still in the nightstand drawer.

Until a heart attack ended her life, Jane had a special cachet in Virginia as a former *Cosmopolitan* cover girl who had worked in Hollywood for Louis B. Mayer. Jane married during her years as a screenwriter, and I had no idea that she had known Fitzgerald. Though she rarely spoke about her career, a few weeks before she died she mentioned to me that she'd had a chance at real happiness between 1935 and 1942, when she'd been productive as an author. For so much of my life, she'd seemed preoccupied by money worries and swamped with business problems; in her later years, she struggled with physical pain from a back injury. I wanted to learn more about the days when her green eyes sparkled, she laughed often, and her wit was razor sharp. What was it like to work as a writer in Hollywood? How did she end up there? Why did she leave? I didn't expect to postpone my search for the answers to these questions for twenty-two years.

On a chilly October morning in 2009, I began, finally, to look through my mother's papers that I'd kept in storage for so long. As a historian, I naturally focused on the years before I was born. As I pored through a scrapbook filled with poems, stories, articles, editorials, and book reviews that she'd published before she was fifteen years old, my heart went out to this young tomboy from an Arizona mining town who wanted passionately to be a novelist. Often she described people on the fringes of life—an elderly lady ignored by a bus driver; the son of a laundress spurned by a pretty, wealthy girl; a lonely street sweeper at midnight; an alcoholic confined to a hospital bed. Her hard work was driven in part by the premature death of her father and idol, Dick Wick Hall, then Arizona's favorite humorist. Jane's fierce ambition and her success as a juvenile author soon led the press to call her a "literary prodigy." But her determination would be diluted for a time after her mother succumbed to breast cancer in 1930.

Once she became an orphan, Jane's circumstances—and, there-
fore, the subjects she wrote about—changed dramatically. She and her
brother traveled east to live with an aunt and uncle as part of a rarefied
segment of Manhattan and Virginia society. Jane brought an outsider's
perspective to her new life among the debutantes and party girls of the
Depression years. She used what she learned to portray and parody this
privileged world in her fiction and screenplays. Her diaries and scores
of letters provide an appealing look at what it was like to be a "woman-
writer" in Depression-era America. Her voice is candid, refreshing, and
at times disturbing as she describes her responses to the demands of editors, producers, studio executives, and the watchdog of the Production
Code Administration, Joseph Breen. Her published stories, articles, and
screenplays depict an absorbing, if narrow, slice of popular culture in
New York City and Hollywood during the turbulent 1930s.

At MGM Jane's days "belonged only to Louis B. Mayer." She worked
long hours for some of his top producers dreaming up scenarios and
clever dialogue that drew on her experiences in Manhattan. Her biggest project came out in print and on the screen. In August 1939, eight
months after *Cosmopolitan* published her "book length novel" *These Glamour Girls*, the movie of the same name premiered in New York City.
The trailer announced "Jane Hall's blistering exposé" of the "platinum-
plated darlings of the smart set"; the *New York Times* called it the "best
college comedy" and the "best social comedy of the year."

Jane not only wrote stories and screenplays during these years but
also reported from Culver City for *Good Housekeeping* and *Cosmopolitan*.
Her editors there (William Bigelow and Harry Burton) loved the way
her buoyant personality came through in her lighthearted interviews
with MGM celebrities and in her account of her visits to the sets of
The Wizard of Oz and *Gone with the Wind*. Her letters home reveal the
fun she had lunching with Rosalind Russell, dining with Walter Pidgeon, dancing with Jimmy Stewart, and sailing to Catalina Island on Joe
Mankiewicz's schooner.

I became intrigued by the way Jane both participated in and observed
the "culture of elegance" that magazine readers and movie audiences
yearned for during the Depression. Historian Morris Dickstein finds

that "a culture's forms of escape, if they can be called escape, are as significant and revealing as its social criticism." The 1930s, a decade often
defined by the suffering and poverty that decimated millions of lives,
was also "rich in the production of popular fantasy and trenchant social
criticism." Jane's storytelling, laced with insight and satire, is a window
into a world that was inaccessible to most Americans then and remains
so today.

What determines who a woman will become? It was only after she
died that I discovered an album of photos from my mother's childhood.
In one image, a tall, proud woman stands with her arms around her two
children in the brilliant sun near Salome, a hardscrabble mining town in
western Arizona. The woman, Daysie Sutton Hall, is the grandmother
I never met. On her right is thirteen-year-old Dickie, Jane's brother, in
scruffy overalls and an oversized sweater, a cloth fedora pulled down
low to shade his eyes. The ten-year-old girl on Daysie's left wears a
pleated skirt and a middy, scuffed shoes, and knee socks pulled up tight.
The light brown bangs of her cropped hair almost reach her eyebrows. It
is the girl's don't-mess-with-me expression that stands out in this 1925
sepia photograph—she is fearless, funny, and proud to be a tomboy who
can ride Killer, the wildest horse in the desert hamlet that her father
cofounded. What thrills her most is that she has just had her first story
accepted by the *Los Angeles Times*.

I grew up with a different image of Jane. The centerpiece of our
living room was Bradshaw Crandell's full-length portrait of Mrs. Robert
Cutler (Jane's married name). In it she is a stunning platinum blonde
in a long black velvet evening dress with a white ermine neckline. She
appears to be a tall woman with a movie-star figure, perfect features,
and ruby lips and nails. The large emerald that sparkles on her left hand
matches her green eyes. The woman in this portrait is as inaccessible as any classic-era star in a publicity photo. The black wool carpet
and ivory upholstered furniture that defined our large, paneled living
room complemented Crandell's work. Many people loved this exquisite
painting—numerous movie stars and other prominent men and women
sat for Crandell, who, in 2006, was inducted posthumously into the

Society of Illustrators Hall of Fame. But looking at it reminds me of the P. D. Eastman book that I once read to my grandsons: *Are You My Mother?*

Such Mad Fun follows a talented small-town girl with grand aspirations who sought to be independent at a time when her family, her friends, and her social and cultural milieu had other expectations for her. It is also a behind-the-scenes look at the messages that popular culture conveys to its audiences. Feminist writer Betty Friedan underscores the critical role that magazines played between the 1930s and the 1950s in defining women's sense of who they were meant to be. Who was the ideal young woman—more specifically, the ideal young, white, middle- or upper-middle-class woman—targeted by so many magazines and movie houses? Whether in print or on the screen, Jane's stories brim with class conflict while providing guidance for her peers on how to navigate the all-important search for the perfect mate.

In the 1950s, my mother was often a mystery to me—if her bedroom was not off-limits, I would head straight for her mirrored dressing table just to look at, not to touch, the artist's tools that she needed to transform herself into a glamour girl before she could be seen in public. She rarely came out of her room without her "face on"; I don't recall ever seeing her with wet hair. I must have sensed that her life was not what she thought it should be. And after her death I wondered how the plucky tomboy in the photo album became the woman in Crandell's portrait. What was lost and gained in the process? Something dramatic happens to little girls as they approach adolescence—many lose their voices. This book is both a coming-of-age story and a cautionary tale set in the cultural and social context of a decade that has surprising parallels with American life today.

Rose and Randolph Hicks at Poplar Springs. Detail from a sketch by Jane Hall circa 1934.

ONE

Passages

IT WOULD HAVE BEEN HARD NOT TO NOTICE THE TWO TEENAGERS AS they boarded the ship alone. At barely five feet tall, the girl looked much younger than fifteen. Her green-eyed gaze was fearless, honest, and at times mischievous. Chestnut hair cut in a short bob framed her round face; a wide smile and ready laugh hid the tragedies that she had faced over the past four years. In the steamy haze of an August dawn, "Little Jane" Hall was off on a journey from Los Angeles to New York City with her older brother, Dick Wick Hall Jr., who towered over most of the other passengers. Dickie's awkward gait, a side effect of the cerebral palsy that had also slowed his speech, must have aroused the curiosity of their fellow travelers. But Jane would look out for him on this voyage, as she always had.

For the most part the seas were smooth, except on the night the S.S. *Virginia* hit the tail end of a hurricane. Even that was not much of a problem for, as Jane told a friend back home, "seasickness on this floating hotel is impossible." One day the captain took them up on the bridge to demonstrate how the electric turbine worked. "It is almost uncanny how much they do by machinery," Jane reported. "The steering is done by some kind of a machine which makes it absolutely automatic. It seems as though all they do on the bridge is regulate the speed of the boat and ring so many bells every half-hour." Jane sent the letter toward the end of the voyage; its high point, she explained, came on the "coolest day of the journey" as they reached the Panama Canal, where she marveled at the ingenuity of it all: "The only machinery is that which opens and shuts the gates of the locks . . . The water is stored up during the rainy season so no pumps are necessary."

After cooking for her arthritic grandmother and her brother all summer, Jane was happy about the superb menus on board. And there was plenty to do on the ship—within a few days she and Dickie had astonished their shipmates with their clever banter and their expertise at the game of chess. Jane said she defeated all the chess players including "a former member of the New York Chess Club." Once the Panama Pacific Line's passenger and cargo ship neared Havana, the oppressive heat led her "to wonder about the relative humidity of Hell."

Late at night, as Jane tried to settle down in their cabin, she thought about the turmoil of the previous twelve weeks. It still seemed impossible that in the middle of another spring, just four years after the children's father had died, breast cancer had taken away their mother, Daysie. In 1927 the three of them had moved from Salome, Arizona, to a rented home in Manhattan Beach, California, near one of the best high schools in the state. "Mother has given up her own existence for Dick and me since Daddy died," Jane confided to her diary. She had not been able to shake off the nagging fear that something might happen to Daysie. "A terrible doubtful feeling" put knots in her stomach once her mother became desperately ill.

And then, on the twelfth of May, 1930, Daysie Sutton Hall lost her two-year battle with breast cancer. A visit in June to Inglewood Park Cemetery, where her mother lay peacefully interred at the bottom of a slope, had made Jane "horribly, achingly, maddeningly lonesome." In the same letter, she admitted to her aunt Rose—who was her mother's sister, and now her guardian—that she had run out of tears: "I just hurt inside. Oh well, maybe it's a good thing. Mother always said to 'take it on the chin' for the sake of those around me, and I hope that's what I'm doing." It helped that she had to take charge of the household during the long, desolate summer before the state of California finally agreed that the minor children of Dick Wick and Daysie Hall could travel unaccompanied to New York to begin their lives with Rose and her husband. The journey would not only mean leaving the wide-open West for a narrower, more constricted world; Jane would no longer have the support of the editors who had helped her launch an already promising writing career.

For the past four years, Jane had compensated for her father's premature death by writing furiously when she wasn't in school. Between 1927 and 1930, she'd been a prolific author with a strong moral compass who urged her peers to develop their talents, work hard, make the most of their lives, and not waste time. She published dozens of stories, poems, articles, and editorials, yet she yearned to write a best seller when she was still in her teens. Newspapers referred to her as a "literary prodigy" who had inherited her father's "genius."

As a new teenager, this sturdy tomboy, who still treasured a brown leather pencil case embossed with the words "Outlaw Jane," felt self-conscious about her looks. Longing to be slender and taller like the models in newspaper and magazine ads, she kept careful track of her height and weight; she worried that her left eyebrow was a touch higher than her right, that her hairstyle never worked, and that her upper lip was too thin. She appeared too smart for the neighborhood boys, who called her a "wisey." And so, during the Roaring Twenties, fearless, sassy, precocious little Jane had no dates, finding solace instead in her work, her pets, and adult companionship. She loved jelly donuts, plunging into the icy Pacific Ocean for a swim, or just running on the beach with her collie mix, Lassie, and she used up some of her boundless energy dancing to pop tunes on the radio. As much as possible, she escaped from her troubles in cool, dark movie houses, imagining that she owned a clever horse like silent-movie star Fred Thomson's Silver King.

Late in June, after Dickie graduated from Redondo Union High School, Jane, her brother, and their maternal grandmother, Rosa Sutton, returned to Salome, Arizona, for the last time. Jane drove most of the 290 miles from Manhattan Beach in Teresa, the Studebaker she and her mother had bought together. As they approached the familiar sand hills populated by greasewood, ocotillo, and saguaro, Jane barely noticed the heat, for this resilient hamlet had been the source of her childhood exuberance, her literary aspirations, and her free spirit.

Salome sits in a valley framed on its northern edge by the Harcuvar and Harquahala Mountains. Sparse vegetation softens the contours
of these jagged ridges that change color by the hour as the sun moves
across a cloudless sky. Clear air, inspiring vistas, and, above all, precious minerals first drew miners to the southwest end of the Harcuvar
range. Jane adored these mountains and the desert atmosphere; most
of all she loved Salome because—when he'd been home—it was where
she'd been closest to her father. Growing up, she and Dickie had been
enchanted by their father's tall tales and his exotic pets—he kept a snake
named Lizzie (to "rattle the tourists"), a roadrunner, and a huge toad in
a tiny "zoo" by the small general store and service station that provided
fuel and sustenance for miners and tourists traveling between Phoenix
and Los Angeles.

For the past three years, Dick's brother Ernie had looked out for the
Halls' modest one-story wooden house. Ernest Hall, a former Arizona
secretary of state and acting governor, had helped found Salome, and he
shared Dick's interest in trying to extract enough copper, gold, or other
precious metals out of the nearby mines to earn a living. Often they'd
come close, with Dick promoting "million-dollar deals" to investors that
never quite panned out.

Memories came rushing back to Jane as she and Dickie packed up
Dick Wick Hall's books and readied his desk, chair, and typewriter to
be shipped to their guardians' Virginia farm. Dick's grave lay next to the
one-room adobe office building where Jane and her father had worked
on their stories together until she'd turned eleven. Her father belonged
with her and Dickie, not next to the roots of the umbrella tree that he
had planted himself. Sometimes Jane thought that she saw his ghost. In
this location, it was impossible to avoid thinking about Dick's unexpected battle with kidney disease, his sudden death in a Los Angeles hospital on April 28, 1926, and the family's grim train ride back to Salome
with his remains—unless, of course, Jane and Dickie concentrated on
the happier times they'd had together and on their father's vivid imagination.

When he was not writing to potential investors for his mines, Dick
Wick Hall created fantasy characters inspired by local personalities and

critters such as horned lizards, Gila monsters, coyotes, jackrabbits, snakes, scorpions, and centipedes. Beginning in 1921, he had used these characters in his *Salome Sun*, a compilation of local "news," humor, and philosophy that poked fun at Eastern tourists, bankers, Wall Street, high-society folks, and all forms of pretension. Hall's imaginary seven-year-old bullfrog that could not swim (it wore a canteen on its back) became Salome's mascot. In the mid-1920s, the syndicated *Salome Sun* introduced Dick's "Laughing Gas Station" to readers across America; his humorous columns and his stories in the *Saturday Evening Post* made the town famous.

Thanks to noted author and humor editor Thomas Masson, Dick's first contribution to the *Saturday Evening Post* was published on August 12, 1922. Over the next two years, dozens of excerpts of varying length from the *Salome Sun* turned up in the *Post*. According to Dick, the magazine paid him twenty-five cents a word. The Halls' income and the welcome publicity for the town of Salome increased even more once *Post* editor in chief George Lorimer began buying Dick's short stories, for the *Post* was one of the top mass-circulation magazines in the United States, with more than 2.75 million readers. "Salome—Where the Green Grass Grew" appeared in the New Year's issue on January 3, 1925. Lorimer published several of Dick's stories that year. The *Post* paid well, and Dick joined authors such as F. Scott Fitzgerald, Ring Lardner, and William Faulkner on its pages.

"Salomey Jane," as her father called her, had been Dick's protégé, and she loved writing stories and poems almost as much as she enjoyed galloping all over the desert on a neighbor's pinto pony. To Jane, her daddy was "a man who made the whole world laugh," and she strove to emulate him. Much had happened in the years since Jane received a money order from the *Los Angeles Times* for her short story about a little boy who learns to control his temper. "Bill's Greatest Victory" appeared on November 8, 1925; it had been her "most thrilling moment." But the money—$2.50—had been as important to her as her first literary success. Jane's clever, capricious father was not the most practical man; he had left the family deeply in debt. Her mother had agonized over their precarious finances for much of Jane's childhood. Jane, though, always refused to dwell on her father's shortcomings. Soon after this bittersweet final week in Arizona, she acknowledged in a poem that she would always be "caught in the mesh of the desert's grip, heart and soul."

That summer, as they'd prepared to leave California, Jane and Dickie received many supportive letters from their aunt Rose, who'd been devoted to her younger sister. She had willingly paid all Daysie's medical bills and did her best to reassure her niece: "I don't want you to be too grown up when you come. I just want a sweet little girl and everyone will love you." Referring to her husband, she added, " I think Randy will be crazy about you." Rose promised Jane that their arrival in New York would bring them all "luck and happiness." Perhaps Jane mulled over these words as the *Virginia* made her way up the Atlantic coast. Finally, on Monday, September 8, the long-awaited sights of the crisp Manhattan skyline and the massive, pale green figure of the Statue of Liberty came into view.

In the Hudson River, on the lower edge of Manhattan's west side, a string of concrete-and-steel piers welcomed ocean liners from across the globe. Once the *Virginia* lowered her gangplanks at Pier 61, near West Twenty-First Street, Jane and Dickie scanned the faces looking up at the arriving passengers and wondered: Did they look presentable? Would their uncle, whom they had never met, truly be happy to see them? Jane wore a white skirt with the new blouse that Aunt Rose had sent her. She wanted to be the first to spot the distinguished older gentleman and his sophisticated wife who would shape their future. From the ship's railing, Rose and Randolph Hicks seemed more formal and dignified than most of the jubilant crowd. What a relief it must have been when they all finally connected on the crowded pier and scrambled into a car that waited to take them across the city and up Fifth Avenue.

For years Jane had fantasized about Manhattan's fashionable shops while she sketched the models in stylish clothes that she saw in newspaper ads. Now here she was, gaping out the car window as they passed B. Altman, Lord & Taylor, Saks Fifth Avenue, and Bonwit Teller. At Forty-Ninth Street, Jane and Dickie could have caught another glimpse of the future. Construction had just begun on John D. Rockefeller's massive building project, much of which would be completed as Jane turned eighteen. The creation of Rockefeller Center provided welcome employment to more than four thousand men whose lives had been turned upside down by the Depression. But Rose had no intention of exposing her niece and nephew to New York's sad and seamy sides—at least not yet.

Randolph Hicks immediately put his new charges at ease. Ten years older than Rose, he had a deep smoker's voice, sympathetic gray eyes over a prominent, straight nose, and thinning brown hair on the verge of turning gray. He had married Rose Sutton Parker in December 1919, at the historic Immanuel Church in New Castle, Delaware, about a year after he lost his first wife. It's unclear how he and Rose met, but they corresponded during World War I while a newly divorced Rose travelled in Europe to study languages and try to launch a writing career. Randolph admired her keen mind, polished manners, and unlimited curiosity. "He loves me because I have a lot of character—he likes that better than anything else," Rose had confided to her niece.

In 1918, Randolph transferred his law practice from Norfolk, Virginia, to the Wall Street firm of Satterlee, Canfield & Stone where he had a number of well-known clients including industrialist William C. Durant, the cofounder of General Motors and Chevrolet. He also remained indispensable to his former partner, Arthur J. Morris, who established the Morris Plan system of industrial banks that gave average Americans installment credit for the first time. Randolph was delighted that Dickie had been accepted at his alma mater, the University of Virginia. In spite of his handicaps, Dickie was a brilliant student with a far more scholastic bent than many of his peers—UVA produced more gentlemen than scholars in those days. But Dickie would still have to work hard to speak clearly and avoid stammering. Between 1930 and 1934, he would have, as *Life* magazine noted, the "finest training for convivial mannerly social intercourse to be found anywhere in the world," whether he cared about social amenities or not. (He did not.)

For eleven years, Rose had divided her time between New York City and Poplar Springs, Randolph's ancestral farm in Virginia. Her life among the privileged elite of Manhattan and Fauquier County could not have been more different from that of her younger (and much taller) sister Daysie. They hardly looked like siblings. Petite in stature, at fifty

Rose had seen most of her ebony hair turn pale gray. Behind round tortoiseshell glasses, her mesmerizing large black eyes struck fear in those around her when her temper flared. A model of decorum in public, in private she could be quite volatile, unlike her gentle, patient sister.

Raised in Oregon as a Catholic, Rose had overcome several handicaps as she sought acceptance among the old-guard arbiters of New York society. She had carefully followed the rules that mattered to them; her years in Europe and her cultivated manners had helped. Through Randolph's connections, Rose became active in volunteer work and as a patroness at events for the New York Southern Society and The Virginians of New York. The Hickses' favorite charitable event was the annual Blue Ridge Ball to benefit an industrial school in Greene County for "country children of limited means" from isolated mountain areas "who do not have the money to attend more expensive schools." Rose had also slipped ambivalently into the Episcopal identity that was so important to her husband, a longtime member of the august Church Club of New York. By 1930, she fit in fairly well with other women who lived at smart addresses and frequently enjoyed the opera or bridge with their friends. Together they planned gala events to help the swelling number of less fortunate Americans, whose voices grew louder each month. These were the women who would determine whether or not Jane would be a social success.

Rose and her courteous, erudite husband now found their future plans upended. Theirs was a second and childless marriage for them both; the pattern of their lives had been quite settled before the size of their family abruptly doubled. Plus there were unforeseen financial pressures: Along with many of their friends, the Hickses had lost most of their savings as a result of the Wall Street crash six months earlier. Their financial situation would worsen over the next two years. Although they were far better off than millions of jobless citizens, for the remainder of the thirties Jane's new guardians lived beyond their means as they tried to hang on to their farm and the life they'd grown accustomed to in New York City while carrying the added expense of being surrogate parents. One thing was certain: Sixty-year-old Randolph Hicks would need to postpone retirement and his dream of pursuing the life of a scholarly gentleman farmer. From now on, much of the time it would be up to his resourceful, fretful wife to manage Poplar Springs on her own.

WHILE THE NEW FAMILY OF four motored past grand and iconic buildings, dodging buses, boxy automobiles, and pedestrians, Jane and Dickie listened raptly as Rose pointed out the Plaza Hotel; the brand new Pierre hotel, which would open in October; and the Metropolitan Club, the Gilded Age edifice where Randolph played poker with his cronies and where he and Rose dined with other couples who were eager to forget their financial reversals. This was the world to which Rose planned to introduce her niece, one that would help Jane meet the right people. She would nurture Jane and prepare her to be a suitable bride for the sort of generous, successful gentleman she had married the second time around. Yet Jane may have wondered if she could be comfortable in this socially competitive world in which good breeding and class took on a Gatsbyesque significance; it was a perspective that did not come naturally to her.

Once their car reached the East Sixties, Central Park provided them all with pastoral views that were treasured by those who inhabited the buildings on their right. Luxury apartments that overlooked Fifth and Park Avenues had recently become more popular than the mansions and townhouses they replaced. They were more cost-effective as well for the majority of residents, who maintained second homes outside the city. Uniformed doormen stood attentively under their canopies to welcome residents and discourage uninvited visitors; they were symbols of a life in which privileged families derived great comfort from social and geographical boundaries.

Such a doorman was probably the first person to greet Jane and Dickie as their car pulled up to a nine-story burgundy-colored brick building on Seventy-Seventh Street near Madison Avenue. Seventy East Seventy-Seventh Street had been built toward the end of the Great War; its eight-room apartments, with their mahogany-paneled libraries, formal dining rooms, and working fireplaces, spoke of another era. Rose and Randolph had lived in this close-knit community for several years. It was a reasonable distance from his club, they knew their neighbors and the building staff, and they were reluctant to leave. But before the end of the month, they would move into a larger apartment near Jane's new school.

Nine days after Daysie Hall died, Randolph Hicks had leased an apartment in a brand-new building, 1100 Park Avenue, at Eighty-Ninth Street. Nineteen stories high (then the building code limit), with a rosy brown masonry exterior over a three-story camel-colored sandstone base, it had terra-cotta balconies and a spacious lobby with marble floors that set a tone of opulence. With Park Avenue views and elevators that opened onto private landings, the A- and B-line apartments were the most desirable. Jane's new home was Apartment 7B, and she'd been enchanted by the prestige of her new address. "I think it's perfectly ripping to live on Park Avenue. Everybody's been asking me what my address will be. Wait till I give them an earful of that. Don't you love living there better than on 77th?" she'd asked her aunt in a letter at the beginning of July, before she learned they had not yet moved. Jane assumed everyone in the world had heard of Park Avenue. A 1931 guidebook by future screenwriter Rian James observed that the avenue "trips daintily along through the center of Manhattan, with its top hat thrust jauntily on the back of its head; its nose in the air; its silver-tipped ebony walking stick flashing gaily in the sunlight. For Park Avenue is the street of streets." Underneath this "Boulevard of the Bigwigs," which began at Thirty-Second Street and extended north of the Hickses' new home into a densely populated squalid world of tenements, New York Central Railroad trains rumbled on through the days and nights.

For the next two years, until she finished high school and the worsening economic crisis made it necessary for them to relocate again, Jane and her aunt and uncle remained in the family-friendly neighborhood known as Carnegie Hill. Stretching from Eighty-Sixth to Ninety-Sixth Streets between Lexington and Fifth Avenues, the area took its name from Andrew Carnegie's mansion (now the Cooper Hewitt, Smithsonian Design Museum) on Fifth Avenue at Ninety-First Street. The Nightingale-Bamford School for girls, which Jane would attend, was just three blocks away from 1100 Park at 20 East Ninety-Second Street. After a short trip to Virginia to be sure that Dickie was settled in Charlottesville, the Hickses and their niece returned to New York to deal with packing boxes and movers.

Three months earlier, Jane had left a spectacular Beaux-Arts campus not far from the Pacific Ocean. There had been 429 students in Jane's co-ed freshman class at Redondo Union High School. During her two years at the school she had made the honor society and set her heart on going to the University of California, Los Angeles. Academics had never been a problem for Jane, but now she would join a class of just sixteen young ladies from some of New York's most fortunate families. These girls already knew each other; Jane prayed that she would not have to reinvent herself.

Jane Hall, Nightingale-Bamford
Yearbook Photo, 1932.

TWO

"Genius Growing Cold"

IN 1920, TWO VISIONARY EDUCATORS, FRANCES NICOLAU NIGHTIN-
gale and Maya Stevens Bamford, had founded The Nightingale-Bamford
School to foster truth, friendship, and loyalty (*Veritas Amicitia Fides*) in
their students, as well as excellence in academics, the arts, and physical
education. The parent-driven social life of their pupils was something
they lived with reluctantly. A decade later, the two town houses that
originally housed the school had been combined into a neo–Federal
style red brick building where Jane would spend most of her time until
she graduated in 1932.

As it turned out, Jane adjusted remarkably well to the small, supportive academic environment at Nightingale-Bamford. School began
on October 2. Before long her classmates applauded her sense of humor
and her "distressing talent for puns," which threw them all "into fits of
extreme melancholy." The seniors would name her the "friendliest" girl
in the school. Tall, poised Jane ("Jamie") Voorhees gladly left Jane "a few
inches from her height" in the tongue-in-cheek 1931 Senior Will. The
bequest must have worked, because Jane grew to be over five feet five
inches tall during her first few years in New York City.

Jane's talent as a wordsmith and amateur artist attracted notice right
away. She became assistant editor of *Chirps*, the school literary magazine,
and would be the art editor of the 1932 yearbook. Her performance in
A. A. Milne's *The Ivory Door*, plus her role as the lamp in "And the Lamp

Went Out, a Pantomime in One Act," inspired her peers to predict she would one day rival the celebrated stage and screen actress Lynn Fontanne. But none of these accomplishments could match her success as a juvenile author and nascent reporter during her years in the West. At fourteen, she'd even been the manager of the Manhattan Beach office of the Redondo Beach *Breeze* where, working from home, she'd covered "City Hall events, service club meetings, births, deaths, weddings and other local happenings."

"There is no sadder story told than of genius growing cold, 'neath the melting pot of fame," Jane lamented in a poem in the spring of 1930. The linen pages of her scrapbook are weighed down with the work she published as a juvenile author: more than four dozen poems; eighteen short stories; thirty-five cooking columns; nineteen articles, essays, and editorials; plus two book reviews. I was astonished by the breadth of her knowledge and the ease with which she switched among genres. I was also deeply moved by the empathy she showed for animals and for her peers. Often she won prizes from the *Los Angeles Times*'s Sunday supplement for young writers, the prestigious *St. Nicholas* magazine, or local papers such as the Redondo Beach *Breeze*. Jane was especially proud of the articles that reporters had written about her unusual talent. The first of these, "Eleven-year-old Salome Girl Is Writer of Fairytale with Most Impressive Moral; Shows Genius," had been published only a month before her father died.

By February 1930, Jane had enough notoriety so that Donovan Roberts, a reporter for the Newspaper Enterprise Associates feature service, showed up at her Manhattan Beach home office to interview fifteen-year-old Jane for an article. Jane did not want to be a humorist like her father: "I want to be a novelist, I guess daddy was the only humorous one of the family," she'd insisted. "And besides, humorists are so glum and work so hard to be funny." No one was going to publish a book of her poetry, she told Roberts, as publishers "don't make much money from them." Around Manhattan Beach, though, editors had been quite convinced that Dick Wick Hall's daughter would be a well-known author one day; it was hard for them to see her go.

Jane's scrapbook of clippings did become a bit thicker during her last two years of high school. In August 1930, she won honorable mention from the St. Nicholas League (an organization of readers of the magazine) for her "Dirge to Mother," composed right after Daysie died. The poem ends with an admission that she'd lost her bearings: "With you my heart and soul have flown, / And that park of ambition's pride / Which means life itself; / There is nothing left, / But the mourn of an ebbing tide." Although she earned a cash award for her vivid "Ode to the Arizona Desert," her poem "Arachne," about a deep love shattered by "stern reality," likewise exposed the cracks in her heart. Even so, she had not totally given up on her mission of making it as an author.

Just before leaving California, Jane had purchased *Where and How to Sell Manuscripts: A Directory for Writers* by William B. McCourtie. Published by the Home Correspondence School (its last edition dates from 1929), it was full of practical advice and an annotated list of periodicals. Jane carefully checked off the names of magazines that might accept what she wrote and penciled in a list of her submissions at the back of the book. During the summer of 1931, sixteen-year-old Jane mailed poems, stories, and articles to *True Confessions, Sweetheart Stories, Love Story, Harper's Magazine, Pictorial Review, Everyday Life, Household Guests, Delineator, Ladies' Home Journal, Vanity Fair, Judge,* the *New Yorker* and even Hearst's *New York American.* None of those efforts made it into print, but in June 1931 *True Confessions* published "Jonquils," another poem about life, death, and love that she had sent in under the pseudonym of "Leah M. West." Because Jane had little success at first in the adult literary world, accolades from her new teachers and friends were vital to her fluctuating morale.

Each of the sixteen graduating seniors had her own page in the Nightingale-Bamford yearbook. Quotations in italics under their profiles drew attention to the girls' personalities. "In righte gude fellowshipe could she laughe and carpe all day," read Jane's (its source was unknown). Her class thanked her for saving the yearbook "more than once this year from utter destruction"; four samples of her writing appeared in the book that year as well.

In the summer of 1932 the stock market hit bottom—down from a high of 381.17 on September 3, 1929 to just 41.22 on July 8 three years later. Although less than three percent of Americans owned stocks, radio programs and the press hounded everyone with grim news of the Depression on a daily basis. Unexpected expenses in Virginia and New York had further depleted Randolph Hicks's savings. It made sense to have Dick at the University of Virginia, as he would be expected to support a family. But Rose had learned in March 1932 that the small savings account Daysie Hall had squirreled away for her children had disappeared—the Guaranty Building and Loan Association of Los Angeles had failed. The expensive women's colleges that appealed to five of Jane's classmates (Sweet Briar, Vassar, and Sarah Lawrence) seemed unnecessary to the Hickses as a choice for their niece. Instead, Randolph encouraged Jane to apply to the all-scholarship Women's Art School of Cooper Union. Known then as a "school for respectable females," it exposed her to a completely different world than the one she knew on the Upper East Side.

EACH WEEKDAY MORNING BEGINNING IN October 1932, Jane headed for an Italianate masonry brownstone on Seventh Street between Third and Fourth Avenues. The Foundation Building of Cooper Union housed the Women's Art School, the School of Engineering, one of the best libraries in Manhattan, and the Great Hall, where Abraham Lincoln gave a speech that set him on the path to the presidency. Most Cooper students worked during the day and studied at night, giving the school its "proletarian" atmosphere. Even at the Day Art School, according to a lengthy 1937 New Yorker profile of the campus, there were "no wealthy pupils."

Jane's commute to Astor Place probably came with warnings from her aunt to stay clear of the Bowery, where the unemployed populated the sidewalks, desperate to pawn, sell, or exchange whatever they could for an illicit beer or something more nourishing. Nonetheless, she was exhilarated by the energy of the neighborhoods that surrounded the school, filled as they were with the scents of ethnic food and people of different national origins—Italians, Slavs, Eastern European Jews, Russians, Poles, Greeks, and Hungarians. These were the shopkeepers, grocers, machinists, and bus and taxi drivers whose labor built New York and kept it moving, and whose wives' and daughters' sewing machines made the clothes that filled the city's department stores. Manhattan's Lower East Side was a mix of pushcarts, tiny shops and larger industrial buildings, squalid cold-water flats, tenements, and a few elegant homes left near Astor Place. Cooper Union was also an easy walk to the East Village, Washington Square, and Union Square, as well as several secondhand bookstores.

Jane loved Cooper Union in spite of the old building's poor ventilation—she caught several nasty colds and even pneumonia during the winter months. The school was open to everyone, regardless of race, creed, or color. Jane's diary reveals that her fellow students' personalities and accents were a constant source of fascination: "Selma Cohen is one of the most unique people I've ever seen. She's a genius. When you ask her age she sez: I'm eighteseen going tso be ninetseen. . . . There are such interesting types at Cooper. Today Desser and I dressed up like 2 lesbians and went to see 'Madchen in Uniform.'" (Virginia Desser would be expelled in April—"non-receptive to teaching," Jane noted in her diary. "Will I be next?")

In her first year, Jane took freehand drawing, modeling (in clay), elementary design, composition, and lettering. She'd joined the class of '36 at a time of transition. Within a year of her entry, the school's new director, Austin M. Purves Jr., who had taught at Yale, would persuade its Ladies Advisory Council of the value of coeducation. Forty percent of the students would now be men; he also got the go-ahead to let male students work in their shirtsleeves. Jane found Mr. Purves to be much more demanding than she expected. She made it through the first year "on probation"—"by the skin of my teeth. Think how awful if I had failed." The problem was that every so often, her life outside of school became much more appealing.

By the winter of 1932–1933 she'd become much more confident socially and begun to have quite a few dates. When her friend "Muggy" (Margaret Gregory) gave a party Jane noted gleefully that "EVERYBODY took my phone number." Her zany humor, sharp wit, unusual candor, and independent streak enchanted several men, especially some in their twenties who were bored with being idolized by college girls.

But Jane saw her dates as pals; she took none of them seriously, and that was dispiriting to those who fell hard for her. Occasionally the boys would disappoint her, too. Billy Rolf from her artists' club seemed to like her: "He wants to make a mask of me. We were all alone in his work room. I had my eyes shut waiting for the plaster and he bent over and kissed me." Then she learned that Billy kissed other girls while he made masks of their faces. More promising was Doug Frank, who spent fifteen dollars to take her to dinner and to see Mae West in *She Done Him Wrong*. A bright, modest Russian boy, Andre Smolianinoff, invited her to a bullfighting comedy, *The Kid from Spain*. She liked him a lot, though not as a potential husband; instead he would become a lifelong friend and eventually her trusted stockbroker.

Jane confided to her diary that she much preferred dating men who were more than six feet tall like her father, such as a "6'3" Princeton smoothie" who asked her to the intercollegiate dance at the new Waldorf Astoria hotel. The forty-seven-story Art Deco landmark on Park Avenue had just reopened in 1931 after being forced to move by the construction of the Empire State Building on its old Fifth Avenue site. Its Starlight Roof was one of many elegant settings where Jane would rumba to the sounds of big bands during the next few years. When they were not dancing or at private parties, Jane and her friends tried out restaurants in Greenwich Village, went to the theater, or drove around the city in someone's roadster with the top down. Their favorite pastime was the movies. Some of the films they saw in the early thirties, before the Motion Picture Production Code was strictly enforced—such as those starring Mae West—were quite risqué. That was not the case with a time-travel fantasy Jane adored, *Berkeley Square:* "It was so beautiful that I didn't even want to speak when we came out. I felt as if I was in another world and I could hardly keep from crying." This touching romance starred Leslie Howard as Peter Standish, a wealthy American who becomes obsessed with the diary and letters of his ancestor of the same name.

They also took advantage of the city's parks, which were populated in the 1930s by the homeless as well as the privileged. Hundreds of the hungry and jobless built shanties—"Hoovervilles" had been scraped together in Central Park; their residents sold apples or waited in breadlines. In sharp contrast to this debilitating poverty, luckier folk found the park ideal for skating, horseback riding, rowing, and romance. On warm summer evenings, Jane and an admirer might drive into the park, turn up the car radio, and dance under the stars. In late spring, before she left for the summer to Virginia, Jane would head for Rye Playland, in Westchester, or take the train to Coney Island. On June 11, 1933, she recorded her first swim in the ocean since leaving California three years earlier. Although she would be invited to posh clubs on Long Island's North Shore, as well as to summer cottages in the Hamptons, almost any place where she could swim and sunbathe appealed. With a new awareness in the culture of the damage caused by the sun's ultraviolet rays, smart women had been advised to avoid deep tans on their faces, but acquiring a golden glow and sun-streaked hair was not only stylish, it was a sign of good health and prosperity.

"Beer is back!" Jane told her diary on April 6, 1933—at least 3.2 percent beer was, and even though the legal drinking age in New York was twenty-one, Jane celebrated with a boy named Jimmy Callaway who took her to the circus a week later. Always wary of alcohol, as her mother had been, Jane nevertheless decided that Prohibition, which would not officially end until 5:32 p.m. on December 5, 1933, was an "asinine law." But unlike her dates, she stuck to milk or ginger ale, rarely trying hard liquor. At a beer party at 535 Park Avenue, one of the boys' fathers bet them five dollars each that "they couldn't drink a soup plate of warm beer with a teaspoon. They all won."

Each year between June and October, Jane stayed with Rose at Poplar Springs while her uncle Randolph worked in New York. She had cultivated a second group of friends in Fauquier County that she now referred to as "the old gang." She'd fallen in love with the landscape just as she had the sand washes and vegetation-free purple mountains near Salome; she wrote often about the rolling hills, the scents and sounds rising from the lush green lawns and creeks, and the brilliant ivory moon in all its phases. Already completely at ease in a Western saddle, she'd quickly learned to ride and jump English style and spent hours schooling horses so that she could foxhunt with her uncle when he found time to come for holidays or for his annual vacation in August.

On evenings and weekends through these hot, humid summers the gang swam at Daniels Mill and in private pools; shared picnics and hayrides; drove to fairs, horse shows, and steeplechase races; canoed on the Rappahannock River; and saw every film that was shown in Warrenton—the Fauquier County seat was about seven miles from Poplar Springs. They sipped sodas at the Village Inn on Main Street and had dinner and drinks at each other's homes. Jane was happiest at Poplar Springs when her brother was there, too. In the fall of 1933, Dickie would be a senior at the University of Virginia; deeply interested in mathematics, he hoped to earn a scholarship so he could remain at the university after he graduated.

Every summer, Jane had definite ideas about all she wanted to accomplish. She sketched, painted, rode horses almost every day, and spent hours with her yellow legal pad or at her typewriter. Her social life in Virginia inspired many of the stories she wrote between 1931 and 1935. She mailed them faithfully to magazine editors from the village of Casanova, which was just a short walk from Poplar Springs. Yet with the advent of crisper days and cool nights at the end of September, she was eager for autumn in New York, where her city beaux had been waiting.

Jane swung right back into juggling school and her social life. She stayed out late so often that Rose issued an ultimatum: no more dates on school nights. By her second year, the Women's Art School at Cooper Union had become the newly coeducational Day Art School. Jane swore to her diary that she would try extra hard to do well despite the many distractions that competed for her time.

THREE

"I'm Coming Out"

"Diary! I'm coming out with Muggy at a tea dance at Pierre's on December 23! I'm so thrilled I'm sick to my stomach. I'll be a new deb." Jane had been ecstatic when she learned that her aunt and uncle had found a way to give a party for her by joining forces with Margaret Gregory's parents. At the height of the 1933 season, between mid-November and Christmas, the Hickses and the Gregorys planned two tea dances for the girls rather than a more pricey dinner dance. The primary one would be at the Pierre hotel in Manhattan, but it would be preceded by a mock foxhunt and tea at Poplar Springs on the weekend before Thanksgiving. Randolph Hicks hailed from a distinguished Old Dominion family; introducing their niece to Warrenton, Middleburg, and even Washington, DC, society was important to him and to Rose.

Celebrating the debutante season was an elite tradition in cities with prominent families such as New York, Boston, Philadelphia, Washington, Atlanta, St. Louis, Chicago, and San Francisco. According to veteran reporter Inez Robb, "Even during the darkest days of the Depression the number of debutantes never varied from the norm," and that norm was "about 350 annually." During the 1930s, as debutantes began to attract great interest from the press, their lives became public property. Each year, about ten of these fortunate females were blessed with the "unbeatable deb combination of beauty, charm, unimpeachable social position and ample family fortune. It would be folly to waste brains on a girl in this category," Robb remarked. Jane's classmates at Nightingale had all prepared for the multiple "coming out" parties that would follow their graduation; they had faithfully attended the right dancing schools ever since they'd been old enough to wear patent-leather shoes and white cotton gloves. In spite of financial strains, parents with daughters in private schools were determined to keep up appearances.

"When a girl comes out, she needs *all* the attention," pronounces Mrs. Connage, mother of the spoiled, gorgeous, vivacious blonde, Rosalind, who captivates and discards her fiancé, Amory Blaine, in F. Scott Fitzgerald's *This Side of Paradise*. For debutantes, little had changed since 1920. (And, in fact, even today in large cities, the "festive tradition continues.") The elaborate process of "coming out" enthralled Jane as she entered a world fueled by publicity and filled with spectacle. Though she was still passionate about becoming an author, the recognition she'd received as a "literary prodigy" on the West Coast had not helped her recently. What she did gain publicity for in 1933 and 1934 was her social life.

Between October 1933 and April 1934 Jane supplemented her diary with "an authentic and unexpurgated record of the haps and mishaps attendant on 'Coming Out.'" She kept this "Debutante's Yearbook" in a hardcover composition book; it is the chronicle of a participant and an observer, a party girl and a reporter who yearns to have her own story matter. It is also a tale of the temptations that are integral to a life of glamour, and of Jane's reaction to the young men who, once she was "out," competed mightily with her mission to become an artist, a writer, or perhaps even both. Jane recounted a series of escapades in the yearbook, addressing it in the second person, as if it was her trusted friend.

One memorable weekend occurred on October 28–29, 1933, when she packed her new suitcase (a recent present from Aunt Rose) and went to visit Doug Frank's family in New Jersey. They headed for the Rutgers–Lehigh football game (Rutgers won 27 to 0), had dinner at Doug's fraternity house, and then drove back into Manhattan to join a small party of about fifteen people at the trendy Sherry's restaurant. They stayed until the management almost threw them out, which was, Jane acknowledged, "bad and so undignified." But they were not done yet. The party moved a few blocks over to the Biarritz, one of many speakeasies in the East Fifties, for about an hour. After being up all night, Jane then accompanied Doug back to East Orange—quite a bit put off because his mother had not wanted him to drive back by himself.

On Sunday morning, at the Franks' house, Jane scanned the society pages for news of the party and was annoyed that their hijinks had not made it into print. Already she had begun "to crave being gossiped about," as did countless other girls of her generation in England and America. Author Joseph Epstein observes that these society publicity seekers perpetually needed reassurance "of their own importance, or at least of their own with-it-ness."

On the way back to the city that afternoon, Jane stopped to see an ailing Thomas Masson and his wife, Fannie, at their home in Glen Ridge, New Jersey. After his protégé Dick Wick Hall died, Masson had been a wise counselor for Daysie, who was baffled as to how to handle her late husband's literary legacy and his considerable debts. Now sixty-six-years-old and bedridden, Masson was much smaller than Jane remembered. She had no idea he had less than eight months to live.

Jane was touched that Masson agreed to see her, "being as how I am my father's daughter," and she noticed the Massons had the Navajo rugs her father had given them on their sun porch. All of her anger and frustration at her father's death came back as Jane sat next to the man who had helped both of her parents so much. "Masson and I were discussing Daddy's temporary fame and his untimely death and he said, 'So, it all goes back into Limbo. But that doesn't matter.'" With the unrestrained hubris of an eighteen-year-old idealist, Jane told her yearbook: "Well I think it does *matter*. I want to be famous and *stay* famous and have everybody and everybody's great-grandchildren know I am and was famous etc. etc. etc., all of which sounds definitely presumptuous, but you should know by now I have an Egotist complex—so what?"

So Jane must have had her ego in place when, earlier that month, she and Muggy sat in front of a Hungarian photographer named Boris as he "leapt around feverishly and did his best to capture the secret of our elusive charms." The girls needed publicity photos for their deb parties. At the time she had been annoyed with Muggy for not telling a man who might have asked her to the Princeton–Columbia game that she was back

in town. "Most girls are rats anyway, so anything like that never disap-
points me," Jane sighed. She abhorred cattiness and backbiting; much of
the time (throughout her life) she thought it wiser to keep to herself or
to confide in men rather than women. At the photo shoot, she reported:
"Muggy struck some sexy Mae West poses which will no doubt be very
'well developed' but I felt I was sticking the Hall bee-stung lower lip out
about a foot, as usual, so mine probably will not be much good. . . . All
in all, Muggy and I really had much fun in having our pictures taken. By
the number we have had, every tabloid in town should be flaunting our
classic features from now until Christmas."

Almost none of these photos show a credit, but several would be
featured in the New York papers in November and December 1933, to
Jane's (and surely Muggy's) satisfaction. Carefully, Jane pasted the clippings in a new scrapbook (at times forgetting to note the date). The first
came out on Wednesday, November 1. Jane eagerly scanned the article
in the *Evening Post:* "Mr. and Mrs. R. Randolph Hicks to Give Hunt for
Niece," as she had dinner with a beaming Uncle Randy at Longchamps.
As usual, she was not satisfied with how she looked. She told her yearbook that it was "a rotten picture but nice to get the publicity." In recognition of the upcoming Virginia event, at least three papers printed
sizable side-by-side headshots of Muggy and Jane with headlines such as
"Feted at Hunt Tea in the South" (*New York World-Telegram,* November
20, 1933) or "To Make Their Debut Together at Tea Dance Saturday"
(*New York Herald Tribune,* undated). A *New York Times* story about Miss
Jane Hall and Miss Margaret Gregory on November 16 noted what a
novel party the Poplar Springs hunt and tea dance in Warrenton would
be at the estate of Mr. and Mrs. R. Randolph Hicks ("of this city").

Hearst's *New York American* ("A Paper for People Who Think") would
feature a large photograph of Jane as one of the season's most "prominent debutantes" on New Year's Eve. It was just more evidence of the
media's and Americans' fascination with the lifestyles of the wealthy, a
propensity that picked up during the Depression, when prosperity for so
many seemed so far out of reach. As society chronicler Cleveland Amory
observed, glamour girls emerged during the Depression because "Publi-
ciety" and celebrity replaced old money as marks of social standing.

Citing Columbia professor Lyman Bryson, Amory mentions the start of a trend that, thanks to a new world of omnipresent media, has increased a hundred fold since the thirties: "The predominant American prestige symbol is the appearance of one's real or professional name in print and in sound on broadcast."

This sort of notoriety was not the fame Jane sought deep in her heart; she would cope with her career when the social dust settled. Nonetheless, her diaries indicate that she got a kick out of the debutante experience, or much of it, while feeling guilty for neglecting her art and her writing. And what she learned in this pretentious new world, one that her father had lampooned royally in his syndicated *Salome Sun,* had become fresh material for her.

In the meantime, Jane thought it was impressive that she had an invitation to the highly selective series of dances known as the Junior Assemblies, even though she was "scared limp when I think of facing that stag line on Dec. 1st with Aunt Rose as a patroness and two boys as dates." She was astonished that she and Muggy attracted notice in the *New York American* at the beginning of Thanksgiving week from none other than the highly paid society editor and bon vivant Maury Paul known to the world as "Cholly Knickerbocker" and credited with coining the term "café society." This was the first of many articles Paul would write in the coming decade about Jane: "How they'll have to step to keep up with things this week! By 'they' I'm referring to those 'glamour girls' of Manhattan—the debbies," he declared, referring to Jane and Muggy as "this season's gold dust twins." He then described a party at the Gregorys' apartment with great alacrity (no doubt because he'd been invited). Paul's reference to "those glamour girls" is almost prophetic in light of Jane's future novel and film on the topic.

With all this press coverage, Jane could hardly expect to keep her two worlds separate. A fellow student at the Day Art School brought the *World-Telegram* article about the upcoming Virginia tea dance to Cooper Union. The word was out, and it travelled fast. Jane documented the response to her frivolity from her fellow students on the Lower East Side: "Mary Breeden—a red haired pedagogue from Richmond—said 'how's the blushing debutante?' Selma Cohen went around looking like a thunder cloud and I hear from Jane Cleveland that there has been much muttering about me being a 'lousy capitalist' pretending to be interested in art etc. etc. One of the girls in Design Class said 'are the debutants and the boys they run with really as bad as you read about?' I shook my head solemnly. 'Well they're pretty bad,' I volunteered. She looked delighted."

She also recorded a remark from one of her closest art school friends: "Little Ruthie, my black-haired Jewish pal, even came up to me and said with a simper, 'Well, give us the lowdown on the upper crust.'" Intense and brown-eyed, Ruth Gikow took almost all the same courses as Jane and proved to be an exceptional student. Each of them chose Pictorial Design as her special subject for advanced work. (One day Ruth's work would be exhibited in major museums including the Museum of Modern Art and the Metropolitan Museum of Art.) It was Ruthie who shared Jane's penchant for wisecracks and first called her "D'zani"—derived from "Janey," as it would sound if pronounced with Selma Cohen's accent. The nickname stuck with her for the rest of her life among her colleagues and closest friends.

No matter how scornful her fellow art students might be, it was up to Jane and her aunt to make the most of her "publi-ciety." Already Jane felt awkward without a man on her arm. One night in early November she and Muggy went to see Jean Harlow in *Blonde Bombshell*. "We literally dodged around pillars for fear someone we knew would see us—the two whirlies of New York debutante society—at the movies by ourselves on a Saturday night."

Jane's and Muggy's first coming-out party sparked a weekend of festivities that began with their overnight train trip to Virginia on November 17. In 1928, just before the Depression decimated their savings, Rose and Randolph had commissioned a ten-thousand-square-foot fieldstone manor house to be built at Poplar Springs Farm. At the end of a decade of excess and optimism, this new home, modeled on those Rose had seen in England, was her modest version of Haddon Hall. After the Wall Street crash, Rose had pale blue Tiffany "Poplar Springs" notecards engraved with a white elephant that came to symbolize the rough years ahead in maintaining this architectural anomaly in the middle of hunt country. Its arched doorways, twenty-inch-thick fieldstone walls, and three-story-high great room astonished family members who were used to traditional Southern architecture. Muggy had never seen anything like it; Jane gleefully stated that she was "absolutely speechless with surprise at its 'size and splendor'——or so it seemed to me."

"At half after three," as the invitation read, the Hickses welcomed about two hundred people to Poplar Springs for the tea dance. Photographers from Washington took pictures of various partygoers as mellow jazz from Chauncey Brown's combo wafted down from one of the balconies above the great room. Chauncey Brown remained a popular attraction at Fauquier County parties until his death in 1974. Although Prohibition did not officially end for three more weeks, Jane's account of the next twelve hours draws on a virtual thesaurus of synonyms for the word "drunk." She didn't indulge, but several merrymakers became "fried," "pie-eyed," "smashed," "plastered," or at least "tight." Most guests—primarily the young ladies—remained under control, and about a hundred stayed until 8:30 for a light supper that would mitigate the effects of excessive alcohol consumption. A veteran hostess, Rose had been prepared.

On Sunday afternoon several local bachelors returned to Poplar Springs to join the family that had gathered around the huge fireplace in the great hall. Jane decided to find out what it was like to get tight and told her yearbook all about it: "When Aunt Rose brot in the cocktails I poured three right down the hatch—presto!—I never drink, you know, so the effect was instantaneous, everybody thought I was pretending but I was really as tite as a size 14. I felt sad and very talkative and my own voice sounded peculiar to me. I also wanted to lecture on the evils of liquor. I could walk quite straight and all that, but as soon as I got out of sight of the people I started to skip. Never again for Hall. I want to be complete mistress of every situation, and it can't be done on three cocktails." After supper, Jane, Muggy, Mrs. Gregory, and Uncle Randy headed to nearby Calverton for the overnight train to New York City. An exhausted Jane recounted that it had been "one of the nicest weekends of my life."

In the debutante season of 1933, Jane and her crowd lived in the moment, and the moment was full of fanciful diversions. Many of her contemporaries seemed oblivious to the rough lives faced by thousands of people within a mile or two of Jane's apartment. John Patrick O'Brien, New York's mayor for a year—he would be replaced by the charismatic Fiorello LaGuardia in January 1934—seemed helpless to take effective action as unemployment lines proliferated, men sold their possessions on the street, and hungry families built shanties in Central Park. Jane's diaries reveal little about how the sight of this crushing poverty affected the precocious teenager who, just a few years earlier, had shown great compassion for an elderly hospital-bound alcoholic ("Jimmy," Appendix I) and composed a tender poem about a lonely urban street sweeper at midnight ("Midnight Seen Through an Open Window," Appendix II).

Speaking from both Los Angeles and New York City on November 12, 1933, two actresses, Marie Dressler and Eleanor Robson (Mrs. August Belmont) used the omnipresent radio to entreat Americans to do everything they could to stop the "hidden suffering" that was all around them. "We are interested in the man who plods the streets day by day, desperately looking for work to support his family, who becomes ill from lack of food and proper clothing. We want to help the woman who bravely tries to keep her home together when there is no money coming in, who washes and irons and cares for her children in a frantic effort to make them know the niceties of home life," Miss Dressler pleaded. For men and women like this, local relief agencies were their main hope; Eleanor Roosevelt was then chairman of the National Women's Committee of the 1933 Mobilization for Human Needs. She "devotes her time and energies to the affairs of humanity," Miss Dressler said. "She is an object lesson to every living woman." If Jane's diaries are any indication of their priorities, this lesson had not yet impressed her or the youngsters in her circle of friends. And she still had to be initiated as a debutante in Manhattan, completing another ritual that would inspire scenes in many future stories.

On the afternoon of December 23, 385 elegantly dressed men and women strolled into the three-year-old Pierre hotel for the tea dance that would proclaim Jane's availability to all marriageable suitors from the right background. Jane thought it all went well, despite the punch being "pretty lousy. Everyone said the four of us made a lovely picture standing on the stairs, Mugs and I in white and Aunt Rose and Mrs. Gregory in black dresses with big black hats." The event was probably held in the expansive hotel ballroom, although an ornate oval rotunda was also used to serve tea at the Pierre. Jane gave few details about the actual party, but after two hours of congenial chatter, dancing, and delicacies, Rose and Randolph escaped to Pennsylvania Station for the overnight train to Virginia. They would spend Christmas with Randolph's family, leaving Jane to enjoy her holiday with the Gregorys and friends her own age.

The evening had just begun for Jane and Muggy, who went out to dinner and to two more parties. By six in the morning on Christmas Eve they had ended up at Child's (a favorite haunt) with a "penniless redheaded boy and a Greek God athletic instructor with the mind of an amorous 10-year-old and no sense of humor." But what a breakfast! "Chocolate ice cream, bacon and eggs, shrimp cocktail, shredded wheat, toasted cheese sandwiches, English muffins, pancakes and buttermilk." Once they returned to Muggy's apartment, the girls slept until four o'clock in the afternoon, when the merriment began once more— dinner with two boys followed by midnight mass. Jane later recalled, "It was lovely driving around Gramercy Park tonight—Christmas Eve— very warm and Holiday Spiritish."

Although she found it strange to be away from her own family on Christmas, Jane told her yearbook she didn't mind. Many more parties followed between Christmas and New Year's Eve; all occurred within a very narrow slice of Manhattan's East Side at the St. Regis, the Plaza, the Pierre, the Waldorf, and the River Club. Jane's blow-by-blow accounts of some of these galas as the year wound to a close reveal more of the same. On one occasion, a drunken fellow, who had evidently forgotten he was engaged, ogled Muggy and simpered: "I won't rest until I crush your beautiful mouth against mine until you swoon with pain"; she "lapped it up like an avid Pekinese." Fed up with the "debutante rat race," Jane became exhausted. Fortunately, her aunt and uncle were in Virginia, so she could sleep in the daytime. Throughout the festivities, she had managed to be warm and flirtatious yet maddeningly aloof, shielding herself from vulnerability and disguising her true feelings behind a mask of merriment. In fact, she was proud of keeping her "ice maiden" reputation intact as she swirled through Gilded Age and Art Deco ballrooms in the winter of 1933. Both she and Muggy had done quite well for themselves, Jane confided to her yearbook, "considering we've had a consistent good time at every party and have yet to even kiss one of these plate-faced stags good night." In spite of it all, she rebuked herself for participating in self-serving, inconsequential frivolity and christened the alcohol-infused revelry of her post-Prohibition contemporaries as "mad fun."

January was an unforgettable month for several reasons. One was Jane's first real kiss, from a newspaper reporter, which she instantly regretted: "I swore I wouldn't let anyone kiss me until I fell in love. Then, like a weak flapper, I succumbed to wind and weather and a roadster." Plenty of other distractions kept her from slipping up again. A unique opportunity arose on the twelfth, when she and Muggy crashed the first ever Butlers' Ball at the Commodore Hotel (now the Grand Hyatt). *Time* magazine gave the details about this unusual event, sponsored by Mrs. Marshall Field: "2,500 butlers, chauffeurs, chefs, valets, cooks, footmen, ladies maids, parlor maids, chambermaids and scullery maids abandoned the houses of their socialite employers to attend." No liquor was served—only water; butlers sat in the ballroom's boxes overseeing the staff they had trained, while footmen and maids danced. Many butlers, footmen, and chauffeurs were British, *Time* testified, "but the rest of the butlers' underlings were Irish. German and Scandinavian [being] more raw boned and clumsy than a good butler likes."

It was "simply wonderful" to see them all dressed up, Jane related, "in everything from 1925 evening gowns to real imports that their mistresses must've given them. Some even wore gardenias. Such gaiety!" There were not enough men to go around, "so little maids danced with each other." The hat-check girl put on snooty airs and gave Jane and Muggy a hard time—as well she should have; in a way, "I felt very much ashamed for going," Jane admitted, "because that was something that really should have belonged to them."

Jane was much more welcome at the first annual ball in honor of Franklin D. Roosevelt's birthday on January 30. Across America, six thousand parties of various sizes paid homage to the president by raising funds for his National Foundation for Infantile Paralysis (now the March of Dimes) in Warm Springs, Georgia. "All kinds of people joined in the celebration—rich and poor, old and young, city man and farmer, Republican and Democrat, conservative and radical, employer and employee, Catholic and Protestant, Jew and Gentile, white man and Negro, the Indian on his reservation," announced the *New York Times* the next day.

At the Waldorf Astoria more than five thousand people thronged into the ballrooms, including Roosevelt's mother, Mrs. James Roosevelt, and New York mayor Fiorello LaGuardia. (Franklin and Eleanor remained in Washington for the festivities there.) After much fanfare, the celebrations across the country united into a "vast radio party" as Roosevelt's voice boomed from invisible speakers: "It is only in recent years that we have come to realize the true significance of the problem of our crippled children. There are so many more of them than we had any idea of." He went on to mention the work done at the Warm Springs facility and express his gratitude to all who had contributed to this worthy cause or sent telegrams, postcards, and letters with birthday greetings on this "happiest birthday I have ever known." And then the real pageant at the Waldorf began.

"I was a candle on the president's birthday cake!" Jane exclaimed to her diary. She and fifty-one other well-rehearsed debutantes (one for each year of the president's life) were "living symbols of a nation's love and admiration for its president," said the *Times:* "Clad all alike in long gowns of shimmering white satin, with huge ruffles of white chiffon about their shoulders and with towering satin-covered hats shaped like triple tiered birthday cakes upon their heads, the girls marched to a lilting tune in a double row across the floor of the grand ballroom. Each carried in her right hand a long pink candle. On the stage the girls formed themselves into the shape of a birthday cake, holding the candles straight up over their heads and lighting them from concealed electric batteries. Meanwhile with fresh, clear voices, they chanted in unison: Happy birthday to you."

Jane had "never had more fun." And by February she'd caught the interest of a Princeton junior she'd seen a few times. She'd been out to Princeton before with a fellow who drove ninety miles an hour in a jazzy six-cylinder roadster—he scared her to death. But Jack Hall seemed far more responsible. A twenty-one-year-old English major, he'd sent her six orchids when he'd been her date at a dance in February. They went roller skating later that month, and Jane hoped he would invite her to Princeton house parties in May. She knew that her uncle Randolph was "worried sick about bills" that winter. Jack's parents lived at 825 Fifth Avenue; he was a more well-established suitor than her other beaux. Plus he had impeccable manners.

On March 9, Jack called Mrs. Hicks from a phone booth on the Princeton campus to reassure her that Jane would be well chaperoned at the Princeton junior prom the following weekend. He had arranged for her to stay at the "house of the family of a chap named Baker" in the sophomore class. So Rose accepted for Jane without consulting her niece. As Jack explained to Jane in his letter officially inviting her on March 11, he suddenly realized that neither he nor Rose "ever discussed whether you really wanted to come. It was all very much as if I were borrowing a shiny new lawnmower for the weekend, and sending adequate assurance that it wouldn't be left out in the rain. So now I'm asking the shiny new lawnmower whether it really wants to be borrowed." If so, Jack wrote hopefully, he would pick Jane up early Friday afternoon, "all ready to whisk you out to Princeton—where there is one lawn that wants cutting so badly—love, Jack."

Jane was elated be going, though she hesitated to ask for new clothes. Rose obliged anyway with a yellow satin flowered evening gown, plus a new tailored suit and a spring hat. "The suit is adorable, very mannish. *What* will people say?!" Jane wondered. Jack picked her up in his beautiful roadster. A Friday evening cocktail party was followed by dinner at his eating club, Cloister Inn; a play; and the dance. "He virtually proposed," Jane wrote, "but I cannot let boys kiss me when it doesn't mean anything." Saturday was filled with lunch at Cloister and a smaller dance. "We had a lot of fun. Jack is such a nice boy," she confided to her diary after he drove her back to New York on Sunday. "Wish I could like him better." Though she may not have realized it then, Jane's experiences at this particular Ivy League campus would one day inform her work at MGM.

Jane did get her bid for house parties and headed to Princeton with Jack on the morning of May 4. However, she lost her nerve once she realized what a riotous time it would be if she remained on campus: "I'm paralyzed at the idea of staying here with him all weekend." So she decided they should drive all the way to Warrenton for the Virginia Gold Cup races. Jack was not happy about this change of plans. They left for Poplar Springs at 5:30 Saturday morning "in a blinding fog. Got to Virginia for the race and to a lousy dance at the Club." By the time they arrived back in New York, Jane realized she would not see Jack Hall again. "But so what?" she recorded defensively. "I'm beyond this college stuff now anyway."

More intriguing was another young man whom she'd seen a few times that winter, Richard Shepard Clarke. A popular Columbia College student, Dick lived with his parents in a four-story turn-of-the-century limestone town house in Hamilton Heights, an upscale Harlem neighborhood named for former resident Alexander Hamilton. He had served on the dance and finance committees of the student board and as a senior was president of a service society called the Blue Key Society. Jane found him very attractive—he was so nice, and good-looking, and lots of fun—but when it became clear that he'd fallen in love with her, she was bothered that there seemed to be no chemistry on her part. She felt confused because she wanted to keep seeing him anyway. "It's such a resigned, baffled feeling!" Dick would not give up easily.

While she enjoyed the attention and the endless gaiety, Jane still struggled with intimacy, treating most of her interactions with the opposite sex as if they were a game. "Diary—is it *possible*—here I am a New York deb and not only that but *popular*? I remember when I was about 14, I was very much disliked by practically all the boys in the neighborhood because I was what is now known as a 'wisey.' But times have changed." They surely had. The list of boys she met on a weekly and sometimes daily basis seemed endless as she went from party to party, as many as three or even four in a single weekend day. But Jane saw through the various lines fed to her by boys who plied her with flattery and pledged their undying affection. "They all leave me cold. Oh, Diary, will I ever fall in love? I'd really like to, just to see how it feels, if nothing else, and I often am attracted to people—just at first—but the idea of any intimacy—with *anybody*—repels me beyond words. And I doubt if I will ever outgrow it. If I do ever have any children (which seems a bit doubtful, after the above paragraph) I shall certainly tell them 'The Facts' in such a way that sex will seem a normal and wonderful thing, and not something to be ashamed of. Shame is probably at the root of all inhibitions or complexes."

Some of this discomfort with physical intimacy likely stemmed from Jane's Catholic girlhood and the influence of her strong-minded maternal grandmother, who had definite ideas about modesty and rules of decorum. There are cultural explanations for Jane's feelings as well: Her guardians lived in a world firmly governed by established social boundaries and romantic conventions. Rose and Randolph Hicks assumed that proper young ladies, good girls, saved themselves until they married. These views fit right in with what cultural historian Molly Haskell calls "the big lie perpetrated on Western society"—"the idea of women's inferiority"—so evident in the films and magazine stories of the mid-1930s and beyond: "A woman's only job was to withhold her favors, to be the eternal virgin—not all that difficult, really, since her repressive conditioning had so buried the urge in the first place."

That reserve may indicate why various men proposed marriage so quickly once they became infatuated with Jane, even if they had no chance with her. But she was not in love, plus she recognized that marriage would likely make it impossible for a woman, especially one in her social milieu, to achieve her professional goals. "A woman can do anything, be anything, as long as she doesn't fall in love," Joan Crawford had cautioned in *Possessed*. Educated women recognized that marriage and motherhood—their "paramount destiny," as Haskell writes—was "an injunction that effectively dilutes intellectual concentration and discourages ambition." Jane had just turned nineteen, and she knew full well that her true mission was to make the most of her creative talent—and, until that bore fruit, to find some way to be less dependent on her guardians.

FOUR

"Someday You'll Get Somewhere"

THE MORE ROSE AND RANDOLPH WRESTLED WITH THEIR FINANCES, the more Jane realized she needed a job. She was also concerned about her standing at art school as she began the second semester of her second year. Fortunately, her life drawing professor, the well-known American Regionalist painter John Steuart Curry, began to show a lot of interest in her work. A Kansas farm boy born in 1897, Curry shared Jane's love for animals and nature. After studying at the Art Institute of Chicago as well as in Paris, he had worked as an illustrator for several publications including the *Saturday Evening Post*; he was at the *Post* between 1921 and 1926, in the days when Tom Masson had seen to it that Dick Wick Hall's work was featured in the magazine. Eager for any validation of her progress, Jane told her diary Curry had said one of her oils was "not bad." She worked even harder and found it "fascinating to try to make an arm show through a sleeve" when the class model dressed as a peasant. Her efforts on a landscape even inspired Curry to tell her that "someday you'll get somewhere."

Jane refers to specific work at Cooper only occasionally: "I'm painting a stunning colored girl" (March 11); "how I hate design" (March 13); "we have a crazy model this week—I put clothes on him and put the bars of a prison behind him and a tear in one eye. Very dramatic" (March 21). Professor Curry—to her delight—thought highly enough of one of Jane's oil paintings to put it on exhibition at the beginning of April. That month, Jane also recorded some good news from her brother, who was about to complete his senior year at the University of Virginia. (Dickie would never be as distractible as Jane had been in her deb year.) He'd earned a fellowship at UVA and was on his way toward a Master of Science degree in mathematics.

Throughout the spring of 1934, Dick Clarke continued to pursue Jane even as they both tried to concentrate on school. In May, as the city parks sprang into full bloom, a near fatal accident put all their cares in perspective. "Death took a holiday tonight," Jane told her diary on the thirteenth. As Dick drove Jane, Muggy, Charlie, and two other boys home from Brooklyn, a car smashed into his convertible at an intersection. "Charlie and I were thrown out directly in the path of a streetcar. We were actually under it—the wheel stopped an inch or two from my legs. The whole thing was a matter of seconds and inches. But by the grace of God, I would be legless. Tonight I lived a lifetime in those 10 seconds." It was a horrifying experience that Jane recalled more than once in later years.

Though she was reluctant to leave Manhattan, she knew Rose expected her in Casanova for the summer. Dick drove her to Virginia at the end of May; immediately he was immersed in her active life of swimming, canoeing, horseback riding, and tennis. After a week, Jane confided to her diary: "Here I am with a man who meets practically every requirement of what one fondly calls one's 'ideal' being very much in love with me. Won't I ever be able to love anyone?" As they sunned on the terrace at Poplar Springs, Dick told her he always got what he wanted, and that someday he was going to marry her. "I told him I would never marry. I told him I liked him, but that it didn't mean a thing. He wasn't fazed." In fact, he delayed his return to New York until June 8, promising to write often.

Jane's letters, telegrams, and postcards to Dick, who would be her closest confidante for the next five years, do much to enrich the portrait of her personal and professional journey from late adolescence to womanhood. Dick was the only child of Dr. A. Vernon Clarke and his wife, Harriet. Every August, the Clarkes spent two or three weeks at the 160-room New Prospect Hotel on Shelter Island (between Long Island's North and South Forks). Before it was destroyed by fire in 1942, the hotel was a hub of gracious social activity. When the Clarkes were not there, their handsome bachelor son was still much in demand as a weekend houseguest of families with summer homes in Locust Valley and other stylish hamlets. More often than not, Dick's hosts had grand houses with swimming pools or club memberships and easy access to the ocean; it was a lifestyle that Jane could only dream about.

Jane and Dick had agreed to tell each other *everything* they did, but that often created tension as they each led their separate summer lives. Jane imagined him at Fitzgerald-like parties in majestic houses on Long Island dancing with other women; Dick worried that she might fall for a gentleman farmer with easy access to Poplar Springs. Jane kept her missives newsy, affectionate, and noncommittal. From the few of his replies that survive, it's clear that Dick was far more romantic and exasperated by her coolness. While he coped with complicated math courses in summer school, she tried to reassure him: "I am very safe down here away from college boys, streetcars and White Castle hamburgers."

On her own at Poplar Springs, Jane settled into a routine of writing, painting, and going out with her Virginia pals as much as possible. Rose had asked her to paint a mural to cover the expanse of bare rocks over the fireplace in the three-story-high living room. So Jane made a studio out of the old Hicks family farmhouse behind their fieldstone garage. She worked on a ten-foot-by-nine-foot canvas—it was a foot taller than the ceiling of her workspace—surrounded by dogs and her sketches from art school for inspiration. This daunting project, a scene of the Casanova Hunt meeting in front of the Poplar Springs manor house, took up the remainder of the season.

Once evening came and the comforting sounds of crickets and bullfrogs drifted up to her windows, Jane invented courtship narratives based on her recent experiences. She wrote in longhand, typing only when the clack of the keys would not disturb her aunt. Early in July, she mailed a story to a New York literary agency run by Charlotte Barbour and Elsie McKeogh. It was a smart move. On July 12, she heard from Mrs. McKeogh that she had done quite a good job; if Jane would just change the title of her story, she would see what she could do with it. "I pray I should be able to sell it but I'm not banking on it at all," Jane admitted. This bit of encouragement served to rid her "of the futile longing for the same sort of summer as my friends are having." Over the next week, she sent two more stories to New York.

Thirty-six-year-old Elsie McKeogh was sharp, savvy, and very knowledgeable about the magazine world. At Jane's age, she'd been deeply involved in literary activities at Smith College, where she'd been elected to Phi Beta Kappa in 1919. She'd also grown up on the Upper East Side as the privileged only child of activist and intellectual Jessica Garretson Finch Cosgrave. In 1900, Elsie's mother established a Manhattan finishing school that, thirty-seven years later, became Finch Junior College. Before she became an agent, Elsie had worked for *Harper's Bazaar* and *McClure's*. Her husband, *Good Housekeeping* managing editor Arthur McKeogh, had been an art editor at the *Saturday Evening Post* in the 1920s and may have known Dick Wick Hall.

Founded in 1930, Barbour & McKeogh was part of a new trend of women starting their own literary agencies, a development duly noted by the *Saturday Review of Literature:* "Eventually we predict all literary agencies will be entirely in the control of the women. Their sex has all the advantage in beguiling publishers and authors. And our experience has been that a woman can 'talk turkey' more remorselessly and more relentlessly than any mere man. It's a terrible combination!" Although she was not as impressed by Jane's second and third stories, Elsie encouraged her to keep writing on a regular basis.

Jane's Upper East Side and Lower East Side worlds competed for her attention again once school started in October. Now in her third year at Cooper Union, she focused on two advanced courses. Pictorial design with Austin Purves still proved difficult, while life drawing and painting with Mr. Curry seemed much more promising. That fall, Jane berated herself for not accomplishing more. "Where is this fun going to get you?" she asked, "and when? Where's all my fine talk of a career? Dear God, give me a sense of values before it is too late." Right after the Christmas holidays, she grappled again with her conflicting selves. "As soon as I have a definite purpose I can make a beeline for success," she assured her diary. All the while, she continued to absorb the sights and sounds of an elite and frivolous world filled with fun, building memories that would inspire the fiction she sent to her new agent.

"Gay Pageant Here Honors President," proclaimed the *New York Times* on Thursday, January 31, 1935. That year Americans held more than 7500 large and small celebrations on the evening President Roosevelt turned fifty-three; two hundred of them took place in the New York metropolitan area. Thirty cents of every dollar raised at these events was slotted for the Commission for Infantile Paralysis Research; the remaining funds would aid the children who had been handicapped by the disease. At 11:35 p.m., participants at all of these events heard the president express his gratitude on the radio, just as they had the year before. Jane and Dick Clarke listened from the grand ballroom at the Waldorf Astoria, which saw "the largest and most brilliant attendance of any social event held in the city so far" that season.

Jane's role in the elaborate "Pageant of America" at this event was quite different than it had been the previous year. The *Times* described the "symbolic presentation in which more than 300 New York debutantes, young society matrons and leading actresses of the stage and screen participated." Revelers appeared in lavish, colorful costumes against a background of mountains in a program that celebrated the nation's natural resources. Some young beauties portrayed the green Atlantic and the blue Pacific oceans, while others represented corn, rye, wheat, and cotton. As the spirit of coal, a Georgian princess, Ketevan "Ketto" Mikeladze, "wore a novel costume of black ciro embellished with enormous lumps of black cellophane." Jane, one of two pick-carrying coal miners, sported a black jumpsuit with a wide gold belt and knee-high gold boots.

For the next few weeks, Jane focused extra hard on an oil painting for Mr. Curry's life drawing class. She may have witnessed the scene that inspired its subject not far from Poplar Springs and been fascinated by a world that contrasted starkly with her own. The crowded, colorful canvas is filled with young, high-energy African-Americans engaged in lively camaraderie and a variety of activities near a gas station and ice cream emporium; at the top of the painting a banner reads "Sons and Daughters of the I Will Arise Oyster Fry." The painting captures a happy moment in the lives of an oppressed portion of Fauquier County's population. Perhaps the service station at the center of the festivities reminded Jane of her father's "laughing gas station" in Salome. In any case, Jane's efforts paid off. The authentic carnival atmosphere impressed Mr. Curry, who said she'd "got something there"; even Austin Purves thought it was "swell," something she'd been waiting three years to hear.

Jane's other work for this class, which she described in a letter to Rose (who was away caring for her ailing mother), indicates the range of Jane's interests: a satirical drawing of four haughty patronesses at a debutante ball; a Chinese New Year celebration; and a 1920s mining camp near Salome, Arizona: "I find that when I try to make memory drawings of things that I haven't seen since I was a little girl, that I can remember the most minute details 100 times better than I can about things now. I haven't been to or seen a mining camp since I was 11 years old, yet I can remember just how the miners hung coats on pegs outside of the cook tent. The pitchers and basins on the makeshift bench outside the door, the swinging olla [cooking pots] etc. etc. and that is what Curry likes."

Jane had been to an exhibition of John Steuart Curry's work at the Ferargil Galleries on East Fifty-Seventh Street, where two years earlier he had shared the stage with Grant Wood and Thomas Hart Benton in an exhibition of leading American Regionalist painters. "He is a wonder," a buoyant Jane told Rose, plus the newspapers now referred to his " 'meteoric rise'; 'single-handedly, John Steuart Curry could probably bring about a renaissance in American art.'. . . Did I tell you that I am his special protégé? . . . I'm studying composition under him in the afternoon instead of the tripe Purves was cramming down our unwilling gullets. I know now what I want to be—a real artist—a painter—an immortal." She'd also earned an A on a written exam. For a brief moment, Jane could fantasize about making it as an artist or perhaps illustrating her own work.

In the spring of 1935, Jane's aunt and uncle seemed more concerned than ever about their shrinking investments. Randolph had still not recouped his losses; even though he worked full time, he'd become hard of hearing and feared that some of the other partners in his law firm might be trying to phase him out. Jane also knew Rose no longer liked her living with them in the city, partly because at the Berkshire she and her aunt shared a twin bedroom. (Privileged couples often had the luxury of separate bedrooms; space was never a problem in Virginia, but in Manhattan, Jane and Rose doubled up so Randolph could have his own room.) Many women her age had already married, but she wanted to find work until she could sell her stories. Advertising seemed an ideal field for someone with writing and artistic talent, and Jane interviewed at numerous companies such as Liggett & Myers, J. Walter Thompson, and the fragrance and cosmetics company Coty, Inc. The consensus of those she spoke to was that more positions would be available at the end of the summer, so she vowed to make the months in Virginia productive "by learning shorthand, breaking two colts, and writing a book." Two pieces of news buoyed her spirits. On May 21st she made it into the *New York Times* for a creative (not social) accomplishment; her *Warrenton Oyster Fry* earned an honorable mention among the fifty-three awards given by Cooper Union's Day Art School. Adding to her joy, her twenty-three-year-old brother won a Philip Francis du Pont fellowship that ensured he could continue on at UVA toward a doctorate in mathematics.

Once again she headed south for the summer at Poplar Springs. Dick Clarke, who had graduated from Columbia and now sold insurance at Penn Mutual, continued to be her close correspondent. Jane shared with him her delight in the sights and sounds around her: "The birds under my window are struggling sweetly with sleep, and every now and then a cricket adds its stubborn anthem. Pretty soon the katydids will start." One evening while driving in the country she saw "sheep standing on green and silver slopes and little whitewashed darky shacks left over from real slave dwellings that hang like hornets nests between the rocks in the valleys with droves of ragged children clamoring over the porches."

The high point of June—and probably the entire summer—was her first flight in a small plane with her uncle's nephew, Randy Carter. She could hardly wait to tell Dick about it: "The feeling of impersonal power it gives you to fly over a city at night is the most wonderful experience I ever have had. Washington lay beneath us like an open box of jewels spilled around the mirror of the Potomac. Or have I read too many Arabian Nights? I think what impressed me most was the prim little pattern of black streets—so dark and quiet—and pathetically unimportant. The wind was enough to turn a face inside out. It filled eyes and ears and throat." By the end of this adventure, Jane had decided she would "never rest until I have a plane of my own, and know how to fly it."

When Jane began her last year at Cooper Union that fall, John Steuart Curry was no longer on the faculty and her pal Ruth Gikow had left to work for the Federal Art Project of the Works Progress Administration (WPA). But she still longed to create ad copy. So she sent a letter to the president of Lord & Taylor, Joseph E. Pridday, who asked for samples of her work. Jane sketched women in elegant dresses, added snappy captions, and brought them in. Weeks passed without an answer. In the meantime, a woman she'd known as a deb, a Mrs. Herbert MacGrey Hanscom, who organized publicity, benefits, and fashion shows for the Carlyle Hotel, offered Jane a full-time job. By December 10, Jane could be found at the Carlyle behind a glass-topped desk, earning ten dollars a week. Jane liked Mrs. Hanscom, but as for promoting society events, she wrote: "I don't like the idea at all—I must get that job copywriting for Lord &Taylor." Something had to give. Two days later, Jane dropped out of art school one semester before she would have graduated. Though she was unhappy about it, Austin Purves thought Jane had made the right decision. According to her diary, he told her that " 'success depends on one's attitude toward the future—whether one welcomes it or fears it.' Well, for a change I'm welcoming it," Jane wrote on New Year's Eve. "Come on, World!"

FIVE

"Good Luck, Little Scribble"

THE YEAR OPENED WITH PROMISING NEWS THAT CHEERED JANE AS she fought laryngitis and the flu for a week after New Year's Day. Elsie McKeogh sent word that *Hearst's International-Cosmopolitan* might be interested in her story about a nineteen-year-old post debutante who had had second thoughts about a suitor she'd spurned a year earlier. On Tuesday, January 7, Jane met with an editor at the Hearst Magazine Building on Fifty-Seventh Street and Eighth Avenue. "They want me to rewrite the story and they like my stuff very much," she told her diary. "The chief editor [Harry Burton] said I'd 'found my happy home' if I could keep on turning out stuff like this story, 'Out a Year.'" Plus "the criticisms from their reading staff were *so* encouraging"—so much so that Jane stayed up late after work for several days making revisions.

She sent the story back a week later with a prayer: "Oh good luck, little scribble. Dear God I hope they take it." On the seventeenth Jane declared: "21 and earning $10 a week! But the difference in outlook! If Cosmo only buys my story—and Diary, I'm going to town—no detours." She soon learned that decisions did not come quickly in the magazine world. In February, she began work on another story, though she'd yet to have news about the first one.

Her day job helping Mrs. Hanscom "was a snap" but had no future. On January 23, Jane's impatience got the best of her; she "burst in" on Mr. Pridday at Lord & Taylor to check on her application to write copy.

Jane had set her sights on one of the oldest and finest retail department stores in the United States. In 1826, Samuel Lord and George Washington Taylor founded a dry goods store on the Lower East Side that gradually expanded over the course of the next century. After several moves to different parts of the city, in 1914 Lord & Taylor finally found its permanent home on Fifth Avenue between Thirty-Eighth and Thirty-Ninth Streets. Two other flagship stores had already opened amidst the avenue's fashionable homes in 1906: Tiffany & Co. on Thirty-Seventh Street and B. Altman on Thirty-Fourth Street. These elite shops were in smaller, more elegant spaces, but Starrett and Van Vleck's dignified, utilitarian design for Lord & Taylor declared to the world that midtown Fifth Avenue "now belonged to commerce."

Known for its large, arched entrance and display windows that took on a special appeal at Christmas, the store's future would be determined in part by the hard work of Dorothy Shaver, an ambitious, innovative woman who had been on the staff since 1921. At the time Jane was applying for a position, Miss Shaver was one of three vice presidents. (In 1937, once Walter Hoving took over as the store's president, she would be made first vice president.) Thanks largely to her leadership, the store flourished even during the Depression among its affluent clientele, who appreciated its well-made clothing and home furnishings by American designers.

As a young teen Jane had carefully copied the silhouettes of elegant women that she saw in magazine illustrations and newspaper advertisements. At fourteen, she'd designed an ad for the opening of the Center Pharmacy in Manhattan Beach that appeared in the Redondo Beach *Breeze*. Now that she'd spent more than three years in art school, she was sure that she could create both the illustrations and the dramatic narrative copy needed to seduce consumers in the late 1930s. But advertising was controlled by men who were experts at selling the American dream; they were the ones with the hiring and purchasing power—and they rarely hired women to write copy.

The first opening offered to Jane at Lord & Taylor was not in the art department but as a comparative shopper and assistant buyer in their Buffalo store. "Of course I can't go to Buffalo," she informed her diary on February 25. Even if she'd wanted to, her aunt and uncle would never sanction such a move. But at the beginning of March, she had an opportunity to sell young women's clothes for eighteen dollars a week at the Fifth Avenue store. Though Jane hated to break the news to Mrs. Hanscom, she could not turn down a job that almost doubled her salary. Besides, Jane's lively personality worked well in sales. She sold $206 worth of clothing during her first week and received lots of praise from her colleagues as well as the buyer. Accustomed to working at an easel or a typewriter, by the time she left the store at six o'clock each day, she was exhausted. But her luck was about to change.

On April 2, Jane learned that while her story didn't quite work for *Cosmopolitan, Delineator* magazine would pay $350 if she would make a few revisions. "A journal of fashion, culture and fine arts," *Delineator* (originally *The Delineator*), a respected periodical since 1873, boasted almost two million subscribers by 1929. Its appeal to white, middle class families in the United States, Canada, and England came in part from its editors' openness to the changing role of women in society. Jane was delighted. "[I] am so excited and glad and everything that I don't know whether I'm coming or going," she exclaimed on April 10. Before he published it in August, *Delineator* editor Oscar Graeve changed her title from "Out a Year" to "Tell Her 'Hey.'"

Jane's narrative focuses on Twinx Larrabie, a post debutante who regrets the way she treated a very attractive beau, Skel Lorimer, during her coming-out parties. Surrounded by so many eligible men, she'd been a bit arrogant with all of them. Twinx and Skel reconnect after her little sister runs into him, but this time Skel plays hard to get. He reminds Twinx how self-centered she'd once been. Through the course of their evening together, at a cocktail party and then a quiet bistro tucked into the cabin of a boat, they stop masquerading behind smug banter and discover that they still care for each other.

The story was not only Jane's debut in the world of adult magazine fiction, it was an attempt by Mr. Graeve to attract younger, well-educated readers for his advertisers. Collegiate and single working women were Jane's target market, not just in *Delineator* but in *Woman's Home Companion*, the *Saturday Evening Post*, *Good Housekeeping*, and *Hearst's International-*

Cosmopolitan, each of which would buy stories from her for between $400 and $650 within the next twelve months. Jane's engaging plots about the romantic predicaments of her contemporaries soon earned a following. Her heroines' privileged backgrounds—which Jane knew so well—added to their appeal to middle- and upper-middle-class readers.

While 1930s protagonists in women's fiction had more career options than they would a decade later, marriage and motherhood were assumed to be the primary objective for women in Jane's age bracket. According to Nancy A. Walker, an expert in the history of women's magazines of the era, "A 1936 Gallup poll revealed that 82 percent of Americans opposed the paid employment of married women, and more than half of the then forty-eight states had laws that prohibited such employment in at least some circumstances." Although millions of American women combined marriage and work during the Great Depression out of necessity, those with husbands who could support them were rebuked for taking jobs that men needed.

Popular fiction from the period reflects this attitude. Prolific author Faith Baldwin targeted the same readers as Jane while combining marriage, motherhood, and a career until she died in 1978. Baldwin's female characters repeatedly weigh the merits of independence and conformity, vocation and marriage. In her best-selling romance, *Skyscraper* (published in 1932), the three key women characters compromise their ambitions even as they try to hold onto their jobs. Each must choose between a man she loves who has modest resources and a wealthy older man who offers a life of luxury. In this and other 1930s novels including *Gone with the Wind,* historian Laura Hapke states, "masculine bitterness" toward ambitious women is pervasive. Even left-wing women novelists chafed at the fact that "all too often husbands and lovers punish [their women] psychologically for having jobs." In describing the "misogynistic laboring or writing environment of the 1930s," Hapke concludes that a "guilt-ridden professionalism"—one that had not yet affected Jane—"informed the negative construction of wage-earning women." As a writer and not a wife, Jane had no misgivings about shirking her responsibilities or taking a wage-paying job away from a man.

Quite the opposite—on her visit to Virginia for a weekend at the end of May, Jane noticed that "everybody is so much nicer to me because I sold a story." In July, at her aunt and uncle's urging, she left her sales job and returned to Poplar Springs to write more stories with "pale short fingernails and no make-up and deeper thoughts than ever." Elsie McKeogh's enthusiasm about her latest submission, "Older than God," had buoyed her spirits. She'd sent it right to *Cosmopolitan*. Jane finally saw a copy of the August *Delineator* in mid-July and confessed to Dick, "I do get a tremendous kick out of seeing my story in print, though it is trivial and superficial. Someday I shall write well." Yet to her dismay, Graeve introduced his new author by saying: "Jane Hall made her debut in New York society in 1933; her story, "Tell Her 'Hey' is her debut in print. She is only twenty-one."

After she saw this surprising comment, she was startled by a special-delivery letter from Dick, who hated the story. Jane's frustration with Graeve's remarks and the editing process is obvious in her response: "What little perspective and point the story had was originally summed up in three or four paragraphs near the end. To have so much cut out, plus a few coy bits that some clown has added, was the crowning whack at a story I have never felt even the least flicker of pride in." She'd assumed neither the magazine nor her agent had known anything about her social life when Mr. Graeve bought the story; Jane had been "floored" at the reference to her own debutante past under the title. Mrs. McKeogh had asked her how she had "created such an authentic debutante atmosphere and she'd obviously told the *Delineator* editor. (I don't think she imagined for a minute that a real Deb would bother her head about writing a story.) Unfortunately, the information seems to have pleased him very much. Or perhaps he doesn't know that New York debs are a dime a dozen." But debs with her talent and outsider perspective were not. Over the next three years, Jane's fiction vividly depicted the world Rose and Randolph Hicks had introduced her to—that niche was where the money was. Selling one story would bring in more income than several months' work in sales, and only with income could she define her life on her own terms.

Dick Clarke, however, had convinced himself that Jane's stories were based on her adventures with other men. Jane countered that she drew from her life and thoughts "to get the best possible atmosphere I could, one that we all KNOW is shallow and superficial. But so valued by women magazine readers everywhere. If you are going to credit me personally with all the thoughts, emotions, and experiences that I try to write about, I fear you will find some pretty disturbing ones. I told you long ago, and repeated it often, that 'Tell Her Hey' was just typical popular magazine *tripe*. Not even just typical and popular. I was glad only because it sold. I knew just what the story was and what any intelligent person would think of it when considering 'writing.'" Jane needed Dick's support, not his criticism: "To have all my own words and thoughts flung at me just when I was feeling so desperately low about it anyway was like a knife in the back. And it came, Special Delivery, from you."

Another source of conflict between them in the summer of 1936 was a new novel by an unknown author named Margaret Mitchell. Though *Gone with the Wind* was the "best modern novel" Jane had ever read, her strong reaction to the character of Scarlett O'Hara triggered a heated debate by mail with Dick, who had immersed himself in Hervey Allen's *Anthony Adverse*. Dick had not read any of Mitchell's work, and Jane had read only parts of the sprawling 1933 novel set in Napoleonic Europe. "Even the good parts of *Anthony Adverse* pale beside Mitchell's sincerity," she told Dick. Jane's friends and family, with the notable exception of her uncle, found the novel "thrilling and absorbing." And Jane loved the fact that Scarlett O'Hara did not dwell on the past like other Southern women, who looked backward for half a century "to dead times, to dead men," and bore "poverty with bitter pride because they have those memories."

But Dick Clarke had apparently implied in a letter to Jane that all women are a bit like Scarlett O'Hara. Scarlett, Jane argued, was "uniquely *bad* among fiction heroines . . . that's why she's making publishers' history right now; she had almost no redeeming features . . . She had no conception of what life was except as a sort of putty she could twist in her own two hands into whatever shape she wanted at the time. She had no sense of humor, of kindliness, of her own shortcomings, or of the spiritual and intellectual side of living. Is this, then, the sort of creature that you (representing all men in the world) would make the earth turnaround for? Would come to for inspiration, understanding, surcease? I'm afraid, unless you want me to believe that all men are equally Rhett Butlers, that you have put your gender in rather bad light. Most women are not like Scarlett O'Hara or All Men Are Dopes. Which is it to be?" Jane was appalled that Scarlett had gone into Melanie's room and read Ashley's letters realizing, at the time, that " 'her mother were rather she were dead than capable of such a thing.' Eliminate all the more feminine hypocrisy of her and her coquettish intrigues and you still have a dyed in the wool she-crook."

Jane held on to Dick's response to this tirade:

Don't be a feminist, Jane, Scarlett was you know. She was among the first of the emancipated women. Her story was " 'the story of the career of a managing woman' "—words not mine but those of some 2-penny reviewer (including all reviewers). I know that you tend to hold their opinions in higher regard than mine so here you are.

Don't run down Scarlett, Jane, in order to fight for the defense of women. They aren't worth it. I thought you knew that. And you'll only get yourself in hot water. . . . Not all women go so far as Scarlett (I'm sure you wouldn't) but the idea is there. I'm sorry that you find me unintelligent because I recognized the S[carlett] in women. It is a pity, for there are few redeeming qualities for unintelligence. But thank you for your frankness; and now you asked for this.

Scarlett is not "uniquely bad" among fiction heroines (unless you are poorly read) but she is like all selfish and conceited young women unutterably [sic] tiresome. Only Ms. Mitchell's genius, her touch and hue to draw amazing portraits, and her knack for stringing incidents together holds the book at the top. Scarlett, as Scarlett, has nothing to do with it. Scarlett in contrast to her surroundings, and Melanie (who is 'uniquely' good) help hold the book [together] as central figures.

Jane's point that Scarlett had no redeeming features annoyed Dick, who not-so-subtly implied that at times she reminded him of Scarlett. They did share the same piercing green eyes, strong will, Catholic background, and contempt for what author and film critic Molly Haskell refers to as "the idiot wellborn." Both had a keen intelligence and charm that proved more seductive to men than classic beauty, although these attributes were complicated by a fear of sexual intimacy and a "very American need to stay in control" in intimate relationships. Haskell also believes that "both Scarlett and Margaret Mitchell desperately need their mothers," as Jane surely did. But these were not the similarities that troubled Dick Clarke as he continued:

Have you never been at fault? I expect very few of your dime-a-dozen debs have any conception of what life is except as a sort of putty. You yourself stand accused in that regard. I think you are too harsh (where have I heard that word before?) on S[carlett]. [Though] she had no sense of humor, but little kindliness (except for Ashley, in her own mind), she did know her own shortcomings, but preferred to think of them 'later.' And her spiritual and intellectual side was neglected through no fault of hers.

I (representing all men) am far from making the earth turnaround for this sort of creature. Don't forget that I had never found a source of 'inspiration, of understanding, of surcease,' until I met you, and now you're turning on me in defense of a worthless sex. It has been because of the S. O'Hara in women that I have been wrapped in my own cellophane. I have been physically attracted, yes, but if that were all I sought Lord help us. Just you think of all the girls you know and see how 'fine' they are. Don't you know that men (the Dopes) fight for and marry these women and then continue fighting the rest of their lives. And just try to deny it.

Left speechless by this missive, Jane suggested they stop any discussion of the war between the sexes until they saw each other in person. Dick had left his car, Mr. Deeds, in Virginia for Jane to drive. Despite this generous gesture, after every visit he returned to New York disheartened because Jane was not responsive to his pleas for a serious romance.

WITH NO SCHOOL OR WORK in Manhattan, it was easy for Jane to settle down at Poplar Springs with Rose, occasional house guests, her father's typewriter, and horses to school and hunt for what turned out to be the remainder of 1936. She'd also been distracted by a dashing blond pilot, Cliff Zieger, who was trying to end a fragile marriage and had been pursuing Jane for about six weeks. Jane kept him at arm's length while enjoying his attentions immensely. She took flying lessons from Cliff in the fall. Aviation fascinated America in the twenties and thirties—Jane had been impressed by the news that Louise Thaden and Blanche Noyes beat their male competitors in the cross-country Bendix Transcontinental Speed Race, and by the story of Beryl Markham, the first woman to fly across the Atlantic solo from east to west.

Jane related all this to Dick, without touching on Cliff's amorous behavior, because "I want to tell you everything." Flying, Jane wrote, was "a deep-seated joyous feeling" that she wanted Dick to share: "If you had the opportunity to fly that I have right now I wouldn't want you to miss it for anything because it's part of the kind of life—the kind of fun—that you and I share the same feeling for." Cliff and his partner Graham piloted people all over the country and taught sixteen- and seventeen-year-olds to fly solo. "It's their business and there is no more risk attached—not as much—as there is when I take one of our green horses out to cub." Besides, her aunt and uncle would never have allowed her to fly had too much risk been involved.

As the bitter cold formed icy crusts over the fields and the frozen muck often made it too lethal to ride very far, Jane focused harder than ever on her writing. At the beginning of October Elsie had sold "Older than God" to *Woman's Home Companion* for four hundred dollars for the January 1937 issue. (Its new title was "Smooth as Glass.") Jane's protagonist in this story is eighteen-year-old Ann Marie Aubrey, who recovers from a broken heart with the help of twenty-eight-year-old Princeton alumnus Pete MacArthur. Once again, *Cosmopolitan* had seen her work first and wanted her to rewrite it, but Elsie knew she could sell it with few changes.

Woman's Home Companion was one of the four most popular women's magazines in America at that time; its forward-thinking editor, Gertrude Battles Lane, had great respect for her busy reader and understood that she wanted to do much more than housework. "She is intelligent and clearheaded. I must tell her the truth," Lane stated. And she was "forever seeking new ideas. I must keep her in touch with the best." During her tenure, from 1919 to 1941, Lane satisfied her readers' voracious appetite for fiction with the best work she could attract from well-known authors of the era including Sinclair Lewis, Ellen Glasgow, and Willa Cather. But "Smooth as Glass" may have been the only story she was offered by Jane Hall, for *Cosmopolitan* recognized Jane's potential and asked Elsie when they could "expect another story." The editor wrote, " 'I'm convinced that Jane Hall is Cosmopolitan material.' Isn't that encouraging?" Jane confided to Dick. "This last letter was just out of a clear sky." It was enough to motivate Jane to keep working at Poplar Springs all fall and through the Christmas holidays.

By December the talk of the town among the socially conscious in Warrenton, Virginia, was the news that Great Britain's king, Edward VIII, had abdicated to marry the twice-divorced Wallis Warfield Simpson. The then Mrs. Spencer had lived in Fauquier County's seat for two years between 1925 and 1927 while divorcing her first husband. Everyone in the Hickses' circle of friends still remembered her days at the Warren Green Hotel on Main Street. "I wonder if it's really to marry Wallis Simpson—or because he doesn't like that King business?" Jane asked her diary on December 11 after she heard the king had given up his throne. She would soon learn it was the former.

At the end of the month, Jane could be found at all the toniest local parties; her family's Christmas Eve festivities took place under a twenty-foot-tall tree festooned with silver tinsel and large colored lightbulbs in the three-story-high great room at Poplar Springs. The following day they all met for Christmas dinner at Randolph's sister Dony's home in Warrenton. A few days later, Jane saw Busby Berkeley's *Gold Diggers of 1937* "with that insipid Dick Powell" and the nineteenth-century period film *Camille,* starring Greta Garbo, Robert Taylor, and Lionel Barrymore. She was deeply moved by the latter, finding some of the scenes "surpassingly beautiful. At times Garbo looks so much like my mother that the resemblance is startling." As the year came to a close, she had the wistful thoughts of a young woman who felt older than her years: "Almost 22 years old—the trouble is one still feels young *inside*. Diary, do you think I have very much to show for all of the Age I've piled up? I've been exceptionally lucky to sell two stories—during this year I've earned myself over $1200 and that's only really 'working' [at Lord & Taylor] four months of the time—but I don't know."

In January, the atmosphere at Poplar Springs was perfect for dreaming up stories. The countryside was bleak and lonesome; the mercurial weather varied from being grim, grisly, and gray to a balmy June in January. "One goes out without coats, and the breeze hits you like a swat of perfume, and you close your eyes and think of warm, windy days on the beach and all the beauty and sadness that spring has ever meant," Jane wrote. Diversions from her male friends were now at a minimum. Randy Carter was preoccupied with flying for the Virginia Air Service; "they have an air news route now and deliver 300 papers from the air." Even Cliff had gone south to fly for the Miami Branch of the VAS; he wrote frequently about how much he missed her, so a wistful Jane began a new story based on her friendship with Cliff.

When she wasn't writing, Jane headed to the movies in Warrenton or occasionally to Washington, DC. Two of her favorite movies were *Libeled Lady*—("Jean extreme-line Harlow is a riot and the dialogue is tops")—and *Three Smart Girls*, featuring "the gorgeous voice of young, simply delightful Deanna Durbin." There were also daily trips to the post office in anticipation of news from New York or a package from Cliff, Dick Clarke, or her brother in Charlottesville, where he'd begun work on his PhD. Dickie sent Jane two records: "Little Old Lady," from the Broadway musical revue *The Show Is On*, and Bing Crosby's "I Can't Escape from You," which could have been Dick Clarke's theme song. Putting the Crosby record on the phonograph was irresistible, even if its melancholy refrain added to Jane's occasional nostalgia for her younger days in Manhattan: "And so you see that I'm really not free/ I'm so afraid you might escape from me/ And yet I can't escape from you."

Finally, on January 25, Jane wrote to Dick that they would be back in New York within a week. She'd had no idea how complicated it was for Rose to close up the big stone house until April and to supervise myriad chores such as turning off the water and locking the silver safely in a vault at the Fauquier National Bank. Rose would supervise her farm manager throughout the winter by mail—letters between Casanova and Manhattan were delivered by train within a day, thanks to the very

efficient train service. On Saturday, January 30, Rose and Jane made it
to Washington's Union Station late in the afternoon. Jane had already
asked Dick to pick her up at their Berkshire Hotel apartment at eleven
o'clock that evening, less than two hours after their train arrived; that
way they could still make it to the third annual President's Birthday
Ball at the Waldorf Astoria. (This year Jane was just a guest.) For Jane,
the new year really took off once she returned to the stimulating atmosphere of Manhattan. Now that she'd appeared in print, she had high
hopes for her future as an author. In 1937, writing about the swirl of café
society became much more important to her than participating in it.

SIX

"So Lucky at Last"

"THIS HAS GOT TO BE A BIG YEAR," JANE PROMISED HERSELF ON HER twenty-second birthday. Financial independence seemed to be within reach as she pounded away at her Royal typewriter, "beating it to a pulp." She wrote quickly—the first draft was often handwritten—and a story would take shape in just a few days. By the end of the year, seven of Jane's stories would be published in mass-circulation magazines, plus she had a contract for three more. Once Elsie sold a story, that usually (but not always) meant it would be published, though months could pass between the time Jane received a check and when she saw her name in a table of contents. If a story was rejected by one periodical, Elsie sent it right off to another.

In 1937, two competing Hearst publications vied for Jane's work: *Good Housekeeping,* the top women's service magazine, and *Hearst's International-Cosmopolitan,* whose editor, Harry Burton, had almost picked up Jane's first two stories. Fiction had long been *Cosmopolitan's* trademark; Burton would boast that "more motion pictures are made from *Cosmopolitan* stories than from any other magazine." In 1929, William Randolph Hearst had promoted a sharp ad sales executive, Richard Berlin, to general manager of his International Magazine Company—soon to be Hearst Magazines. Berlin knew how to manage a budget, increase advertising sales, and cut editorial expenses, which he'd done when Burton took over the editorship from Ray Long in 1931.

Per Berlin's wishes, Burton pulled back a bit from acquiring new material by best-selling authors. Some had long-standing contracts, but Burton did not renew many of them in the volatile economy of the 1930s. Instead he bought fiction "on a story-by-story and serial-by-serial basis." All that belt-tightening increased the appeal of a talented new writer whose agent would settle for less than a thousand dollars a story. Jane had earned $350 for her first published story in *Delineator,* but by the summer of 1937, according to her diary, *Cosmopolitan* offered eight hundred dollars apiece for her sixth and seventh. The magazine's approximately 1.7 million readers came from households with above-average income and above-average education. Each issue included several nonfiction pieces, at least a half a dozen short stories, up to three serials, and a book-length novel. Jane was in good company in 1937 and 1938, sharing the magazine's pages with Faith Baldwin, Pearl Buck, Edna Ferber, Paul Gallico, Erle Stanley Gardner, W. Somerset Maugham, Ogden Nash, Ursula Parrott, and Adela Rogers St. Johns, to name just a few.

In mid-March, Jane sent Elsie "The Snow Queen Type," a story told primarily from the point of view of its male protagonist. The following month, after meeting editors at Elsie's literary cocktail party, she was invited back to *Cosmopolitan's* offices in the Hearst building, where, her diary notes, Mr. Burton agreed to buy her latest story for his December issue if she would change the ending, which, of course, she did. Jane's protagonist in this adventure, fledgling attorney Robert ("Rusty") Michael, is infatuated with gorgeous, nineteen-year-old Evan Guathmie, who does not return his affection. No longer a good sport, she's become arrogant and condescending. She looks at him "with that sort of wistful-but-well-fed expression that women use on people who are in love with them."

To resolve his one-sided love affair, Rusty immerses himself in books about how to understand the feminine mind. He uses his newfound insight when a pretty Mississippi belle named Marilee Ellis arrives to visit Evan's family for the weekend. Evan's houseguest is easy to flirt with and loaded with Southern charm.

The settings for this story are the smart-set hangouts Jane frequented: El Morocco, where Evan watches as Rusty and Marilee rumba "under a ceiling that twinkled with dozens of electric stars"; the Tavern on the Green in Central Park, where Evan and another beau, Gregory Smith, enjoy cocktails and the mellow sound of swing tunes from the orchestra; and the Warwick Hotel, where Marilee is enchanted by the new Dean Cornwell murals. In one of them, Sir Walter Raleigh spreads his cape on the ground for Queen Elizabeth: "That's when men were men and knew how to prove it!" she observes. A photograph of the mural appears in the body of Jane's story along with three-color modernist watercolor illustrations by Jaro Fabry. (The murals—restored in 2004—are still in the restaurant at the Warwick.)

Rusty's plan to make Evan jealous has unintended consequences: She's so distraught that she agrees to marry an inebriated Greg Smith. The four take off on a hilarious car trip to the tiny town of Elkton, Maryland, where a couple can get married any time of the day or night. Of course, Evan learns a lesson in humility. The impulsive nuptials are aborted, and Rusty gets his girl. Even Marilee's future looks promising, for she has a fiancé back home in Mississippi.

While Jane's protagonists always learn valuable lessons about how not to behave in the dating game, her editors and her readers still expected everything would turn out well for them. To keep her readers interested in this engaging yet flawed segment of the upper crust, Jane inserts some of the same characters in more than one tale. Set in or near Manhattan, or in the gentrified parts of northern Virginia, Jane's narratives are filled with high-energy, plucky young men and women who are constantly on the move—on the dance floor, on horseback, in small airplanes or convertibles, and on top of double-decker buses.

In 1936 and 1937, Jane wrote several stories based on her dating experiences in Fauquier County. They provide an animated picture of genteel Southern life among young men and women who mingle at the Gold Cup races, at a hunt breakfast, at a box at one of many horse shows, or at a party in the manor house at the historic North Wales plantation. "With Moonlight on His Wings" (*Good Housekeeping*, August 1937) is the first story in a trilogy about the adventures of appealing, resourceful Elizabeth Lee (Liz) McKelvey.

Liz is sixteen and on summer break from her girls' prep school in "Ridgeville," a fictional town derived from Warrenton—even some

of the street names are the same. Liz and her best girlfriend, Jeanie
Landon (very "likeable" though she is "the richest girl in town") are
eager to meet the handsome pilots Pell Loomis and Cary Shriver, who
have turned some farmland not far from Ridgeville into a small airport.
The plot revolves around Liz's unsuccessful attempt to snag tall, blond
Pell by taking flying lessons behind her parents' backs. Pell—whose
character is based on Cliff—seems so glamorous, so sophisticated, and
so beautifully dressed compared to boys Liz's own age. Once it is clear
that Pell is immune to her amorous advances—he refers to Liz and her
friends as "kids"—she realizes that her crush is a mere episode in her
journey toward adulthood.

That realization doesn't stop Liz from succumbing to two more in-
fatuations with older professional men at seventeen and eighteen. In "A
Lion on the Tree," a Christmas story commissioned by *Good Housekeeping* for its December 1937 issue, Liz has a yen for New York theatrical
producer, Crosby Starr, the houseguest of one of her friends. Liz is an
aspiring actor and does a superb job in a corny school play despite a nasty
cold that turns into pneumonia. Unfortunately (but not surprisingly),
while Crosby loves her performance, he has only a mentor's interest in
Liz. But she does learn that should she ever come to New York to pursue
a career on the stage, he will try to help her out.

Liz's third "Grande Passion" for an older professional man is the basis
of "Elizabeth, Femme Fatale," (*Cosmopolitan*, July 1939). In this installment, Liz focuses her romantic aspirations on Taylor Cooper, a Manhattan magazine illustrator whom she meets at the Orange Horse Show in
Virginia. He confides to Liz that he finds many New York girls a disappointment, as they so often appear "pseudo-sophisticated and bored,"
while she seems more "frank and genuine." But Liz juggles two other
boyfriends while flirting with Taylor; she makes several missteps as she
plays with all three men's emotions. Once they discover her fickle behavior, she learns a lesson about treating her suitors honestly. And Jane's
readers can take comfort in the fact that this time Liz has another chance
at romance because Taylor, who still likes her, receives a commission to
work in nearby Washington, DC.

"Venetian Blind" (*Cosmopolitan,* March 1938) also includes locations derived from Jane's life at Poplar Springs. Socialite Pamela Fielding is torn between an Italian financier from Manhattan and a wealthy, modest Virginia gentleman farmer who flies a plane. Pam meets Ike Kendall during a summer at her grandmother's farm, "Viewtree." After several mishaps, Pam chooses Ike over the sophisticated New Yorker. She decides it could work out well to remain in Virginia because she has no career. In fact, she wishes she had been "born the Mental Type. If only she could have painted or written or researched on Topology—just anything to keep the stagnance out of her soul." This remark, a direct reference to Jane's and her brother's careers, reflects her impression that not having a passion or being able to pursue a calling could be debilitating for many women.

By March 1937, Elsie was confident enough in Jane's work to contact Hollywood's star literary agent, H. N. (Harold Norling) Swanson, known worldwide as "Swanie." Born in Iowa in 1899, for eight years during the 1920s he'd been editor and part owner of the popular Chicago-based magazine *College Humor.* "The years spent in running *College Humor* were without a doubt the happiest of my life," Swanie admitted in his short late-life memoir, *Sprinkled with Ruby Dust.* He'd first come to Hollywood in the early 1930s to work as a producer for his friend David O. Selznick, then the head of RKO (Radio-Keith-Orpheum) Pictures. (He had sold Selznick the film rights to Fitzgerald's *Tender Is the Night.*) Selznick "loaded" him with lots of projects, and Swanie immersed himself in the film world. He found the business "laced with stress and anxiety. Apparently everybody in the field understood this and simply lived with it." In the magazine business, by contrast, "writers were the main concern: how to find them and how to get their best work. In Hollywood, I quickly discovered that in the movie business, the important people were the star, the director, the producer . . . And, of course, the source of the production money. The writer was far down on the list, perhaps under 'Miscellaneous.' "

So it wasn't surprising that Swanie concluded the best way he could help writers was to be his own boss. In 1934 he set up shop as an agent "in a modest little building at 9018 Sunset"; at the time the boulevard was "still a half paved and half dirt road." He had the "ear and respect of the studio bosses," a producer noted many years later. "You never needed a contract with him—just a handshake." Swanie propelled many well-known authors into lucrative second careers as screenwriters. In fact, it was Swanie who suggested to F. Scott Fitzgerald in 1924 that *The Great Gatsby* would be a better title for his iconic novel than *Trimalchio in West Egg*. Swanie's other clients included Raymond Chandler, Pearl Buck, William Faulkner, and Thornton Wilder.

Swanie first read Jane's story "Smooth as Glass" in *Women's Home Companion* in mid-March. He found the plot was "too slight for a picture," but Elsie held his interest in her young client's work. At the beginning of June, after reading three other stories by Jane on the train back to Los Angeles from New York, Swanie wrote to Elsie that he was "delighted with this author's work." On the fifth, he sent "You Can't Laugh All Night," a story that was bought by *Cosmopolitan* (but may never have been published), to story editor and head of Paramount's writer's department Manny Wolf.

Over the next three weeks, samples of Jane's work arrived at the story departments of Metro, Twentieth Century Fox, Universal Studios, Warner Bros., Columbia Pictures, and RKO with Swanie's strong endorsement: "We feel we have made another writing discovery here and hope you can recognize in this young girl's work the charm and freshness that we found. Her ear is attuned to the modern flapper slang and we think she could write picture material for the subdeb as she has never had written before." Often Swanie made specific suggestions. He wrote to Warren Groat at Metro: "The writer would be excellent on 'Broadway Co-ed' as her college kid dialogue is the last word. She is in the East now and is selling her stories to top magazines."

In July, he told Elsie, "You know how much I like Jane Hall's work"—he'd "put on a campaign for her"—but the studios wondered, given the narrow scope of her stories, whether she could "develop into an all-around screen person." Elsie reassured him that Jane was indeed interested in a contract, "and it seems to me with the vogue for sophisticated and amusing dialogue something might be arranged." Swanie then urged

Elsie to encourage Jane to do a serial that would have enough plot to sell to the pictures. On August 18, Swanie took another tack and offered Jane "at an attractive salary" to a dozen scenario heads including MGM's Edwin H. "Eddie" Knopf "as a staff writer, specializing in the dialogue and point of view of our young moderns in love."

As all this lobbying went on in Los Angeles, both Jane and Elsie faced tragedies at home. In April, a man Jane had been out with a few times as a favor to a friend committed suicide by jumping out a fourteenth-story window. It had been clear he was depressed and having a hard time getting used to New York. "Dear diary, if only I had called him to see how he was," Jane lamented. She was mortified that she had not been as sensitive as she should have been. "I can't forget Bob standing by the revolving door downstairs! Smiling like a lost child—and after all he told me I didn't even phone him? I 'intended' to." For weeks, she kept thinking about this catastrophe.

In May, her grandmother's fragile health had begun to deteriorate further. Jane felt terrible that Rosa was so far away in San Francisco. "Gram is desperately ill and sinking fast. I wanted to fly to California this afternoon but the Rs [Rose and Randolph] think I better not. I should have gone six months ago," she moaned to her diary. On her late mother's birthday, May 20, Jane reported that "Gram is in a coma—so I suppose she would not recognize me anyway—oh but I missed the boat this time." She definitely had; Rosa Sutton died on May 23. She is buried in the San Francisco National Cemetery (the Presidio), surrounded by acres of identical white military headstones that overlook San Francisco Bay. Jane would always regret that she had not gone to see her earlier in the year.

Jane owed her eventual publishing success that summer to the fact that her thirty-nine-year-old agent kept right on working despite the tragic loss of her husband. Major Arthur McKeogh died of pneumonia on June 15 at New York's Mount Sinai Hospital. A member of the American Expeditionary Forces in World War I, his lungs had been badly damaged in 1918 during the Battle of the Argonne Forest. In its August issue, Good Housekeeping editor William Bigelow printed a moving tribute to his highly regarded colleague's heroism and condemned the futility of war.

FOR THE REST OF THE year Jane continued to be productive while enjoying nights out at El Morocco, the Rainbow Grill, and her new favorite, the Stork Club, on Fifty-Third Street near Fifth Avenue. She still saw Dick Clarke, but Cliff was also a frequent companion now that he was an Eastern Air Lines pilot based in New York. Jane had flown down to Virginia with him for the Gold Cup races and marveled at how beautiful the farm looked thanks to her aunt's gardening and landscaping skills. The high point of the visit was a chance to see Dickie, who after two years of postgraduate work in topology was about to leave for California to become a teaching assistant at UCLA.

In 1937, *Cosmopolitan* became the exclusive publisher for Jane's fiction, primarily by tying her up with contracts for lots of work. On June 11, *Cosmo* had bought "Sidewalk Café" for five hundred dollars. It had been the magazine's idea to have her first *Cosmo* story set in the world of alfresco dining. During July and August, Mr. Burton commissioned five more stories—two for six hundred dollars apiece and three more at eight hundred dollars apiece. Jane had apparently come to terms with her status as a post-debutante author, perhaps because *Cosmopolitan* emphasized her professional achievements in its Over the Editor's Shoulder column:

A deb with a difference is Jane Hall, whose story, "Sidewalk Café," is in this issue. Miss Hall is extremely pretty, enjoyed coming out, loves to dance and play and flutters a mean eyelash. All that is according to pattern. But from that point on Miss Hall is different. She is the only debutante we ever heard of who was a newspaper reporter at 13. (Her editor didn't know her age because she painted crows' feet around her eyes.) She sold her first story at ten for $2.50. She went to art school for three years because she is determined to be an illustrator as well as a writer. And she wrote advertising copy for a big department store. How she could do all these things, as well as learn to write, while growing up to the advanced age of twenty-one, is a mystery.

Under the story's title, the magazine added: "Love—in the great open spaces of Manhattan's sidewalk cafés! Here is a story of the smart young set as gay as a striped awning, as sparkling as a champagne cocktail, and as funny as next year's slang." This was a perfect introduction for those who enjoyed romances as an escape from their troubles in the 1930s. But the story also explores the difficult question that Jane (along with millions of other women) wrestled with throughout the decade: Could a determined young woman have a profession *and* succeed in marriage?

Twenty-one-year-old former debutante Penny Raymond wants to be a writer. Until she can sell her stories, she's selling clothes at Hess & Gaynor, a big department store modeled on Lord & Taylor, where, of course, she really hopes to work in advertising. Her fiancé, Chris Grimes, who wants to get married as soon as possible, offers to use his contacts at the store to help her get promoted. Penny insists she can advance on her own and won't commit to a wedding date. One afternoon Bill Alexander, a man Penny had seen at Princeton house parties, comes into the store to buy a sharkskin jacket for his wife, Margot. The heat in New York is brutal that July, and Margot is in Newport—she often travels to see friends, leaving Bill to his own devices and their six-month-old daughter with her mother. Penny and Bill end up having dinner together at the Brevoort Hotel's sidewalk café on Fifth Avenue and Ninth Street to commiserate about their respective significant others.

Penny's fiancé seems to want to tie her down too much; Bill's complaint is that his wife "runs all over the country, flies, sails, drives exactly as if she were a deb again." After they've had a few drinks, two other couples they know join them. Well-nourished with alcohol, the six jovial members of café society head off to Coney Island for a thrill ride on the famous wooden roller coaster, the Thunderbolt. Later that night, the group of revelers returns to Manhattan, only to be caught on Park Avenue hijacking a horse-drawn milk wagon for fun. Penny and Bill spend the rest of the night in a detention center. Even worse, she's in the news following day: "Prudence Raymond follows Milky Way" . . . "Sun Rises on Post Debutante Theft of Milk Wagon." She feels ridiculous about their zany antics and embarrassed to be late for work. Naturally, Bill's wife and Penny's fiancé see the articles. The evening after Bill's attorney father gets them out of jail, he and Penny return to the Café Brevoort, where they brainstorm about how they will save their relationships.

To their great surprise, Margot and Chris suddenly turn up at the Brevoort, too. Margot swears she will never leave Bill alone again, and Penny has decided to marry Chris as long as he doesn't mind that she's just been offered the job she wanted in Hess & Gaynor's advertising department. As they ride a double-decker bus back up Fifth Avenue, Chris jokes that he may become Mr. Prudence Raymond after their wedding in August.

"WHAT ARE THE HABITS THAT American popular culture encourages audiences to pursue?" film historian Jeanine Basinger asks in her history of marriage in the movies. As was often true of 1930s magazine fiction and the movies, "Sidewalk Café" has a message. Married mothers like Margot were expected to stick close to their husbands, and while Penny's fiancé takes her job seriously, should they have children, his career will come first. Most of Jane's readers expected their single state to be temporary, and once they were parents, the assumption was that a woman would stay home to raise a family or at least to supervise any household help she could afford.

On June 6, 1938, *Life* magazine published the results of a comprehensive survey of the habits of sixteen- to twenty-four-year-olds: American youth "preferred cities to towns and country," they "want more education than they have and they don't always like what they get. They aim for the professions and rarely attain them. Their morals are no worse than their elders'." They like "movies, dancing, music, reading, 'cokes' and sodas at the corner drugstore." Many of them are discouraged because they can't find a job. The magazine's profile of Betty Fulton, a typical "rich girl" of twenty-one, describes her as a "beautiful and intelligent girl, touched with sensitivity and charm, she takes her art seriously, studies hard, is proud of the money she makes from modeling, though she does it mainly for fun. She is not averse to a career for herself." Betty and her friends may well have enjoyed Jane's stories, but they did not share the values of some of Jane's most ostentatious characters. The *Life* pictograph illustrates that

56 percent of girls and 38 percent of boys either did not drink or were opposed to drinking generally. And the "top crust" of young women at big eastern women's colleges saw themselves as "preparing, usually, for a healthy, comforting marriage." The fiction they read and the films they saw both encouraged and reflected that assumption.

Many young women and men, however, worried about whether to marry for love, money, social standing, or some combination of the three. Jane tackled this timeless question openly in the third of the five stories she'd promised *Cosmopolitan*, "Such Mad, Mad Fun" (May 1938). This melodrama clearly reflects the tension between Jane's ambition and that of her aunt Rose for her. The story opens at a cocktail party as the guests pile their minks on top of the hostess's bed until it looks like a "fur trapper's teepee." Veronica ("Rocky") Alcott, last year's premiere debutante, plows her way through "gin-vigorated voices" and her boisterous peers until she notices "a thin man with a nondescript brown suit" whose face "might have come straight from an Italian portrait, dark and serious and intense."

A composer eager to make a name for himself, Gordon Kelva is the opposite of a high-society stag. He approaches Rocky, and, in an effort to convince her that popular music is culturally significant, he puts a 1931 hit, "Dancing in the Dark," on the phonograph. Veronica thinks back half a dozen years to: "Miss Chapin's green surge uniforms; playing records after school with Ann Marie, wondering what it would be like to be grown up enough for dates with boys—for dancing in the dark with one!" Memories crowd out other thoughts until Gordon accuses her of being too caught up with her own picturesqueness, of never having had a chance "to see or do anything that wasn't artificially colored and flavored." To him, those in the crowd of wealthy revelers at the party talk "a lot of drivel that doesn't mean a thing." They have walled themselves off from a chance at living a full life. It's clear from their verbal sparring that there is already a strong attraction between Rocky and Gordon; he's still on her mind when she and her steady date, Kenneth, head for Child's on Coney Island with three other couples. When, Rocky asks herself, has there ever been more "mad, mad fun?"

She invites Gordon to be one of her escorts at a dance so he can see "how the other half lives." Observing the strong contrast between

Gordon's unaffected manner and that of the other pompous men, Rocky assures him that dances usually are more "mad fun" than this one, where society matrons perched in a gilded balcony air their long gloves "and hope all the eligible gals will meet all the eligible men." Gordon's aloofness intrigues her, so Rocky flouts protocol and leaves the dance with him and without Ken. The poignant dialogue that follows as they walk up Fifth Avenue touches on class distinctions that had been on Jane's mind ever since she'd arrived in Manhattan from Los Angeles. Gordon observes that the two of them are from "different halves of the world," so what good would it do if he liked her?

> "Gordon, what are you *talking* about? I don't care if you haven't any money. You don't seem any different from the people I know." She bit her lip. Of course he did; wasn't that the reason she liked him?
>
> For an instant his dark, harassed face was almost paternal. "Listen you dumb little deb, do we *both* have to lose our perspective? Of course I'm different and you know it. What's more, in the past twelve hours I seem to have developed a bad case of class consciousness. Last night I saw your picture in the paper, 'Socialite Runs Booth for Charity.' *Charity!* Do you know how that feels? When I was thirteen the church gave us the clothes we went to school in. I'll never forget it."
>
> "But I don't *care* about that." Things were moving too fast. "Why do you tell me? What's this all *about?*" This wasn't just another stag asking for a date. This was *awful.* Veronica shivered. "Wh-what's any of that got to do with our seeing each other again?"
>
> "Just this. I seem to have fallen in love with you."
>
> Naturally, there wasn't anything either of them could do about it, after that.

So Veronica determines to learn about the music world. She listens to the song Gordon has published and sees him at every opportunity.

"Who is this man?" asks Mrs. Alcott—a character clearly derived from Rose Hicks—and Veronica is ready with her answer: " 'He's Middle Western; his family are just farmers, and they're not anybody at all, so there's no use you trying to look them up in the Social Register. He went to public school and night school—and he writes the best songs I ever heard.' Veronica jumped up. 'And I *am* going to marry him!' "

Veronica knows just what her mother is thinking: "Of all the eligible men in New York that we've bankrupt ourselves to have you meet—A person doesn't grow up in a Miss Chapin's—Cholly Knickerbocker—Tuxedo Ball atmosphere without a slight realization of what they are supposed to marry. And Gordon Kelva wasn't any part of it." She also knows what her mother hopes to hear: " 'He's with his father's firm on Wall Street—yes, Harvard 'thirty-five. You remember, his sister married Wilcox Tremaine.' That's what Mrs. Alcott wanted to be able to say about her future son-in-law—that sort of thing. Lots of money, definitely. Lots of family, preferably. But at least one of the two—imperatively!"

Rocky's parents decide that Mrs. Alcott will take her to California for six months while her husband lives at his club. If she's still in love with Gordon after that, they will open the discussion again. Rocky has a great time with her mother in Los Angeles and San Francisco while Gordon works hard to launch his musical. But she misses being part of a couple. In the interim, Ken, who has "made a minor killing in the stock market," ventures west to see her. Everything they do in this new setting seems exciting and so romantic; they even buy a car to match her hair. To her mother's delight, the two become engaged after a fun-filled weekend cruise with one of Ken's Harvard classmates. Rocky, Ken, and Mrs. Alcott drive back across the United States in the new car. Soon wedding plans begin to fall into place at the Alcotts' summer home in East Hampton.

Kenneth comes out every weekend, but Rocky still thinks about Gordon, who, she assumes, must have learned about their engagement in the papers. One day Ken buys tickets to the opening of a Broadway musical that turns out to be Gordon's show. Not only is the show a great hit, Rocky realizes that the theme song, "Do I Still Love You?" is based on their past relationship. Recognizing that she's still in love with

Gordon, she calls off the marriage to Ken. She and Gordon reconcile at a party given by one of her friends. And thanks to the success of Gordon's show, Jane's readers can assume that the couple will ultimately marry and be fine financially and socially, to the delight of Rocky's parents.

"Sunrise over Newark," Jane's only piece for the *Saturday Evening Post* (October 9, 1937), is another vote for emotional honesty over self-delusion. In this plot, Manhattan socialite Carol Cameron falls for a married man, Hyatt Rhodes, while ignoring Jeff, her more reliable beau. Again, Jane's self-knowledge helped her transform her own experiences into fiction: Carol's father (like Jane's Uncle Randy) has lost too much in the Depression to send her off on a trip. She's twenty, and he wants her to figure out on her own that she's made a mistake. Several dates with Hyatt in New York City and in Virginia convince Carol that she's been foolish—especially once she meets the rich wife who supports Hyatt at a party over Gold Cup weekend.

Jane's male characters frequently talk sense into vapid and occasionally wayward but salvageable well-off girls for whom accumulating material assets, displaying high-fashion hats, and being seen at the Stork Club are top priorities. Jane left her readers to wonder why so many women seemed to find it hard to act natural around men. As Carol proclaims, "A woman can be deep and emotional and still cover it up with flippancy." During the Depression, as Dickstein finds, popular culture gave "hard-pressed audiences . . . pleasure, escape, illumination and hope when they were most needed." In Jane's fiction, the illumination and hope come as soon as her protagonists recognize that solid values rather than great wealth are the real key to self-respect.

In 1937, Jane's confidence grew with every sale until she told her diary, "I feel so lucky at last." Her good fortune would increase in the early fall when Swanie's lobbying resulted in an exciting deal. Eddie Knopf, the thirty-seven-year-old younger brother of publisher Alfred A. Knopf, had been an actor and theater producer before he took charge of the MGM writers' department in 1936. Not long afterwards, Knopf had a run-in with Swanie, who recalled that Knopf told him: "I just discovered that one third of the material we acquired last year was from you or the New York agents you represent. That's not a healthy situation for us to be in." So Mr. Knopf had gone to New York to visit "every agency that used" H. N. Swanson as its Hollywood correspondent.

One of these was Elsie's agency, now called McKeogh & Boyd, at 542 Fifth Avenue. When he met with Jane and Elsie on October 7, 1937, Knopf had already ascertained that Jane would be an asset for Metro. Swanie had kept the pressure on at various studios all summer. Although none of her stories had been snapped up for a movie plot, Knopf offered Jane $350 per week for six months as a scenario writer. By the time the MGM contract finally reached Elsie's office on November 4, though, a new player had entered the picture. Randolph Hicks insisted on reviewing the agreement and did not like what he saw. The Loews, Inc. contract (MGM belonged to the theater chain) stipulated that Jane was entitled to three months off each year without pay but that she would commit to MGM for five years, assuming the studio renewed her contract every six months. Five years seemed much too long.

Swanie replied by Western Union that Jane's and her uncle's request for a shorter time commitment would be a "complete reversal" of studio policy. He wired Elsie that "whenever writer wishes to leave picture business studio always grants release," adding that "in all of our agency experience we have never found studio willing to make this deal in writing but always found they will grant this any time writer wishes leave." Swanie knew that MGM could give Jane a great start and a lot of security. Once she had worked there, she would have no problem finding another job.

"Metro Signs Jane Hall," the four-year-old Hollywood trade paper *Daily Variety* announced on October 22. "Jane Hall, 22-year-old magazine fiction writer, has been signed by Edwin Knopf at Metro. H. N. Swanson agented." Although Jane expected to continue her career as a freelance writer, Metro wanted options on all the fiction and nonfiction that she wrote while under contract. Elsie was disappointed that the studio took such a tough stance on work Jane did on her own time, which meant that before she left New York, Jane would need to complete the work that she owed *Cosmopolitan*. It seemed hard to believe she would be off to Hollywood in a matter of weeks.

Swanie, who never vacationed, expected a lot from his clients. He urged Jane to keep on writing a "whole bunch of short stories so the name will be plastered on every magazine worthwhile during the spring months. This will be very helpful to you, not only if we want to sell you at another studio but in raising your standing on the Metro lot." Once her contract was signed, Elsie tried to interest Swanie in pitching more of Jane's stories as movie scenarios. She suggested "A Lion on the Tree" as a possible vehicle for Deanna Durbin; he found it too "slight." Although "Venetian Blind" and "Such Mad, Mad Fun" were "very charming," the plots were also "pretty slight for pictures."

However, Swanie would continue to keep a close eye on Jane in the coming months while his new associate, Edgar Carter, handled most of the administrative details and the correspondence. One of the first things Mr. Carter accomplished was getting MGM to reimburse Jane $129.61 for what would have been the cost of the one-way rail fare in a lower berth if she'd come west right after Thanksgiving. Jane could hardly survive in Los Angeles without a car, and she'd insisted on bringing Hi Toots, the black Chrysler convertible she'd bought in July, by ship. A seagoing voyage would take longer, so Elsie and Swanie worked out a new deal with Knopf that gave Jane until Monday, December 20, to show up in Culver City. "I am delighted that Miss Hall is to be with Metro," Elsie told Knopf, "and I have every expectation that she will prove to be a real picture find."

SEVEN

"Darned Attractive on the Surface"

IN EARLY DECEMBER, JUST AS JANE CLIMBED INTO A TAXI TO HEAD for Chelsea Piers, where she would take off for the West Coast, a bell-boy rushed out to the curb with a spray of orchids from Dick Clarke. Now that she would be so far away from home, Dick's devotion, and Cliff Zieger's too, took on a new significance. Both men hoped to marry Jane, and both were distraught over her departure. For the next two and half years she would write them scores of newsy letters, eagerly anticipating their more amorous responses. Dick's orchids lasted for three days, after which Jane reported from the ship, "the memory lingers on in a bunch of green ribbon over my mirror."

Though the full-color ads for the S.S. *Santa Paula* promised passengers that they would "[l]ive luxuriously in a gracious Georgian country house afloat in tropic seas," Jane told Dick that this smaller ship offered "nothing like the luxury" of the *Virginia*, which had brought her to New York in 1930, "perhaps . . . because that was pre-Depression." Still, passengers could swim in the "largest outdoor tiled pool on any American ship" and dine under the stars when it was warm and dry enough to retract the roof on the promenade deck. And Jane appreciated the thoughtful service as well as the country-club décor created by veteran marine designer Dorothy Marckwald.

As the *Santa Paula* steamed toward California, stopping along the way at Havana, Colombia, Panama, El Salvador, Guatemala, and Mexico,

Jane detailed what she had seen and done. At the start, choppy seas made most of the passengers sick—but not Jane, who bragged, "I'm a really good sailor I guess." In one rough patch, her trunk had fallen flat, almost obliterating her; a steamer basket filled with chocolates, pepper-mints, and candied ginger from Dick's parents bounced off a shelf and flew across the room. Once the ship left Puerto Colombia, the voyage became smoother, the water bluer, and the breeze much warmer. On December 13, Jane wrote Dick from El Salvador that "the sun has come out at last and I am sunburned to a misery—how I wish you were! I read that the temperature was 18 in New York." About halfway through the voyage, a fellow passenger let her care for a four-month-old tiger cub—"the cutest thing you ever saw—just like a kitten." She was also intrigued by one of her shipmates, George Arliss—the first British actor to win an Academy Award, for his performance as Disraeli in the 1929 movie of the same name. The "charming" sixty-nine-year-old gentleman advised Jane not to try to compete with all of the people who lived a luxurious life in Hollywood, "as it can't be done in the first place and nobody cares in the second."

When the ship pulled into Los Angeles Harbor on December 19, it was a relief to see her brother, who had started his job at UCLA. Jane and Dickie had not been in California together since their mother, Daysie, had died. Yet Jane was suddenly filled with a "ghastly lost feel-ing" that persisted throughout her first two weeks on the West Coast. Her surviving letters from Hollywood never refer to Daysie, who lay nearby in the stillness of Inglewood Park Cemetery. But her new office was not far from Manhattan Beach, where the encouragement she'd received as a juvenile author had been overshadowed by her mother's lengthy battle with breast cancer.

At first, she was put off by her new surroundings: "The people in the acting part (and others, too!) look so awfully cheap—and the at-mosphere is absolutely cutthroat," she complained to Dick Clarke, who longed to be there with her. He'd even thought about trying to write for the movies, but she warned him not to consider switching careers for this "tinsel niche" where writers "develop hardening of the arteries waiting to hear if [their] options are going to be taken up." Sociologist

Leo Rosten, who spoke to several people in the movie colony between 1938 and 1941, confirmed Jane's impressions. He found that many of her neighbors and colleagues were "characterized by showmanship, not breeding; glibness, not wisdom; audacity, not poise." Producer David O. Selznick once observed that "so much of Hollywood is a façade," and Jane felt this acutely.

"Hollywoodland"—as the fifty-foot-high sign then asserted—was as much a state of mind in those days as a location. It was known for its department stores, beauty parlors, luxury hotels, Grauman's Chinese and Egyptian Theatres, dozens of booking agents, and highly publicized restaurants and night clubs like the Brown Derby and La Conga, where, the 1940 WPA guide to Los Angeles observed, "the consumption of food and drink is incidental to seeing and being seen by 'the right people.'"

In November, Swanie had encouraged Jane to rent living quarters at the Garden of Allah, a popular Spanish Revival apartment complex at the east end of Sunset Boulevard. Though notorious since the mid-1920s for booze-fueled parties that continued until the early morning hours, it remained a favorite nesting place for recently arrived writers from Manhattan. Years earlier, the main building had been the mansion of Alla Nazimova, a stage and film star from Yalta, who supposedly built the pool in the shape of the Black Sea. The pool was surrounded on three sides by two-story bungalows; units on each floor contained a kitchen, dinette, living room, bedroom, and bath. Lush gardens and exotic plantings gave the entire place a tropical feel, and an enthusiastic chorus of birds would wake those who had imbibed too much the night before. The long waiting list at the Garden prompted Jane to snatch up a single room in the main building rather than a villa. Room 108 was the smallest place she'd ever lived, but at first she didn't mind too much because of the appeal of her new surroundings—plus the room (and the rug) had been Beatrice Lillie's just a few months earlier.

Through the holidays, Jane's time was "practically [her] own with no specific hours to be on the 'Lot.'" Though she missed being with her family for Christmas, she made a real effort to have fun. Within a week she could be found at the popular three-year-old Café Trocadero on Sunset, a sidewalk café and supper club complete with scenes of Paris and the Eiffel Tower at the end of the main corridor above a staircase that led down to the bar and grill. Jane appeared there with the one "young and fun" person she'd met on the ship and a couple of his friends. In the main dining room on the ground floor, a sumptuous meal with white tablecloths and live jazz awaited those who preferred a more elegant evening. The Troc had been the place to be seen since 1934. Until he sold it in 1938, its founder, Billy Wilkerson, never missed a chance to advertise his restaurant in the trade paper he owned, the *Hollywood Reporter*, or to pick up the latest gossip from those who sought the spotlight at the Troc, which was near the *Reporter's* offices.

The scene of Jane's first "real" Hollywood party was the Brentwood home of Gary Cooper and his wife, former Park Avenue debutante Veronica ("Rocky") Balfe. After meeting the Tom Browns, Lana Turner, Cesar Romero, and Ann Sheridan, among others, Jane wrote: "They couldn't have been nicer (outwardly). The Coopers are charming—the others—I don't seem to be able to write coherently about it—but, Dick, there is an undercurrent that literally makes my blood run cold. Everybody knifing everybody else as soon as they turn around and talking differently to their faces. It was a lovely party; I don't know why it made me feel so sick. I came home at 11:30. I want to be with real people with real senses of values . . . It's so darned attractive on the surface . . . but with all my heart—I don't want to 'GO HOLLYWOOD.'"

Back in New York, the holiday mood at the Berkshire apartment hotel was mixed as Rose and Randolph Hicks coped with the fact that both their niece and nephew were three thousand miles away. They made and drank quite a bit of eggnog and tried to picture what Jane and Dickie were up to. "Uncle Randy kept track of what time it was in Hollywood. He really can't overcome the fact that you are both out there," Rose confided to Jane. It helped that Dick Clarke and Cliff Zieger came by with candy and flowers. And they were thrilled with the books from Dickie, and with the surprises that Jane had left, including a rose-colored satin bed jacket for her aunt. On Christmas Eve they joined their close friends, the William C. Durants, for dinner. The founder of General Motors, Chevrolet, and ultimately Durant Motors, Inc. had declared bankruptcy in 1936, but Rose found him "in fine feathers" in spite of his huge stock-market losses. Mrs. Durant, on the other hand, looked "very badly. The loss of a great fortune nearly finished her."

While dining at the Metropolitan Club on Christmas Day, the Hickses ran into a friend who, on hearing of Jane's new life, "said he always knew you would do something big. It's the old women who are unable to stomach your success. That does amaze me," Rose wrote, "why any old woman should object or show the green eye I cannot understand."

Rose was genuinely proud of Jane; she was also relieved that her niece could now support herself since finding a husband did not interest her at all. In response to Jane's dispirited early letters from Hollywood, she offered a pep talk: "Just try your wise cracks on your 'plaster paradise' surroundings until your imprint is all over the place. To be as young as you are and as talented with your chance! Jane you *can* do anything. You want a career and you have it." Rose thought Jane might even earn a thousand dollars or more a week someday, and assured her that her "nostalgia" would pass. "I want you to show the world you can do this job. . . .*You have it in you.*"

Jane still had misgivings about her new surroundings on December 30, but she recognized that this was a time in her life that would not come again. She began "doing Hollywood," just as Dick went out to parties and nightclubs in Manhattan. She assured Dick she always came home by midnight. How much fun it would be, she wrote, if he came out to "drive my car down the sunny roads, and have breakfast by the swimming pool—and tell me what you think. I want to stare at the Big Shot Cinema-ites, and make fun of Show-Window Hollywood and watch the lights from the hill at night—with you."

Though she didn't warm to her neighbors right away, Jane did find herself exhilarated by the wide-open Western terrain that had shaped her life as a child. She was sure she was the only person with the top down on her car in December. "These people drive like maniacs. 60 miles an hour on the main streets—and in traffic—no exaggeration," she told Dick. While Hollywood had close to 185,000 residents, Los Angeles was still relatively small, with just under one and a half million residents in total. The natural landscape asserted itself throughout a city characterized by low-lying buildings, or "whiteness, flatness, and spread." The WPA guide describes the area at the end of the 1930s as an "exotic land of lofty purple mountains, azure ocean, and mild, seductive climate, where the romance of old Spain is nurtured and blends with the gaudiness of Hollywood." Lemon, orange, olive, eucalyptus, palm, and pepper trees and native birds brought back sense memories that had lain dormant during Jane's seven years as an easterner.

By mid-January Jane's initial panic had ended—work took up most of her time. She spent her daylight hours and many evenings in Culver City (population about nine thousand), one of several towns near Los Angeles. MGM had officially come into existence in 1924, thanks largely to the initiative of theater owner and shrewd businessman Marcus Loew, who had been looking for a source for his pictures. In 1938, the studio had more than four thousand employees. With its thirty huge sound stages, sets that might include whole city blocks, and multiple administrative and auxiliary buildings, this "complete city" was spread out on well over a hundred acres. Most employees stayed a long time—Louis B. Mayer's biographer, Scott Eyman, believes they felt a "sense of security unparalleled in the movie industry."

Jane settled in on the second floor of the brand new Thalberg Building, often referred to as the "Iron Lung"—primitive air-conditioning made it impossible to open the windows. The massive granite tribute to Irving Thalberg, who had died in 1936, marked a new era for the studio; Louis B. Mayer would remain in charge until 1951. Up on the third floor, the diminutive, high-energy, and volatile Mayer held court in a white office where his huge, kidney-shaped desk stood on a platform so no one could look down on him. From there, this son of Russian Jewish peasants controlled a cultural empire and, according to Mickey Rooney, used MGM "as a pulpit to establish values for the whole nation."

MGM employees took great pride in the fact that their studio was the most successful one in Hollywood during the 1930s. But life and work in Culver City was unpredictable, and Jane was never sure exactly when she might return home. Some MGM screenwriters admired Warner Bros. more than their own studio because its pictures tackled real issues confronting the nation rather than the "florid spectacles" Mayer preferred. As Eyman remarks, Mayer "fervently believed that movies were not a reflection of life, but an escape from life. He believed in beauty, glamour, the star system, and materialism." Plus he knew his audience: Americans liked "stars, spectacle, and optimism, if possible with a little sentiment attached." He wanted everyone in his pictures to look gorgeous all the time—including women who had just rolled out of bed. A showman and a consummate actor who could "be whatever he needed to be," Mayer loved melodrama. He valued his stars above all, next his producers, then the writers, and finally, the directors.

MGM boasted that its great team of executives and producers made for unparalleled stability. All of these movie movers and shakers would become familiar faces to Jane over the next three years. She learned how to work with men such as John W. Considine, Jr., Joseph Mankiewicz, Mervyn LeRoy, Merian C. Cooper, Sam Zimbalist, and Joe Pasternak who protected their stars and kept their projects on track and on time. At first, though, she was baffled by the studio system. She told Cliff Zieger, "the system is too ridiculous—a producer is allowed just so much on budget—and you may be doing nothing at all and getting paid for it —but if he can't afford your salary he won't put you on his working list until everything is set!" Jane would have to get used to input from colleagues she might or might not like, and to being a good sport about who got the credit for a script, no matter how much work she put into it.

The year 1937 had been a banner one for MGM—as of November, its stable of ninety-seven writers had churned out treatments and dialogue for fifty-five pictures, exceeding its goal of fifty-two pictures per year. A multipage advertisement in the *Hollywood Reporter* in 1938—"MGM's Writing Staff is Tops!"—indicates how appealing the lucrative picture business had become for those with literary skills. Jane's colleagues included Robert Benchley, F. Scott Fitzgerald, Everett Freeman, Dashiell Hammett, Ben Hecht, Anita Loos, Frances Marion, Ogden Nash, Dorothy Parker, George Oppenheimer, and John Lee Mahin, to name a few. Several of them had known each other for years. To Jane they all seemed so "Bright and Sparkling . . .the talk is all like dialogue . . .The only real person is a young Jewish writer who is very silent and still surprised by his success, with fine eyes and a fine mind and a friend to the death . . . Everybody is so damn CLEVER." Jane knew she would need to work hard to keep up; she was at least a decade younger than most of her colleagues, whose median age was thirty-seven.

Some of the writers who lived at the Garden of Allah stayed for weeks, others for months or even years at a time. Jane liked "the picturesque side of Hollywood life." One morning as she left for work, she noticed F. Scott Fitzgerald "climbing into his battered little 1932 Ford amidst the English jobs a mile long, red, grey and silver, Benzes, Cords etc. It was a very warming thought that someone who has done some really good writing and probably never made much money would be so simple and unpretentious among all the Get-Rich phonies."

In June 1937—four months before he hired Jane—Eddie Knopf had persuaded the executive team at MGM to let Fitzgerald have another chance at screenwriting. H. N. Swanson was his Hollywood agent, too, at least while he was in Culver City. Determined to make it on his third stint in Hollywood, Fitzgerald watched dozens of films and took prodigious notes. He loved the movies. A writer who collaborated with Fitzgerald on a film treatment for *Tender Is the Night* recalled, "Scott would rather have written a movie than the Bible, than a best-seller."

But Fitzgerald's eagerness to succeed was also due to serious financial strain; like Jane and so many of his literary colleagues from the East, he had come for the money. After the publication of *The Great Gatsby* in 1925, he depended for income on the sales of his short stories to the *Saturday Evening Post*—just as Jane's father had done up until he died. Fitzgerald had fought hard for a $1,000-per-week contract at MGM; after six months it was raised to $1,250, far more than most screenwriters received at the time.

The stakes were high for Fitzgerald and his anxiety great. He had hit a low point between 1935 and 1937, just as Jane's stories had begun to sell. Three essays, collectively known as *The Crack-Up*, describe this period of desperation: His wife, Zelda, had been institutionalized for her fragile mental health; their previously extravagant lifestyle had emptied the coffers; no one wanted to publish his short stories; and his debts mounted up. He owed large sums to his literary agent, Harold Ober, and his editor at Scribner's, Maxwell Perkins. Fitzgerald also worried constantly about how he would pay to send his daughter, Scottie, to

The Ethel Walker School, and before long he would have to consider her college tuition. But his biggest expense was Zelda's care at a mental hospital in Asheville, North Carolina. In spite of meticulous financial record-keeping, Fitzgerald was never able to keep his spending in line with his income. On top of everything else, he feared that Scottie would lead an idle, frivolous life as a glamour girl or a playgirl. While at MGM, he wrote her many heartfelt and firm letters cautioning her to stay away from alcohol, debutantes, and high-society debauchery (in other words, mad fun).

MGM had originally hired Fitzgerald because the screenplay for *A Yank at Oxford* required polishing and, in *This Side of Paradise*, he had proven how skillfully he could write about upper-crust college life. But his producers knew he had broader experience than that. The studio declared that it had amassed "the greatest library of celebrated stage hits, best-selling popular books and unusual original stories ever owned by any one company." One of these was the German novel *Three Comrades*, Erich Maria Remarque's story of three World War I veterans and the terminally ill woman who is in love with one of them. In late 1937, Fitzgerald had a chance to adapt it for the screen.

Like Jane, Fitzgerald struggled to find a place in Hollywood. Instead of being authors, they were both now just employees. Leo Rosten found in his study that screenwriters were "engaged in the manufacture of an extremely expensive commodity"; they had traded prestige for money, and their clever dialogue and story ideas were now being targeted at a mass market. Writers who might have previously seen themselves as "the unofficial oracles of society" were now in the entertainment business, where theatricality, showmanship, and role-playing were fundamental. In *Life: The Movie: How Entertainment Conquered Reality*, Neal Gabler observes that for serious writers in Hollywood, grappling with the difference between art and entertainment was a major obstacle. Popular entertainment "was primarily about fun. It was about gratification rather than edification, indulgence rather than transcendence, reaction rather than contemplation, escape from moral instruction rather than submission to it." Above all, it "dealt with its audience as a mass"; it was sensational, effortless, and mindless, and people loved it.

Because he was such an experienced author, Fitzgerald hated the assembly-line system of producing a script even more than Jane. Theatrical producer Irene Mayer Selznick (Louis's daughter and David's wife) observed that "sometimes [the writers] worked in teams—or several writers worked separately on the same script, and each one thought he was alone on it. Sometimes one writer did the outline, someone else did the synopsis, someone did the dialogue, someone did the revision, someone did a complete rewrite. Who the hell knows who wrote anything?" This collaborative process grated on Fitzgerald's nerves. Nevertheless, as he told Scottie, this go-round he would try to be tactful and "malleable among the collaborators" until he could find a way "to work alone on a picture."

Fitzgerald did his best to work within the system as he tried to adapt Remarque's novel for the screen. Alone on the project at first, he was optimistic as he carefully studied the history of post–World War I Germany so he could describe the setting in detail. He submitted a good part of the script to producer Joe Mankiewicz, "a member of the palace guard," early in September; Mankiewicz "wired that the screenplay was 'simply swell.'" Even so, after Fitzgerald returned from a week in South Carolina with his wife and daughter, Mankiewicz, who was also an accomplished screenwriter, insisted that he collaborate with the more experienced Edward E. "Ted" Paramore Jr. Fitzgerald found it hard to refrain from revealing how much he resented the process.

Nevertheless, despite his recurrent drinking problem, Fitzgerald managed to work with Paramore to submit six more drafts of the screenplay, the final one in early February 1938. Even though Mankiewicz rewrote much of it, Fitzgerald received his only screen credit on *Three Comrades*. In addition to whatever stylistic issues there might have been, the author's truculent attitude while he worked on *Three Comrades* did not augur well for his long-term future at MGM.

Meanwhile, Jane had hit the ground running, and her agents were optimistic from the get-go. She found it much easier than Fitzgerald to come up with screen-friendly banter; she was also young and accommodating, and that helped a lot. "Jane Hall is fat and sassy and getting along great over at Metro. Her producer is Laurence Schwab, whom you undoubtedly know," Swanie had informed Elsie in early January. "She is impressed by the great amount of time on everybody's hands out here, especially the writers. I have urged her to employ it for herself. I don't know what luck I will have because this country seems very interesting to her." Elsie was relieved to have news from her West Coast counterpart, but she needn't have worried about Jane's work ethic. She was now in her own office with a typewriter, an ample supply of yellow legal pads, erasers, and pencils (and a secretarial pool to sharpen them). While other writers sometimes sat around for weeks waiting for work, Jane, with more than enough to do, was "working like a Trojan."

Autographed photo "To D'zani" from Jim Stewart in the author's collection.

EIGHT

"A Luxurious, Amusing, and Stimulating Place"

OVER THE NEXT FEW MONTHS, JANE'S INSECURITY FADED AS SHE grew more familiar with her colleagues and developed a lively social life. Her long days at work were followed by nights out at cafés, nightclubs, and small, informal parties; once in a while she went bowling with her new pals. She continued to write frequent letters to her two beaux back east, always gleefully reporting when she'd gone to Dave Chasen's for barbecue or a steak, or to some other fashionable spot. Often she joined her fellow writers "from the Lion's Club" at one of the many private showings of the latest films. On weekends, she could be found on horseback in pine-scented hills or at the Santa Anita racetrack with actress Claire Dodd.

Betting on the horses at Santa Anita, Del Mar, or Hollywood Park was a favorite pastime for moviemakers. On Saturday afternoons, movie-colony types and racing aficionados from across the world could be found in the large, elegant clubhouse at Santa Anita. A number of Hollywood notables—including Robert Taylor, Barbara Stanwyck, Spencer Tracy, and John Considine, Jr.—owned racehorses. Louis B. Mayer was renowned for his interest in racing; he'd bought dozens of horses with fine bloodlines and took great pride in his spectacular horse farm seventy-five miles from Los Angeles. Jane enjoyed going to the races, but she couldn't afford to lose much at the track.

Occasionally, there were weekends away. Jane might end up two hours north of Hollywood at Lake Arrowhead, or a hundred miles east in the desert at Palm Springs. She was beginning to make friends, though she was conscious of, and amused by, how she stood out among her many Jewish bosses and colleagues; she referred to herself as "D'zani the Gentile Girl." The land of make-believe was much more compelling than it had seemed at first. Perhaps in an effort to soothe his despair at her absence, she sent reassuring letters to Dick, telling him that while her new life was "very attractive," she did not find "all the glamour very much fun."

But Jane loved the relative informality at MGM. Hats were not required. Women often wore slacks—she'd picked up a tobacco-colored pair at Bullocks Wilshire, the famous department store on Wilshire Boulevard—and pipes and tweeds were so popular among men that she sent Dick Clarke a pipe with a pigskin pouch. Her good friend, illustrator Jon Whitcomb, was more flamboyant. Jon made a pilgrimage to Hollywood at least once a year to scout for beauties to use as models for his illustrations. "Wish you could see the clothes he wears," Jane wrote, "red linen slacks, belted yellow coats, he calls that making Hollywood Whitcomb conscious."

It was heartwarming that so many people she met remembered her father. One of her colleagues said Dick Wick Hall "was to fiction what Will Rogers was to the newspaper world." The year 1938 marked the thirteenth anniversary of the celebrated Salome Frog's first appearance in the *Saturday Evening Post*; to Jane's great surprise, the *Post* placed a two-page spread about Dick Wick Hall and his most famous character in *Time* magazine on January 3 in honor of the occasion. In a tribute titled "Birthday of 'That Salome Frog,'" the *Post* boasted that even though Hall had died in 1926, the frog that came to life in the magazine's pages lived on. (It still does: Today, the high school football team in Salome is named the Fighting Frogs.) Swanie knew this publicity would help Jane. On January 11, he sent a copy of the tribute to Eddie Knopf at MGM, and a warm letter to Jane at the Garden of Allah mentioning the spread. "Elsie hopes I've been looking after you," he added. And he clearly was, in all sorts of ways. His agency had even helped Jane get new license plates from the Virginia Department of Motor Vehicles for Hi Toots.

MGM's huge chrome-and-green Art Deco commissary, which seated more than 2500, brimmed with star power and was renowned for its chocolate malts and chicken soup (the recipe for which came from L. B. Mayer's mother). Early in January, Jane was introduced to Rosalind Russell; shortly after they met, the warm and friendly Roz called to invite her for cocktails at her home followed by dinner at the Clover Club with a group of her friends. Jane was eager to see a movie star's house and astonished to be included, as "writers (especially new ones) are so unimportant out here." Afterwards, she admitted to Dick that she'd had "an awful lot of fun," and "Rosalind herself couldn't be more charming—she is a lovely person." Jimmy Stewart had been there—"of course, because he and 'Roz' are semi-engaged—we danced a lot and talked, nice, natural, but absolutely no stuff." And she'd had a choice celebrity sighting as they were leaving the Clover Club: "La Dietrich [Marlene] was just coming in with the deadpan Earl of Warwick [who acted under the stage name Michael Brooke]" and Loretta Young. "Can't hand Miss D a thing now that I've seen her under the lights. But Loretta looked bewd-i-ful."

Jane eagerly welcomed Roz's warmth, for she found many of the women around her "hard-boiled and appraising and 'jaded' looking— makes one's arteries chill to cope with them." Although the lifestyle was attractive, she assured Dick, "that doesn't mean I approve of this way of living or that I'm not thinking every moment of how to be in it but not of it." She'd thought she was fairly sophisticated until confronted by the "utter lack of idealism" around her. In some cases, she just found people pretentious and unappealing. When she was introduced to the powerful gossip columnist Louella Parsons, for instance, she noticed Parsons "was so TIGHT she could hardly see my hand to shake it—at 4 p.m.'"

Yet Jane seems to have found an ally in the thirty-year-old Russell. A few days after their dinner, they met again at the Vendome Café, a "gourmet paradise" that had become "the most important place to lunch in town." It was gratifying to be welcomed to MGM by a woman who was "truly a nice person, not one of these floozies who vamp their way to fame." Rosalind had always been down to earth and pragmatic about her place in Hollywood; in her short autobiography, *Life Is a Banquet*, she

confessed, "I wasn't a sex symbol and never could be." As fiercely independent interlopers among the glitterati of Hollywood, Jane and Rosalind shared Catholic roots, a background filled with advantages (though
Jane's were more recently acquired), and a love for horses, as well as
great senses of humor and plenty of grit.

As the weeks passed, Jane encountered more celebrities, including
the prolific screenwriter John Lee Mahin, whose credits already included *Treasure Island, Small Town Girl,* and *Captains Courageous.* One day
Mahin introduced her to Clark Gable and Victor Fleming. She'd seen
the still married Gable with Carole Lombard at the Clover Club and
concluded that they made a great pair. Not long afterwards, at a party at
fellow screenwriter Dashiell Hammett's house, she met the "charming"
forty-four-year-old author and critic Dorothy Parker. Miss Parker asked
Jane to call her from the lot so she could lunch with her and her much
younger second husband, writer Alan Campbell, but Jane was hesitant
to do so and probably never did. They both had sharp wits, though Jane's
was far less caustic, and she was much more socially reserved.

Dottie and Alan were Hollywood veterans who had just settled in
at MGM, as Jane did, in January 1938. They'd been hired at close to
two thousand dollars a week to replace another couple on a project for
producer Hunt Stromberg. It was Alan who kept his feisty, moody wife
disciplined and, when he could, away from too much alcohol. But no
one could distract her from her passionate political activism, strong
communist sympathies, and recent despair about the Spanish Civil War.

February 1938 was gray, wet, and, after Jane caught a terrible cold,
downright depressing. She'd already had a persistent ear infection not
easily cured by her well-respected otolaryngologist, Joel Pressman,
whose wife was Claudette Colbert. But what really made things grim
were the layoffs. Everybody at MGM spoke in "hushed whispers because
heads are falling left and right." So many writers were let go that Jane
feared she would be one of them. "From over 100 writers in January
there are now less than 60," she confided to Dick on February 23. The
studio is "getting rid of all the contract people as fast as possible." Each
day more people were gone, though some layoffs were just temporary—
all the writers' contracts, including hers, gave the studio the right to

"make anybody take a six-week layoff without pay any time." To Jane the studio felt like a "morgue" and the writers' offices like a "deserted battlefield."

It didn't help that her first assignment, with the former Broadway producer Laurence Schwab, had gone nowhere, through no fault of her own. Schwab had come to MGM as a specialist in musicals; his best-known picture was 1930's *Good News*, a musical comedy about a college football star who falls for his studious tutor. For about three weeks, Jane pored over various scripts with him, but the executive in charge of musicals, Sam Katz, would not let him produce any of them. So Schwab told her the studio was "giving him the runaround and he would not be making any pictures anytime soon."

But Jane had no reason to fear for her job security. At the end of February, she'd been assigned to a Luise Rainier picture with the working title *Frou Frou*; it was later released, to excellent reviews, as *The Toy Wife*. (Zoe Akins, who had won the Pulitzer Prize for Drama in 1935, wrote the screenplay.) The dialogue Jane contributed made a good impression, and word spread about the talented, industrious new writer on the project. Veteran producer Merian C. Cooper (*King Kong, Little Women*) "liked what he saw" and told her he wanted her to work on a project he was "going to bat for," a story that had run as a serial in the *Saturday Evening Post*.

But then more rains came: "California is the wettest place—when wet—of any I've ever seen," Jane decided in early March, at the beginning of what would turn out to be one of the most severe storms in half a century. "STORM HITS PIX HARD" a *Hollywood Reporter* headline shouted on March 3, after "torrential rains and raging floodwaters swept the studio area of Southern California" creating "widespread havoc in the film industry." An eyewitness to all this mayhem, Jane was shocked by the devastation the storm created in some communities; amused by a huge Warner Bros. rubber whale prop that cascaded down the Los Angeles River; and frustrated without mail, phone, or telegraph service for days. MGM had stopped production when heavy rain "threatened to isolate Culver City completely." Several people were marooned at home or at work, but fortunately there were no fatalities. When the rain finally stopped, five days after the storm began, Jane noticed that California looked "clean and tired. There was a landslide right in the midst of Sunset Boulevard that took two days to clear away—buried a car to the roof, about a block below the Garden of Allah. But now the waters have subsided and the streets are dry again, and the golf courses look less like lakes."

For Jane, the storm turned out to be one of the luckier events of her Hollywood days. "I am doing flood relief in the form of the most draggled little wire haired fox terrier you ever saw," she informed her East Coast beaux. "She was running up and down frantically, looking lost, when I came out of Dave Chasen's restaurant and the doorman said she'd been there since afternoon. I took her home and looked in all the want ads with no sign of an owner. She is a Dream Pup though so I don't mind if I don't find one." For some time, Jane had been extremely eager to have a dog again; as a child she had never been without one. Nevertheless, she kept checking the ads in case the pup belonged to a child. She would never forget how she'd felt when her collie pup, Lassie, died just before she and Dickie left California. In the end, no owner turned up, and Jane fell in love.

The bedraggled dog was unrecognizable once she'd been shampooed and clipped. The groomer said she'd found a real thoroughbred, about a year and a half old, "an exceptionally fine one." The pup was loaded with guts and crazy about the water, diving to the bottom of the hotel pool for rocks. Before long, she was running up and down the halls of the Garden of Allah's main building as if she owned the place. In honor of the ongoing search for the right Scarlett for *Gone with the Wind*, which had preoccupied studio executives and the trades for months, Jane named her new pal Katherine Scarlett O'Hara, and called her Kate.

Dog ownership was integral to the good life in Hollywood, and Kate must have helped Jane feel like she belonged in her new town. Fox terriers were especially popular—Rosalind Russell had one named Cracker, and everyone loved Asta, the canine star of the Thin Man movies. More importantly, Kate put an end to any lingering loneliness Jane might have felt; she had a new best friend who would accompany her everywhere for more than a decade. At times she trusted Kate more than she trusted the people in her life.

With more incentive to find a larger place to live, on March 18 Jane sublet an apartment from a fellow writer at 1414 North Havenhurst Drive. Just a block away from the Garden of Allah, La Ronda (known today as Mi Casa) was an attractive 1927 courtyard complex that had been designed by a distinguished Los Angeles husband-and-wife team, Nina and Arthur Zwebell. Many celebrities had stayed in the building, including Cary Grant in 1934 and 1935 during his short marriage to Virginia Cherrill. Jane's apartment was small, but at least it had a kitchen, and a separate bedroom; she described it as "darling, with an arched ceiling in the drawing room" and a fireplace. "Now I'm spared the acute unhappiness of living in a bedroom. I shall begin staying home and I am reading and writing in earnest," she assured Dick, for she had just been given her first substantial project.

Louis B. Mayer reveled in refined settings, "drawing room comedies," and happy endings, and Jane had been hired for her expertise in this ambiance. In April she started work on *Hold That Kiss*, a romantic comedy starring Maureen O'Sullivan, Dennis O'Keefe, and Mickey Rooney. The project was in production under the seasoned eye of John W. Considine Jr., the producer of *Boys Town*, soon to be one of the most successful films of 1938. *Hold that Kiss* (and the book it was based on) had a simple and time-worn premise: "Hero and heroine both pose as socialites, but all comes out well for they discover they both work for a living." Several hilarious action-packed scenes and misunderstandings occupy a cast of eleven plus a Saint Bernard. Jane felt intense pressure, and seemed happy about it, reporting that "every afternoon we change the dialogue." Edgar J. "Eddie" Mannix (aka "The Fixer"), a key player on Mayer's powerful executive team and vice president of Loew's Inc., would approve the final script on May 13, 1938, less than two weeks before the picture was released.

Two mimeographed copies of Jane's 110-page script for *Hold That Kiss* reveal the work she put into it. One is accompanied by a note asking Edith Farrell, head of the secretarial pool, to "divide this among several girls so I can get it back this afternoon." Nonetheless, the "Original Story and Screen Play" credit went solely to a man named Stanley Rauh. Jane had this to say on April 22: "The little blue serge picture is finished at last and no credit lines for anybody except the man who wrote the original story . . . He came and wept and put on an act and so the rest of us (Brad Foote, Ogden Nash and I) just signed the waiver and that was that. Rauh is trying very hard to get a job [contract] with MGM and seems to think that if he has total credit he will get one. Not that it's much of a picture to want one's name on any-how." Among other things, she wished the movie had a stronger cast. Jane knew enough not to complain at work, but the lack of credit must have bothered her because she filed away a tiny unidentified clipping: "That great dialogue job, uncredited, on MGM's 'Hold that Kiss' is the work of a 22-year-old mag writer, Jane Hall—and she's a doll." However, critics found much more to like in the film than Jane had, even if they did give Rauh credit for dialogue that she had written.

Swanie again urged Jane to keep up with her own writing whenever she had a break between projects. He suggested she turn several of her stories into a collection, perhaps using the character of Virginia teen-ager Liz McKelvey as a unifying element. A "cute title" for the book, he thought, might be "Elizabeth—Maker of Men." "It would help her no end out here," Swanie observed, "because a book is always more impressive than scattered magazine stories." Jane seemed open to the idea, but she also reminded Swanie that she could hardly report "any new sales of stories when it's not in my contract to sell anything to anybody but Metro." She could, however, showcase her nonfiction skills, with the studio's approval. Her first opportunity to be a Hollywood reporter came that spring.

Although the editor of *Good Housekeeping*, William Bigelow, felt Jane had compromised her future as a serious author by moving to the West Coast, he decided to try her out on a new assignment: He wanted an article from the set of *Three Comrades,* the film on which F. Scott Fitzgerald had labored so unhappily. The novel had been serialized in *Good Housekeeping* in 1937. Elsie wired Jane on March 29: BIGELOW GETTING HOLLYWOOD ARTICLES FREE FROM STAFF WRITERS THROUGH

PUBLICITY DEPARTMENTS BUT AGREES TO PAY YOU TWO HUNDRED FIFTY DOLLARS FOR THREE THOUSAND WORD ARTICLE. DOES NOT WANT USUAL PRESS AGENT STUFF OR FAN MAGAZINE STYLE MUST HAVE JANE HALL PERSNALITY [*sic*]. GREAT RUSH. MONDAY APRIL FOURTH DEADLINE HERE BETTER SEND AIR MAIL. Jane had barely a week to turn it in.

Jane's article "Three Comrades—and a Girl," told in the spirited, friendly voice that Mr. Bigelow knew would appeal to his readers, appeared in June 1938, just as the movie was released. Readers meet Jane at her desk in a stucco cubicle shaded by Venetian blinds in the "new writers building" which, she said, those in the know call the "neuritis building." Jane admitted that she'd started to feel like a "literary Zombie" until she received word that Mr. Bigelow "thought it would be fine if one of his exiled writers could whip down to the *Three Comrades* set and find out what was happening."

The first thing Jane learned was that "movie publicity departments have definite ideas about just what is safe to tell a Reading Public . . . Anything really *intime* that penetrates these careful lines will simply be the power of mine over Metro's." On the way to Stage 12 to interview the *Three Comrades* stars, she encountered Clark Gable: "Clark goes out of his way to be a good gent to everybody on the campus; he stopped his gleaming wooden [station] wagon and said well, how was everything Working Out?" Jane felt self-conscious—she'd not worn her smoothest clothes that day—and she "muttered something unintelligible" as she dug her foot into a pansy bed. "Mr. Gable is the one movie big shot I've met who is really taller, tanner, and terrificer than even the fan mag pluggers would have you believe," she gushed. (Many considered Gable to be "the rock upon which MGM was built.")

Director Frank Borzage met her on Stage 12. "Chummy," "paternal," and sunburned from playing polo, he took her over to speak with Robert Taylor, a "killeroo" who was about to film "the first bathing suit sequence of his cinematic career." Jane's reaction to Taylor in blue swim trunks was just the sort of tidbit that Bigelow liked: "In spite of being one of H-Wood's best dressed men—the Taylor lad is really Built. From the floor on up. I kept reminding myself that I was Jane. Everyone in the world knows—to meet Robert Taylor *in the flesh*—that something practically anatomical is supposed to happen to you. I clutched my folding canvas chair and watched the fog roll in." In the spring of 1938, Robert Taylor was seriously involved with Barbara Stanwyck, whom he would marry a year later. Stanwyck biographer Victoria Wilson confirms Jane's impression: "Women moviegoers found him irresistibly handsome and romantic, the epitome of physical perfection: handsomely poised, handsomely dressed, handsomely scrubbed and polished. Bob was called 'pretty boy' and 'beautiful Robert Taylor.' "

Jane decided that Taylor was not luscious in an artificial way, but just very photogenic. She deplored the fan magazines that overwhelmed young actors such as Taylor, one of many small-town boys "turned into a Legend overnight." "I guess the topsoil of their casual conversation has been so eroded by dramatizing every triviality for an avid public," she decided when he appeared somewhat reticent. She was surprised to find that many stars "hardly know what to say in an interview." Taylor, who tossed on a yellow robe for his meeting with Jane, acknowledged that he was not good at this sort of thing. Wilson finds that he was, in fact, innately reserved—as a child he had much preferred to play by himself or care for his animals. So Jane didn't get any great scoops from Taylor. She was impressed nevertheless by the rugged-looking "answer to a Prom girl's prayer." He seemed perfectly cast as the "young, idealistic but bitter Erich Lohkamp," and he liked the role.

Jane spoke next with Margaret Sullavan, whose "streamlined chassis was clad in a Navy polka-dotted swimsuit." Taylor and Sullavan made a great on-screen couple, she thought, even though Margaret's character, Patricia Hollman, died during the film. Jane was relieved that Margaret was "not a Glamour Girl. She has wide, frank eyes, a tucked-in upper lip, and a great deal of self-confidence. She combines beauty and character, humor and arrogance, with really rather special results." Her husky voice was one of her most striking qualities. She seemed surprisingly natural, sporting a soft pageboy that had not acquired the "texture of horsehair" from too much dying and bleaching.

Margaret told Jane that she loved working with Taylor but she, too, did not enjoy talking about herself. She would have preferred to interview Jane, she said, just as she was called away to do another scene. Jane learned a bit more about her during a lunch with photographer Johnny Swope, who worked for Sullavan's husband, Broadway agent and producer Leland Hayward. Even though Miss Sullavan seemed to be "the sort of person who gives nothing second-best," Swope confirmed that her work was never more important to her than her husband and her nine-month-old baby, Brooke.

"My Big Regret in doing this production slant was not getting a quote from Robert Young," Jane explained to her readers; Young was "one of the handsomest and most popular men on the Lot." But on the last day of shooting (this time on Stage 29), Borzage introduced her to Franchot Tone, in "dirty overalls and a crew haircut," playing the part of "intense, controlled, self-sacrificing" Otto Koster. Tone, like the other actors, was tough to interview. He felt sick and exhausted by the time Jane got to him, which was unfortunate, because in Wilson's estimation Tone was a "handsome, erudite, socially prominent young actor, potentially the best actor of his generation," who "loved the New York stage and hated Hollywood." Jane had seen him the night before with his wife, "Joanie" (Joan Crawford), at the Café La Maze. He "sighed at me unhappily," she admitted, as they took off toward a trailer that served as his dressing room. Confronted by his "tense-tired-boyish" look, Jane was speechless. The most he would reveal was that he liked playing Koster, and low comedy, but he did not enjoy sophisticated high-life roles. Now that shooting had ended, all he wanted to do was go home and go to bed—so she let him. Even had Jane known that Tone's marriage to Crawford was falling apart—they would divorce in 1939—that was not information she would have (or could have) added to the article.

Jane's piece concluded with the disclosure that she'd learned "a great Truth about the movie tribe": These stars were not average people underneath their dramatic craftsmanship. "They aren't human at all; they're pixies. You have to see it to believe it." Sullavan was the perfect example, "wisecracking and chewing gum a mile a minute, and then stepping into the life of a girl in war-wrecked Germany and making her suffering and courage a real and thrilling thing." Jane volunteered that

Taylor and Tone were equally adept at playing heartbreaking scenes with "a special kind of magic." She had, she wrote, "found out what actors and actresses are All About."

Embittered after his disappointing experience working on the *Three Comrades* screenplay, F. Scott Fitzgerald had, perhaps hopefully, predicted that the movie would be " 'the most colossal disappointment of Metro's year.' " He was mistaken. It grossed more than $2 million, and netted $472,000. Plus, Margaret Sullavan received a Best Actress nomination from the Academy. (She lost to Bette Davis, who had the title role in *Jezebel*).

It was true that reviews of the film were mixed; both *Variety* and the *Hollywood Reporter* were critical. However, *New York Times* critic Frank Nugent thought *Three Comrades* was both "beautiful" and "memorable"; he was especially taken with Sullavan's "almost unendurably lovely performance" and Tone's "beautifully shaded portrait of Otto Koster." He was disappointed only by Taylor, who "has his moments of sincerity, but shares them with those suggesting again the charming, well fed, carefully hair-groomed leading man of the glamour school of cinema."

Dick Clarke apparently became quite jealous on reading Jane's description of Robert Taylor. She would only concede that the interview was superficial, and that she "wrote it as I knew Mr. Bigelow, 'the women of America,' and the MGM publicity department wanted it done. Otherwise, I couldn't have sold it at all under my present contract. You are much better built than Taylor my friend."

Jane was also on the defensive with Cliff, who chided her about her session in Franchot Tone's trailer. "Your letter amused me mightily. Is there any comparison between a hotel bedroom and a dressing room trailer in the middle of a set teeming with people?" Later that summer she would add, "the *Three Comrades* blurb I wrote for G. Housekeeping, was, I know, not good—I disliked it intensely in the writing. But I had a letter from my agent today saying that Mr. Bigelow, the editor, told one of his other clients that it was the *best* Hollywood article they had ever had. Isn't that swell? And—I guess I told you—Cosmo wants a series of them." Harry Burton, the editor of *Cosmopolitan*, was not about to be outdone by *Good Housekeeping*.

DICK AND CLIFF WERE BOTH frustrated that Jane would not be back in New York in June as she'd originally planned. Her letters to them (it's likely neither one knew much about the other) indicate that they were both floundering as they tried to succeed in very different careers, though Cliff stayed on a steadier track as a pilot than Dick did in the insurance business. In her letters, Jane frequently emphasized how much she valued their friendship, yet she urged them both to get out and enjoy themselves just as she was doing. Clearly what she also craved was their admiration, perhaps not even realizing how much the early loss of her father had left a permanent vacuum in her heart.

By April, it was obvious how much Jane enjoyed her new home. "There is such contrast out here Dick, it is sort of fun. Friday night I had dinner with Liz and Jock Whitney [John Hay Whitney, son of Payne, horseman, diplomat, financier, art collector and much more] and last night with Mr. and Mrs. Groucho Marx! . . . I'm having lunch with 'Liz' [Whitney] tomorrow. She's one of the most charming women I've ever met." A couple of weeks later Jane mentions meeting Robert Benchley at a dinner. "He's quite a riot and so funny looking, wish you could have met him with me." (Benchley spent the spring and summer as a fixture at the Garden of Allah while acting—and drinking—in Hollywood. A prolific writer, he returned east to his family in the fall; he was the *New Yorker*'s theatre critic until 1940.)

Perhaps most unsettling to Dick was this bit of news: "I'm going to pose for [well-known illustrator and *Cosmopolitan* cover artist] Brad Crandell this afternoon for a sketch. If I had had the time to pose for a full portrait he said he would put me on the cover but I didn't have the time. It would be exciting as I lost 8 pounds." When Jane sent Dick a copy of Brad's sketch, he objected to her new appearance. Brad (who, along with his wife, became a lifelong friend of Jane's) had given her a gorgeous, full-lipped mouth, as he did all his models. Like Margaret Sullavan, Jane had a tucked-in upper lip, but during this period she learned to make it seem fuller with lipstick and a brush, and she never appeared thin-lipped in public again. She shrugged off Dick's disapproval, telling him, "The mouth job is just a matter of lipstick, and of course it's a typical Brad Crandell feat of glamidizing."

Somewhat breathlessly, she added more tales of her escapades that were guaranteed to make Dick jealous, if she'd thought about it: "I've been riding horseback quite a bit with one of the writers [Marion Parsonnet] who has a ranch in San Fernando Valley. I rode about 20 miles on Saturday in dungarees and red leather boots then came back and jumped into evening clothes and had dinner with Jimmy Stewart, Johnny Swope, Hank and Francis Fonda . . .then Johnny and Jim and I went up to Ginger Rogers' (she has an ice cream soda bar) and home about 5 a.m. Sunday to a rodeo and on Sunday night to Venice for heaven's sake which is like Coney [Island] on a slightly nicer scale and home about 11. Meeting all these people naturally makes me very much of a career woman at the moment and no other kind of life seems as attractive. You can understand that can't you?"

Accepting all Jane's fun with good grace was a lot to ask of Dick. Her letters were peppered with mentions of the men she encountered frequently, including Jimmy Stewart's roommate, the photographer Johnny Swope. Jane also commented on how attractive Walter Pidgeon was, their drive in his Lincoln Zephyr, the times she invited him to group dinners. Walter was six foot two, eighteen years her senior, and both elegant and dignified. Jane also found him "realer" than many of the other men she met. Tall, dark, handsome, and older men appealed to her the most. For Walter's part, his interest in her may have been almost paternal—he'd been married to his secretary, Ruth Walker, since 1931 and would remain so until he died in 1984. Jane was a bit naïve and infatuated; her letters to Dick and Cliff do not mention his wife.

Cliff was more worried about the extent of Jane's friendship with her new colleague, Marion Parsonnet. He was ten years older than Jane and still unmarried; she'd admitted to Cliff that he had more than a collegial interest in her. Jane found him "one of the most interesting men she had met in Hollywood but I'm not going in for moonlight these nights." Instead she kept focused on her work, digging into a screenplay idea she had come up with at the beginning of May. She and Marion tossed it around for about three weeks before submitting a twenty-four page summary of "Such Mad Fun" to producer Sam Zimbalist. This was the first project Jane had initiated, and she saw it as her chance to prove herself. The setting for this comedy-drama was a world Jane had known well in Manhattan and at Princeton University: An inebriated student invites a dance-hall hostess to Princeton house parties and there are poignant and hilarious consequences when—to his astonishment—she shows up.

Film exhibitors clamored for better product during the spring and summer of 1938; too many of them had used up the pictures they had bought on double-feature programs. They wanted more and higher-quality stories that would appeal to audiences across the country, not just on the coasts. *Hollywood Reporter* editor and publisher Billy Wilkerson, argued that "people are starved for entertainment and, depression or not, still have enough money to buy admissions to be entertained." Meanwhile, the Screen Writers Guild, revived in 1936, competed fiercely for members with the Screen Playwrights to control the bargaining power of writers. On June 14, Wilkerson warned writers to stop fighting with each other and do their jobs: "If the writer were writing instead of fighting, he easily would recognize the requirements of almost any lot and then could sit down to create a story to fit this or that star, or this or that picture demand, take it into his producer and receive a swell reward for the creation." Jane had received a telegram at MGM on June 27 asking her to join the SWG, of which Dorothy Parker was one of the founders, but she couldn't imagine getting involved in anything "so undignified as organized labor"—"It kills me," she exclaimed to Dick, "Dorothy Parker picketed the other day!" In fact, the leftist Dottie had been furious with writers like Jane who "wouldn't join because they were individuals, they were artists, because it wasn't genteel, because they were ladies, they were gentlemen."

Fortunately, Sam Zimbalist read the synopsis of "Such Mad Fun" immediately and, Jane crowed, he "was 'NUTS' about it." This was an important coup—Zimbalist was one of a handful of producers with considerable clout at the studio. During his eighteen years at MGM—where he'd started when he was sixteen—he had produced an array of impressive films. His most recent pictures included *The Crowd Roars*, *Tarzan Finds a Son!*, and *Lady of the Tropics*. Zimbalist would later produce *King Solomon's Mines* and *Quo Vadis* (both of which received Best Picture nominations) before dying of a heart attack in 1958 while filming *Ben-Hur*. He was confident enough in Jane to ask her to write a 150-page treatment of the story on her own.

"My gosh – a book!" she exclaimed to Dick, who wondered whether she would ever return to Manhattan. It was a big responsibility that sounded even more official once the *Hollywood Reporter* stated on its front page, on June 14, "Jane Hall Scripts 'Fun.'" Jane hastily bought a brand-new Royal Portable and started typing. She worked feverishly for the next several weeks, often continuing to work at home after hours, with Kate curled up in a green leather chair nearby. In Culver City, she had shifted gears to create action-packed scenes, a faster-paced narrative, and more screen-friendly dialogue, with lots of noisy input from her colleagues. She wondered how much her original story would need to change for a medium that provided such an important escape for Depression-era audiences.

During this time, Metro offered to extend her six-month contract, which was about to expire. Jane now earned more than most writers— five hundred dollars a week, retroactive to June 28—though quibbling over the details of her new contract between Swanie and Floyd Hendrickson in MGM's legal department would drag on through August.

While she churned out the pages of her treatment, Jane sent ever more cheerful missives to Dick and Cliff about her busy life. In a letter to Dick typed in red "from Siberia," she acknowledged that she no longer felt like an outsider; she "genuinely liked Hollywood (with the tolerance that one feels for anything that's pleasant but that they can't admire). People whose stock in trade is their looks, their actions etc. are not the world's most interesting companions or truest friends by a long shot. But Hollywood is a luxurious, amusing, and stimulating place." In mid-July, Jane turned in her treatment, but there was no time for a break. *Cosmopolitan* wanted a profile of one of the magazine's favorite authors, Viña Delmar, for a Cosmopolite of the Month column. Delmar's new novel, *Hollywood Dynasty*, was about to be serialized in the magazine. Elsie wired the details: I HAVE JUST HAD WORD FROM MRS. DELMAR ASKING YOU TO TELEPHONE HER CRESTVIEW 59998. COSMOPOLITAN WILL PAY FOUR HUNDRED DOLLARS FOR TWENTY FIVE HUNDRED

TO THREE THOUSAND WORDS, AND WANTS COPY BY AUGUST TENTH. Although in the end this piece would not come out until a year later, thanks to the unpredictable nature of publishing, Jane had been given only a few weeks to finish the job.

She wasn't quite sure how to begin, but Mrs. Delmar made it easy by suggesting they go out to the races at Hollywood Park in her chauffeur-driven car. "Pert, and dark and sunburned," with a shoulder-length bob pulled behind the ears, Mrs. Delmar didn't seem like a writer, and "this is the nicest thing you can say about anybody," Jane told her readers. At thirty-five, Viña Delmar was "one of America's most successful fiction-eers." She was also a success in Hollywood: In 1937 she'd been nominated for an Academy Award for her screen adaptation of the play *The Awful Truth*. Naturally, Jane was curious about her perspective on Hollywood. Mrs. Delmar swore that most of the people she knew were "fairly normal." "I was all set for a debate on how you can write realistically about a place as fabulous as the movie colony without a satirical punch. But as soon as Mrs. Delmar began to talk I realized that she is too intently sincere, not only about her writing but about the people in it, to rule her characters with the modern rod-of-Irony." Viña Delmar's primary complaint about writing for the movies was that "it takes the fun away when you have to work with one eye on the censors."

Mrs. Delmar's straight-shooting manner and simplicity appealed to Jane. She wore three charm bracelets; one held "a tiny golden cross fastened next to a miniature Hebraic mezuzah." Both were gifts from her husband, Eugene, "as foils—to protect her Jewish blood from Gentile and vice versa." Jane took Marion Parsonnet with her to visit the Delmars' Monterey colonial on Rodeo Drive. They settled in at the playhouse near the swimming pool and learned that Viña Delmar much preferred bridge and anagrams to "food, parties and active sports of any kind." But the real center of her life was her husband and their thirteen-year-old son, Gray. "She's really just one third of a very happy family," Jane concluded, in much the same way that she had written about Margaret Sullavan. Meeting these two women who seemed to have it all may have given Jane some encouraging thoughts on the feasibility of combining marriage with a career.

Throughout the summer she remained quite social, going to occasional small parties, to see *The Barber of Seville* at the Hollywood Bowl ("a wonderful setting for music of any kind"), and to Ensenada, where she fell in love with the bright blue sky and pristine white beach. A high point of July was her weekend trip to Catalina on Joe Mankiewicz's eighty-five-foot schooner. She described Mankiewicz as "the boy wonder of Hollywood" and told her aunt Rose that at only twenty-nine, he "makes 3Gs a week and a 10G bonus on every picture." Marion was there, as were composer Franz Waxman and his wife, plus the Viennese actress Rose Stradner, whom Mankiewicz would marry in 1939.

Her most thrilling news came at the end of the month, when MGM executives responded to her film treatment. "That story I did was accepted with enthusiasm beyond anything I had imagined or expected—and they want me to do the screenplay and go into production immediately. . . . [Eddie] Knopf 'thanking me' for 'coming thru for him' etc. etc. . . . [I]t is a great satisfaction to be the white-haired girl for a change, after six months of being just 'that girl writer.' (I mean that WOMAN writer!! At what age does one stop and the other begin?)" Her letters home were filled with excitement as well as misgivings. "Mr. Zimbalist feels that I can do the screenplay by myself—with a solo credit—but I'm very anxious to have Marion work on it with me. . . . He was such a help on the synopsis and is so literally 'simpatico' and I don't feel at all positive about my ability as a playwright. However, it is almost frightening to find these other people so enthusiastic, frankly—I wish I had half as much confidence in the story as they have." Nonetheless, she'd been shuttled from one producer to the next since arriving at Metro, and felt greatly relieved to have her own project. "It is such a great SPIRITUAL satisfaction to have had this treatment accepted so enthusiastically after being pushed around for so many months." Women screenwriters had done quite well at MGM in the early 1930s—especially when Irving Thalberg had been alive. Though Mayer was less supportive of writers, it seemed that Jane had now found her niche in Hollywood.

That fall, *Daily Variety* concluded that moviegoers had tired of "sophisticated comedies . . . the glittering, heartless smartcrackeries that detoured from the common touch." Film historian Catherine Jurca remarks that glamour and glitz alone were no longer enough to hold the interest of moviegoers, who now sought more "ordinary, true-to-life characters and situations." Although the two biggest moneymakers in 1938 were Walt Disney's animated fairy tale *Snow White* and Fox's *Alexander's Ragtime Band*, there was more than enough room for comedy-dramas like "Such Mad Fun." Besides, this genre had long served as the mainstay of Hollywood's box-office appeal, especially for middle-class audiences.

Jane cautioned her aunt and uncle against expecting to see her any-time soon: "If Zimbalist is the slave driver they say he is I'll be eating dinner in the commissary." She explained to Dick that she hoped to see him in another two months—in the end, he would have to wait until Christmas. But Jane had never been happier. She wrote and revised all summer and into the fall. Finally she could head to the commissary for lunch with the self-confidence of a writer with a mission—one who had also been accepted in the professional and social circles of scenarists and producers. Colleagues recognized her; they smiled at her and laughed at her wisecracks. And she was going to write a great script, one that would not only have plenty of snappy witticisms and satirical twists but would have characters with soul and heart, some of whom learned important lessons. Jane had fashioned several true-to-life and down-to-earth characters for the movie and felt thrilled, if a bit apprehensive, about the work ahead. She was blissfully unaware of the many challenges she and Marion would face over the next nine months.

*Marion Parsonnet at Metro-Goldwyn-Mayer. From
the Collections of the Margaret Herrick Library.*

NINE

"Everything You Are and Do"

THE SYNOPSIS OF "SUCH MAD FUN" OPENS WITH A SCENE THAT IS rife with class division on the train from New York's Penn Station to Princeton Junction. The eighteen-year-old protagonist, a working girl from Corn Falls, Kansas, serves as a foil for the pampered socialites she meets on the way to Princeton University, where much of the movie will take place:

The sign on the door of the train compartment says: "Ladies."

Inside the washroom, combing her hair in front of a mirror, is Daphne Graves, a New York debutramp. She has chic, breeding, a certain amount of beauty, and a great deal of self-satisfaction. In marked contrast is the girl at the adjoining basin, Lana Peters. Lana is prettier and more appealing, but definitely—flashy. She is a ten-cents-a dance hostess—asked to Princeton House Parties by a shnapped-up campus wisey who finished his last weekend's bender at the Orpheum "Dance Palais." Friendly and direct, she speaks to Daphne. Daphne, much more formal, realizes after two minutes conversation that this girl does not Belong. She cannot orient her, but she *does* recognize this little twitch's effervescence and enthusiasm (about her date and bid to Princeton) as positive earmarks of an Alien. However, she is intrigued by Lana's in- genuousness. With the subtle malice of one pretty girl toward another, she takes her back and introduces her to some of the crowd.

. . . The attitude of these girls (sensing that Lana is an outsider) is tolerant and amused. Quite unbeknownst to her, they put her through a course of very feminine and sophisticated heckling. . . . Let it be mentioned here that Lana is not the typical New York "babe"—she has but recently arrived from Podunk. She's only eighteen, and her hard-boiled knowingness is mostly surface.

When the train reaches its destination, Lana's date never picks her up—he's passed out after drinking too much. What follows is a scornful portrait of drinking, debauchery, and callous behavior among some members of the smart young set during Princeton House Parties: "Every successful prom-trotter in New York counts her bid as a fitting climax to the season's manhunt. Bars are down, rules are off, and for three days of college festivities the campus is virtually uninhibited. The boys start tying on their jugs on Thursday and are well along by Friday." Jane's summary goes on to say: "In a series of flashes at the tea dance [at Princeton's Cloister Inn] late Saturday afternoon we get a very clear-cut picture of the intrigue, cutthroat competition, and actual heartbreak that form the strata underneath this Mad Mad Fun." The phrase encapsulates the glamour and pleasure of these melees, and also their inherent rottenness. Jane's description may also indicate why she had been so reluctant to stay at house parties with Jack Hall for the entire weekend.

By late August, Jane had turned her treatment into 190 heavily annotated pages; she and Marion began to collaborate on the first of several drafts of what would become a shooting script. The work became "trying physically and mentally," for Jane unexpectedly received another assignment. Elsie had shown her August treatment to *Cosmopolitan,* and Harry Burton contracted to buy it as a "book-length novel" for his December issue. Jane had less than three weeks to convert the treatment into a second new format. She worked on it "at odd moments and at night." "Today I was at Metro from 9 a.m. to 7 p.m. in conference and dictating," she complained, and "now I must write some more thousands of words . . . it kills me not to have the time to do anything LIKE a good job on the novel."

The work for *Cosmopolitan* exposed a knotty problem. Back in April, the magazine had finally published Jane's 1937 story with a similar title, "Such Mad, Mad Fun." Because that tale had nothing to do with her Hollywood narrative, the title for both the movie and the novel had to be changed, and that caused considerable friction. MGM decided to rename the movie "Maiden's Prayer." On September 7, Elsie wired Jane: COSMO SCHEDULING STORY FOR DECEMBER ISSUE OUT NOVEMBER TENTH WOULD HELP TREMENDOUSLY TO GET MANUSCRIPT BY WEDNESDAY [SEPT] THE FOURTEENTH AS TIME VERY SHORT. SEND TWO COPIES AS WANT TO TRY ONE WITH BOOK PUBLISHER. PLEASE WIRE WHETHER PICTURE DEFINITELY TO BE CALLED "MAIDENS PRAYER" AS WILL USE SAME TITLE IF NO LIKELIHOOD OF CHANGE. Jane airmailed her novel over the Rockies on September 13. *Cosmo* loved the story, but not the new title. Without telling the studio, the editors changed "Maiden's Prayer" to "College Weekend" and put Jane's name on the about-to-be-released cover.

MGM was not pleased. The studio insisted that the magazine revert to "Maiden's Prayer" to match the film. At great expense, *Cosmo* had the cover plates destroyed and changed the title. Then MGM reversed its decision a third and final time; the movie would be called *These Glamour Girls*. *Cosmo* complied again at the last minute, leaving Jane's name off the cover and her to wonder whether the magazine would ever look at anything she wrote again. "The reason Metro was so damn difficult about it," she told Cliff, "is because they want all the publicity, naturally, since they are making it into a movie—but I would have been so thrilled to see my name on a magazine cover on every newsstand in the country."

There was little time for regrets. Sam Zimbalist drove his writers hard, and this project was no exception; he wanted to go into production in five or six weeks. He assured Jane the movie would be "an IMPORTANT picture—not a B!" Jane had settled into his suite of offices and now spent long days with him, dictating, writing, and brainstorming in endless script conferences. But what a surprise she had on finding F. Scott Fitzgerald in the office next door toiling away on an adaptation of Clare Boothe's hit play *The Women*. The play had several elements in common with *These Glamour Girls*, In both stories elite Manhattan women—middle-aged in Boothe's, college-aged in Jane's—are seen at their worst as they compete for men and revel in catty gossip and shallow values. Jane and Fitzgerald had both been hired, in part, because of their experience with the refined WASP milieu that so intrigued L. B. Mayer, and for their talent in looking below its surface.

Pale, still good-looking, and surprisingly diffident, Fitzgerald appealed to Jane, and they became quite friendly. She was only six years older than his daughter, Scottie, and just the sort of "independent, determined young American woman" who appeared in "Bernice Bobs Her Hair" and Fitzgerald's other commercial stories from early in his career. Though they came from different generations, these two ambitious, hard-working scenarists had similar sensibilities and quite a bit in common: Both had been precocious Catholic children from middle-class homes who enjoyed reading and writing poetry. Throughout high school and college, they were the kind of students who contributed frequently to school publications. In late adolescence, both already yearned to be famous authors—and by then both had been exposed to American upper-class life. At Princeton, as Maureen Corrigan points out in her analysis of *The Great Gatsby*, Fitzgerald, who had acquired a "permanent feeling of never quite measuring up" in his childhood, already hoped to be "one of the greatest writers who ever lived."

Jane and Fitzgerald both regarded high-society decadence with wariness and even contempt, but nonetheless had been seduced by it. Fitzgerald, though, had "felt that he was a member of the lower class" among all the prep-school graduates at Princeton, whereas by the time she entered art school on Manhattan's Lower East Side, Jane had joined the elite and experienced the class divide from the opposite perspective. At Jane's age, Fitzgerald had also written a novel based in part on his experiences at Princeton and with the debutante world—*This Side of Paradise*, which, in 1920, launched his career. His cynical portrait of Princeton appealed to young readers, but it did not please the university's faculty or its president, John Grier Hibben. Fitzgerald responded to Hibben's critique in a letter in which he acknowledged that his years at Princeton had not been "the happiest time in his life." He admitted that the novel "does over accentuate the gayiety + country club atmosphere of Princeton. It is the Princeton of Saturday night in May." In many respects, it is also the Princeton of *These Glamour Girls*: The entitled high-society undergraduates at pre–World War I Princeton in *This Side of Paradise* closely resemble the Park Avenue crowd of young men and women who frequented the university twenty years later in Jane's story.

In both *Paradise* and *Glamour Girls*, the eighteen-year-old protagonist is a participant observer and an outsider through whom the author speaks. *This Side of Paradise* introduces two debutantes, one of whom is derived from a real-life failed romance of Fitzgerald's; the other one, a beautiful, self-centered Manhattan deb named Rosalind, is based partly on Zelda. Like those of Jane's glamour girls, Rosalind's parents insist that she marry someone with money and an upper-class background. She breaks Amory Blaine's Midwestern, middle-class heart, just as Zelda had almost done to Fitzgerald by refusing to marry him until he became more established; his first book contract had finally reassured her that he could give her the lifestyle she felt she deserved.

As soon as his novel was published, Fitzgerald and Zelda embarked on a riotous, decadent life of parties, travel, and continuous boozing; for a time, they had seemed an ideal match. Fitzgerald scholar Matthew J. Bruccoli observed that Scott "shared the responsibility for the way they lived because it was what part of him wanted. They were collaborators in extravagance." Throughout the mid-twenties, Fitzgerald worked as hard as he played, in spite of his wild, somewhat unpredictable life with Zelda. In fact, as is well-documented by Zelda's biographer Nancy Milford, in those early years his productivity increased because of, not in spite of, his wife, who was herself an author, as well as an artist and a dancer. Zelda's collected writings include magazine stories, a play, a novel, and multiple short stories. She acted as a sounding board for Fitzgerald, and, at times, he drew on her letters and diaries in his own work.

Starting in 1925, after the publication of *The Great Gatsby*, he'd found it harder to focus over long periods of time. Alcohol took its toll, as did the ups and downs of life with Zelda, whose mental health declined dramatically until it truly disintegrated after 1930. In his biography, Bruccoli pointed to "a subject that runs through Fitzgerald's work—the servitude of a man to a woman." Though he now began to feel trapped in Zelda's tragic circumstances, he would never abandon her. He understood the meaning of mad fun more than anyone else Jane would meet in Hollywood; for years he had suffered its consequences. Often reluctant to socialize, he felt like an outsider in Hollywood, which he called "a Jewish holiday, a Gentile's tragedy."

Yet Fitzgerald was glad to be working on *The Women*—he admired Clare Boothe's work and found Hunt Stromberg to be one of "the pleasantest people in the industry." Fitzgerald wanted to understand the characters' motivations, and tried to turn the play's protagonist, Mary Haines, into a woman who was " 'active, intelligent, and courageous,' rather than 'passive, simple, and easily influenced.' " Neither Stromberg nor director George Cukor wanted major changes made to Boothe's Broadway hit, and the script would be turned over to Jane Murfin and Anita Loos, who received credit on the film.

While Fitzgerald created dialogue that "was not regarded as bitchy enough" for *The Women*, the perimeter of his office floor was lined with empty bottles of Coke that he used as a stimulant and sugar fix while on the wagon. Jane found him to be "a charming burned-out genius of 40 or so—and the only celeb I have met outside of possibly Gable, who does not disappoint acutely." Late that summer, as she produced her own acerbic banter for the glamour girls, Jane enjoyed their camaraderie. Writers often spent time in each other's offices, and even if Jane and Fitzgerald didn't actually discuss the concerns that weighed on them—both were very private, and it's impossible to know if they did—they surely acknowledged the parallels in their past experiences.

In September 1938, right after Jane mailed her novel to *Cosmopolitan*, Fitzgerald had a short, troubling visit from Scottie, who was about to enter Vassar. They "had some pretty hot talk" and, Fitzgerald told Harold Ober, he "wasn't at all pleased with her attitude on anything." Elsewhere he noted that she already showed "tendencies toward being a play-girl." His hopes for his daughter were revealing and ambitious; he'd given her weighty advice in a letter that summer:

When I was your age I lived with a great dream. The dream grew and I
learned how to speak of it and make people listen. Then the dream divided
one day when I decided to marry your mother after all, even though I knew
she was spoiled and meant no good to me. I was sorry immediately I had
married her, but being patient in those days, made the best of it and got to
love her in another way. You came along and for a long time we made quite
a lot of happiness out of our lives. But I was a man divided—she wanted me
to work too much for her and not enough for my dream . . . . She realized
too late that work was dignity and the only dignity and tried to atone for it
by working herself but it was too late and she broke and is broken forever.

He told Scottie he had made a mistake in marrying her mother because they belonged to "different worlds." What really scared him, he
wrote, was that Zelda "never knew how to use her energy—she's passed
that failing on to you." For a long time, he had hated Zelda's mother for
giving her such bad habits. He "never wanted to see again in this world
women who were brought up as idlers. . . . I think idlers seem to be a
special class for whom nothing can be planned, plead as one will with
them—their only contributions to the human family is to warm a seat
at the common table." Fitzgerald was convinced that Zelda had cheated
him out of his dream. His main hope was that Scottie would use her talents wisely. He warned her not to take a drink before she turned twenty
or people would assume she was just like her parents. Above all, he hated
the thought that she might start running around with the debutante
crowd: "Never boast to a soul that you're going to the Bachelors' Cotillion. I can't tell you how important this is. For one hour of vainglory you
will create a different attitude about yourself. Nothing is as obnoxious as
other people's luck." All that fall he kept honing in on this same theme,
that "debutante parties in New York are the rendezvous of a gang of professional idlers, parasites, pansies, failures . . . the very riffraff of social
New York." Had he and Jane discussed this subject, she would have had
a lot to say about the dangers of alcohol, or about immersing oneself in
a hedonistic lifestyle instead of focusing on more worthwhile pursuits.

In researching this book, I was struck by the fact that so many of
the challenges Jane would one day confront were ones that Fitzgerald

thought about often as he tried to steer his daughter toward a mean-
ingful life and away from the extravagant and destructive behavior that
had defined his early years with Zelda. Had they lived, Jane's parents
could have cautioned her about the choices that she would make; their
priorities were quite different from those of Jane's guardians. But then
again, had her parents lived, Jane's life would have taken a totally different path.

In late September, Fitzgerald brought Jane a copy of *Tender Is the Night*.
For nine years, between 1925 and 1934, he had struggled to write this
psychological novel of Dick Diver's harrowing journey toward disinte-
gration after he marries the wealthy Nicole "out of his need to be needed,
and to be used." At several points in the book, Fitzgerald "mercilessly exposed" the details of Zelda's mental condition as he developed the character of Nicole Diver; the book is a cautionary tale pervaded by a "mood
of loss and waste." Morris Dickstein believes it is "primarily about money
and society as a trap, a temptation, especially for the gifted man." As
Fitzgerald and Jane both knew firsthand, phony values and a flamboyant
lifestyle of glamour and glitz could likewise ensnare a gifted woman.

The copy he gave Jane had a sunny, arresting cover image of a hill-
side village overlooking the Mediterranean. The brilliant primary colors
and tranquil scene belie the book's somber contents. Jane was deeply
affected by the inscription:

> *For Jane Hall*
> *In memory of those years together while I was writing this book—*
> *her tireless help and encouragement—*
> *the way she slaved for me at menial chores to make it possible—*
> *I dedicate this little sheaf of woodland pipings*
> *from her Chattel*
> F. Scott *("Pretty Boy")* Fitzgerald Metro-Goldwyn-Mayer 1938

Writing about it the next day, she mused: "Just think, Dick, being
able to joke when one has had the tragic life that his has been, and the
book, of course, is one of the saddest ever written. (Or so they tell

me—I haven't had a chance to read it yet.)" What did Fitzgerald say when he gave his fellow screenwriter this book? Did he apologize for its flaws? Or was he in an instructive mood, as he always was with Scottie? If so, the book may have been his warning to Jane about the consequences of marrying the wrong person, and the seductive power of wealth, alcohol, and a world of superficiality and showiness.

Fitzgerald used the words "from her Chattel" above his signature at least a few other times in messages to women. He presented *Tender Is the Night* to Lillian Gish in 1937 with the inscription, "For Lillian Gish My Favorite Actress On the occasion of her 1st visit to New York, of which this book, is a practical guide from Her Chattel, F. Scott Fitzgerald." In 1939, while Fitzgerald struggled with tuberculosis, he presented *Tales of the Jazz Age* (1922) to his nurse, Anne Wilson, "from her chattel," adding in facetious quotation marks, "We were happy in Switzerland—will we ever be so happy again?"

During his sojourn in Hollywood, Fitzgerald found companionship and solace with the gossip columnist Sheilah Graham, though their relationship became volatile when he drank. According to Bruccoli, his "feelings about his liaison with Sheilah were ambivalent. . . . He needed Sheilah and loved her; yet his Puritan streak disapproved of their arrangement, which was circumspect by Hollywood standards." Though he'd sent her a bouquet of violets with a card that likewise read "from her Chattel," Sheilah believed that Scott was still "very much in love" with Zelda while he worked in Hollywood.

To be someone's chattel—their personal property or slave— suggests tongue-in-cheek humility or, more likely, Fitzgerald's genuine gratitude to the recipient. Maureen Corrigan emphasizes Fitzgerald's lifelong self-deprecating behavior, and believes he "always prostrated himself before those he revered or thought were his betters." Therein may lie one key as to why he used the word "chattel." Or the word could be related to Fitzgerald's theme of the subservience of men to women. But Jane could not have known during the exhilarating and yet lonesome summer and fall of 1938 how many life-altering decisions she and Fitzgerald would share.

The addition of "Pretty Boy" to Fitzgerald's signature may have been inspired by Fitzgerald's interest in his own appearance, or by the fact that Jane's effusive interview with Hollywood's "Pretty Boy," Robert Taylor, had just been published that summer in *Good Housekeeping*. Given their shared experiences with *Three Comrades*, a discussion about the film and its cast would have been natural.

Early in November, Fitzgerald related to Harold Ober that he was "back at work on a new job that may be something really good—Mme Curie for Greta Garbo. It was quite a plum and I'm delighted after the thankless months spent on fixing up leprous stories." However, on the day after Christmas, he wired Ober: METRO NOT RENEWING TO MY GREAT PLEASURE BUT WILL FINISH CURIE THERE'S LOTS OF OTHER WORK OFFERED. He claimed he did not know why MGM had let him go and ranted: "Baby am I glad to get out! I've hated the place ever since Monkeybitch [Mankiewicz] rewrote 3 Comrades!" A year later, Fitzgerald admitted to Leland Hayward that he "didn't get along with some of the big boys at Metro."

Fitzgerald never did receive a credit on *Madame Curie*; the movie went through several transformations before it was finally released in 1943 with Greer Garson as the star. His official end date at MGM was January 27, 1939. By then he was no longer Jane's office neighbor; since January 6 he had been on loan to David O. Selznick as one of many writers who at various times worked on *Gone with the Wind*.

During the last two years of his life, Fitzgerald would have a rough time making it as a freelancer, in part because of his bouts of heavy drinking. He found it hard to believe that neither Harold Ober nor Maxwell Perkins would advance him any more loans. He did manage to produce *The Pat Hobby Stories*, which chronicled the life of a depressed hack screenwriter in Hollywood, for *Esquire* magazine, though money remained a constant worry. And he made considerable progress on a working draft of the first novel he had written since *Tender Is the Night*. Based on the career of Irving Thalberg, *The Love of the Last Tycoon* is the story of Hollywood mogul Monroe Stahr; Matthew Bruccoli notes that the book is now considered to be "the best novel written about the movies." Stahr, he writes, "is an archetypal American hero, the embodiment of the American Dream; A Jay Gatsby with genius." Despite his best efforts, Fitzgerald's health became increasingly precarious, as did his relationship with Sheilah—it was so hard for him to stay away from alcohol. In 1940 he would give Frances Kroll, his young secretary during the last twenty months of his life, a copy of *Tender Is the Night* with a humorous inscription that read: "In memory of those happy years together on the Rivierra [*sic*] which inspired this book from her admirer." The handwriting is not as firm as it was in his inscription to Jane two years earlier, but in 1940 Fitzgerald's hold on life was not as steady either.

In September 1938, Jane decided that her temporary sublet at La Ronda had "gotten so junky" she "couldn't stand it any longer." She leased another new apartment in the same neighborhood, in a more elegant, somewhat more expensive complex called Brandon Hall where she enjoyed "a grand bedroom looking down three stories into a clump of pepper trees." At night, the Hollywood lights twinkled in the distance. It looked like " 'House-Beautiful' and not cheap and pseudo-Spanish like most of these places."

By then, Jane had been in Hollywood for nine months without a visit home. Her brother Dickie, who now had his doctorate, boasted that he was "the only new National Science Fellow in Mathematics in the United States"; between September 1938 and June 1939 he could be found at the University of Pennsylvania, leaving Jane on her own in California. She continued to correspond with Dick Clarke, trying without success to boost his morale after his efforts to launch his own insurance business failed. Still living with his parents, Dick's low spirits intensified after the Clarkes sold their large home in Hamilton Heights to move to an apartment on East Eightieth Street. Even with the pressure at work, Jane vowed that she hadn't been drinking anything except sherry or the occasional cocktail; she pleaded with Dick not to drink too much. "Have you still got such a hot, unreasonable temper?" She knew alcohol had a terrible impact on Dick, though not as devastating as it had on Scott Fitzgerald.

When she'd come to Manhattan in 1930, at age fifteen, Jane had entered a world that Fitzgerald had been immersed in for more than a decade. His warning to Scottie that "everything you are and do" during late adolescence will define the rest of your life came only ten days before he brought Jane his book. She was living proof that his forecast had some merit, for the experiences she had had at Scottie's age informed most of what she wrote—and at twenty-three she still struggled with whether or not those years had not only changed her material but altered the core of her being.

TEN

"The Accent on Youth"

"THE FIRST RULE OF WRITING SALABLE MATERIAL IS TO REMEMBER to write not what you want to say but what other people want to hear. Which is why so few young writers sell their stuff," Jane explained to Dick in October 1938, as she and Marion labored over the script for *These Glamour Girls*. On the twentieth, she had hopeful news: "We are licking the screenplay at long last into completion by next weekend." The only problem was that Sam Zimbalist had come down with a virus and needed a break. He thought about taking three writers with him to Palm Springs. Jane had her hopes up, but there's no indication she escaped to her beloved desert.

Two weeks later, Jane was convinced that "the movie of this story is going to be much better than *Cosmo*'s novelized 'treatment.' We have kicked the story around for months now but as a result have better angles for dramatization than I ever thought of having." Jane may have been too tough on herself; her novel is a much more in-depth portrait of the glamour girls and their families than would be possible in a fast-paced seventy-nine-minute film. Besides, the print version was not subject to the critical eye of Joseph Breen and his Production Code Administration. It already had hundreds of thousands of likely readers who in November 1938 eagerly looked in their mailboxes or on newsstands for the December *Cosmopolitan* with its iconic Bradshaw Crandell glamour girl on the cover.

WHAT COULD BE MORE DAZZLING than a beautiful blonde in evening attire who looks as if she's expecting her dream prince? Her Art Moderne gold earrings, necklace, and matching bracelet studded with diamonds and rubies complement the rose-colored background and the top of her strapless dress; elbow-length dark violet gloves cover the elegant hands that are folded under her chin. Lee Russell's Fashions in Fiction column in the Over the Editor's Shoulder pages reveals that Crandell's "Cosmopolitan Lady" of December 1938 is Miriam Jordan, "who has appeared on the London stage and in American movies." Miss Jordan's dress and gloves are from Bergdorf Goodman, her jewelry from Marcus & Co. The words "THESE GLAMOUR GIRLS—A COMPLETE BOOK LENGTH NOVEL" have just made it onto the bottom edge of the cover.

As they opened the magazine, readers could select any one of several articles; they might learn what it is like to vote for the first time, or about job opportunities in Alaska or the Philippines; or they could explore the reasons why boys find playing G-man (federal agent) more appealing than playing soldier. They could turn to Elsa Maxwell's insights on heiress Barbara Hutton or to the most recent encouraging research from Stanford University about marital happiness. But if they longed to escape from their worries at work or home through mysteries or romance, they dove into one of the magazines eight short stories or three serials, or Jane's novel, which was listed at the top of the table of contents. That December, *Cosmopolitan*'s contributors included W. Somerset Maugham, Bob Considine, and Adela Rogers St. Johns, who was also profiled by Paul Gallico as the Cosmopolite of the Month. Jane, the editor noted, is "hard at work on the film version of 'These Glamour Girls.'"

In this era before television or the Internet, mass-circulation magazines played a singular role in defining and reflecting women's aspirations. No one knew this better than the sponsors whose ads were the fuel that kept the 160 to 200 pages of *Cosmopolitan* in the mail and on the newsstands each month. Just imagine how Ivory Flakes, Mum deodorant, Pond's cold cream, a Remington or Corona portable typewriter, or a new "glamorous" Plymouth could improve your life. Several of the ads included edifying information: On the back cover of the December *Cosmo*, readers learned that their cocker spaniels (whose origins date back to 1386) have complicated nervous systems just like theirs. The "highly strung" dogs stop frequently to rest, and *Cosmo* readers might try that as well. So "ease up and smoke a Camel," the ad suggests—like reporter Estelle Karon or U.S. Open golf champion Ralph Guldahl, both of whom know that true relaxation comes from puffing on a cigarette.

It was not the purveyors of nicotine but the producers of alcohol who made the biggest investment in persuading *Cosmopolitan*'s readers to buy their goods in 1938. Ads for bourbon are the most prevalent: Schenley's Belmont Kentucky Straight, Four Roses, Paul Jones, and Golden Wedding join Budweiser, Hennessy Cognac, Martini & Rossi vermouth, and Heublein's Club Cocktails in the December issue. Jane's novel, unpaginated and printed in three columns on yellow non-glossy paper, is bracketed by two full-page color ads that are impossible to miss: The first illustration, inside the novel's title page, depicts Samuel de Champlain, who founded Quebec in 1608. Canada's finest explorer is paired with another of "Canada's Finest": Seagram's VO, "deliciously delicate—yet deeply satisfying." At the end of *These Glamour Girls* is an image of the Temple of the Sun in Baalbek, Syria. There, a local curio dealer arranges supper for two Florida businessmen. The "guest of honor?" Canadian Club, of course—"a favorite in 87 countries of the world." Did Jane's readers catch the irony in the placement of these ads on either side of her parody about the pitfalls of drinking too much at a college weekend that "rolled along in its alcoholic way?" (For a full synopsis of the novel *These Glamour Girls*, see Appendix III.)

"Here is the accent on youth that only Jane Hall can give," editor Harry Burton promised on the first page of the novel. In November, he'd already advised his readers to look for Jane's story about "Princeton promtrotters," as well as the forthcoming movie. However, personal names and real place names such as Princeton, Princeton Junction, and Cloister Inn were changed in print, as they would be in the film. Jane had originally called her male protagonist Richard ("Dick") Griswold rather than Philip, and she'd given "Dick's" father a high-profile position as president of the New York Stock Exchange. That job description would not hold sway with either her editor or her producer who may have been wary of alienating Wall Street.

In the 1930s, Jane (and her fellow magazine writers) frequently wrote about class conflict, income disparity, and the criteria that should determine a young woman's (and, to a lesser extent, a young man's) choice of a life partner. The opening paragraphs of *These Glamour Girls* reveal the distinctive personalities and backgrounds of four post debutantes with more than a soupçon of satire. Wide-eyed, dimwitted Mary Rose has a mother who is a blatant social climber—she epitomizes the nouveau riche. Daphne is the season's popular killer debutante, she, too, has a thoroughly pretentious mother. Ann, who is tall, ungainly, and not very pretty, has a mother defined by her WASP roots who feels contempt for anyone not listed in the Social Register. The fourth and most appealing post debutante is Carol Christy, whose situation and unaffected temperament resemble Jane's. Her father has lost his savings in the volatile stock market. Mrs. Christy—an intriguing combination of Daysie Hall and Rose Hicks—is a more empathetic character than the other girls' mothers, but she still hopes Carol will marry her long-standing beau, Phil Griswold, a congenial, wealthy fellow and a big shot on campus who can provide her with long-term financial security. Carol has grown up with Phil, and they are fond of each other but not in love. During the previous summer she fell for Joe Whitbeck, an engaging, down-to-earth young man working his way through Kingston [aka Princeton] University. Joe—her mother insists—will never provide the lifestyle for Carol or her future children to which she has been accustomed.

Jane's female protagonist, Lana Peters, is a vivacious singer and dancer from Kansas. She works as a dime-a-dance girl only because other opportunities have fallen through. Lana also hopes to meet the right man; her small-town roots and plainspoken personality provide a foil for the self-important Park Avenue girls. While some of Jane's male characters are snobs, fortune hunters, or alcoholics, narcissistic women with social power who engage in constant backbiting and lack compassion for the less fortunate are the primary target of her satire. Her novel highlights the widening gulf between the average American family and those who held onto their wealth and sense of entitlement through the Depression.

Lana's initial excitement at being invited to House Parties crumbles once she realizes her invitation came from an inebriated young man who subsequently forgot he asked her. During a weekend where heavy drinking, female backstabbing, and male bemusement define the atmosphere, both she and Carol face difficult choices. Much of the action takes place at "Sanctuary," an undergraduate eating club frequented by upperclassmen that is based on Jane's experiences at Cloister Inn. The debutantes—with the exception of Carol—feel nothing but scorn for Lana's humble rural roots.

As the festivities begin, twenty-three-year-old Betty Ainsbridge, a regular at house parties for years, arrives at Kingston in a custom-made yellow car that, perhaps not coincidentally, evokes Jay Gatsby's car, the ultimate symbol of crass materialism. Eye-catching but worn out, Betty provides pathos for the story. The nineteen-year-olds think she is much too old to be there—it's obvious she's desperate to find a husband. Betty overhears the other girls making fun of her and becomes increasingly depressed. After her frantic attempt to marry an inebriated Kingston boy fails, she commits suicide, much to the debutantes' dismay and embarrassment. Further anguish occurs when the revelers learn through a headline that Phil's father has been indicted for fraud and lost his fortune. Carol and Phil decide to split up, but in the end she does not choose modest Joe, despite her feelings for him. Instead, in the *Cosmopolitan* version, Jane has Carol seek the financial security her parents feel she must have over true love. She drives off in rich Charley Torgler's "yellow dream sled." Readers can take comfort in the fact that Phil and Lana, who have hit it off over the weekend, together head for Manhattan where he will—like an everyman—look for a job.

THROUGH THE FALL, Jane and Marion kept working to shape this story into a viable film. As the scripts were kicked around in story conferences, Jane became so tense that she began smoking cigarettes "while closeted with two or three men all yelling ideas at each other. "Now listen this isn't it," they shouted, "but this may give you something, here is how it is." Through rewrite after rewrite (and retype after retype by the large MGM typing pool) they added dialogue, created film-worthy, action-packed scenes spiced with gags and physical hijinks, deleted anecdotes that would not film well, eliminated some minor characters, and changed names and spellings as well as the ending in response to guidance from Sam Zimbalist and studio executives.

The change that would be most noticeable to those who read the story in *Cosmo* and later saw the movie was the creation of a stronger lead role for the actor who played Phillip Griswold III. Phil wants to be master of his own destiny, to leave the "glittering, inarticulate, so-called civilization" of New York and "Kingsford College" (the screen name is a slight change from the print version's "Kingston"). As the script develops, his character provides a moral center for the story.

In the final shooting script, *These Glamour Girls* opens as a postman arrives at the front door of Ann Van Reichton's lavishly appointed mansion. To the delight of the staff and of Ann, the mail includes an invitation to Kingsford House Parties. Ann is thrilled; her overbearing mother, whom the film audience meets as she enjoys breakfast in bed surrounded by silk and satin, is not. How, she asks, could Ann possibly be interested in "an unregistered nobody" from the Midwest? Although the movie version of Ann remains shy and less sophisticated than Daphne, Mary Rose, or Carol, on screen, not surprisingly, she will be blond and good-looking rather than a plain girl. Ann wins her case to go to Kingsford and the glamour girls are introduced quickly to viewers as they phone each other about the status of their bids to house parties. Carol answers her telephone pretending to be the Christys' nonexistent maid, so the audience instantly realizes that she is in a different financial situation from that of her friends.

Meanwhile, Phil and two of his Kingsford buddies decide to visit the Joylane, a Manhattan dance emporium where he immediately notices attractive, redheaded Lana. In this fast-paced medium of show-don't-tell, slapstick and physicality replace the inner monologue of one character at a time used in the printed version of the story. A fight breaks out between Phil and one of the regulars, a rugged seaman who also has his eye on Lana. The Joylane bouncer throws Phil down the stairs, and Lana comes to his rescue. Lana is more open about her interest in Phil than she had been in the novel because in the movie he's not officially engaged to Carol Christy. Lana admits that this is the first time in six months she's danced with anyone and enjoyed it. Phil returns her interest, and, after warning her that he does not think much of the debauchery at Kingsford during House Party weekend, he invites her to come as his date. The evolution of their friendship is a key part of the movie's narrative. But throughout the weekend Lana is not treated well by Daphne or Mary Rose. At one point, she and Joe, who also wants to escape the Park Avenue crowd, head for an amusement park. Soon they all end up there; Daphne scoffs that they came to see how "Mr. and Mrs. South Brooklyn spend their weekends." Lana is fed up with Daphne's arrogance. As the gang gathers outside the Hall of Mirrors, she starts to walk away.

DAPHNE

You'll learn to love us as the years go by. Stay and have some fun.

LANA

Listen you wisecracking, back-knifing glamour girl. I've had all of your kind of fun that I can use. Why I wouldn't breathe the same air with you and your pedigreed polo shirts for another five minutes. The glamour girls and their men! Men, this herd of calves? Well you can give me the mugs at the Joylane. Mr. and Mrs. South Brooklyn know more about living than you and your whole phony crowd. Champagne for breakfast; two-timing for lunch. It's family and background that matter. Well listen upper crust, you go home to your families and rest on your backgrounds. With a pedigree and a nickel you can buy a cup of coffee in Kansas. Boy, what a sucker I was. I wanted to meet you, the nice people.

CAROL

Well, I think she's got something there.

And Carol's world is about to be upended as well. A newspaper boy
runs through the crowd selling copies of *The New York Chronicle*. The
headline shouts PHILIP S. GRISWOLD INDICTED FOR FRAUD.
FINANCIER JAILED. CHARGE IS EMBEZZLEMENT. The glam-
our boys and girls are stunned—no one more so than Phil, who missed
the call from his father earlier that day. Jane and Marion wrestled with
various options as to how to end the movie after this dramatic scene. As
the holidays approached, they still had not found the answer.

Unfortunately, Jane came down with strep throat in mid-December
plus a virus that hung on for more than two weeks. But she'd promised to
be home for Christmas. She still felt lousy when Marion put her on a plane
with her hair up in a twist and false eyelashes on to "astonish the Virginia
natives." The trip east was grueling—so much seemed to go wrong. After
four days at Poplar Springs, she dragged herself to Manhattan on the train
with Aunt Rose and Uncle Randy for New Year's Eve. She tried to be
festive, with little success, though she told her diary that Dick Clarke was
wonderful to her after she fainted in the powder room at the St. Regis.

Jane spent New Year's Eve in bed fielding phone calls from Cliff and
Marion while Dick sat by her side. Still not well enough to fly, she'd
booked a sleeping car back to California that would connect in Chicago
with a "speed crazed streamliner"—the Santa Fe Railway's deluxe Super
Chief. On the layover, Jane hired a taxi to drive her around the city.
Though her heart would remain in Manhattan, she decided that Chicago could be a great place to live, despite the frigid temperature. That
night she boarded a deluxe all-Pullman train which raced to LA's Union
Station in less than thirty-seven hours. She arrived at her apartment exhausted, only to find that her best friend was now in dire straits.

"KATE IS VERY ILL THEY LET HER CATCH A COLD WHICH IS VERG-
ING ON PNEUMONIA THE DOCTOR HAS HER IN A DIATHERMY MA-
CHINE AND I AM WORRIED TO DEATH," she wired Dick on January 6.
Kate remained in a pneumonia jacket for the rest of the month. As her
twenty-fourth birthday approached, Jane confessed to Dick, "my pocket

is not as full of dreams as it was twenty years ago but maybe that's because some of them have come true. Not many—but a few—so how are
you—I'm rather blue." Already she missed New York and the change of
seasons that California lacked; Manhattan is "so thrilling and so stimulating," she told Dick, because the city reminded her of the fun they'd
had "from the first warm yellow mists of April to the snows outside the
'Crystal Room.'"

UPON REACHING HER OFFICE IN Culver City, she telegraphed that
she'd been hit by a "TERRIFIC AMOUNT OF WORK IMMEDIATELY"
because Sam's deadline was coming up. On Friday, January 13, Jane,
Marion, Sam, and possibly a couple of other executives from the Metro
team had another of the brainstorming conferences that Jane usually
detested. This one was worth it: They realized the "last fifth of the picture was falling flat because of something wrongly done somewhere. We
talked and argued and figured and got quite desperate—then suddenly
(at exactly 6:17) a shape formed itself in the mist. Eureka! So now we
have to rewrite the last 30 pages!!!! The deadline was a noose. Still even
though it means more work (no Santa Anita) gosh, Dick, it's a relief to
get what we have been lacking all along. This picture has a million times
better plot than the *Cosmo* story and a definite premise—which we had
lost utterly. Now I believe we have got some suggestion of it back in
the picture. Endings are by far the easiest part of a short story, and the
hardest part of a movie. Haven't you noticed that most of the ones you've
seen fall apart either in the middle or at the end?"

Jane worked "THROUGH DARK AND THROUGH DAYLIGHT," accord-
ing to the wire, and straight through weekends until January 24; even
Rose began to wonder what had happened to her niece until she received
a telegram on January 22. "FRONT OFFICE HAS TURNED ON THE HEAT
ALAS NO TIME TO WRITE A LINE OF ANYTHING BUT SCRIPT WORKED
AT STUDIO UNTIL MIDNITE AND WORKING ALL DAY SUNDAY. HOPE
YOUR FLU IS BETTER TAKE CARE OF YOURSELF DARLING YOU ARE
VERY PRECIOUS."

The January 24 script put a new emphasis on Phil's relationship with
his father, and on his recognition, in the face of his father's corruption,

that doing honest work is far more rewarding than an easy life fueled by inherited money. This next-to-last script ends with Phil and Lana rushing to meet each other after the devastating news about his father's arrest. Phil tells her "I'm going to get a job. I'm going to work! On my own, and if it's okay with you . . . I won't have a cent, Red [his nickname for Lana]. But it's a cinch! All I have to do is work!" A ragged Bowery bum watches them; he moves with great dignity as he picks up a new cigarette that Phil has tossed away. " 'Work! What is this modern generation coming to?' " the bum asks no one in particular as he pulls a "magnificent silver cigarette lighter" out of his pocket and lights up. Clearly he is a man who has seen better times.

At the close of a decade of extreme economic uncertainty, the premise that financial integrity, hard work, and, of course, true love matter much more than class and wealth had to resonate with America's audiences. Mayer had little interest in making films with a social message, yet this point would be made even clearer in the final version of *These Glamour Girls*, which has another ending: Phil and his father have a heart-to-heart talk in an office at the Manhattan House of Detention (the Tombs). At first, Mr. Griswold assures Phil that once the financial scandal blows over, "there is plenty of money I can get at."

"But they said you were bankrupt," Phil counters.

"The Griswold-Snead investment company is bankrupt. You've got nothing to worry about. I made sure of that. There's quite a good chunk in your name. No one can touch that. You can finish college . . ."

"Father, if there's any money in my name it's going back to your stockholders."

"There's no legal . . ."

"I'm not thinking about the law."

"This is no time for schoolboy heroics. Listen son, ever since you were a child, all I wanted was for you to have every possible advantage."

"Father, I want to thank you for everything you've done for me. But we've had the wrong ideas about advantages. It's all so clear in my mind, but I can't quite express it. All I know is I don't want any further part of this wacky, selfish, upper crust business."

Phil explains to his dad that he and Carol had really been a phony setup, that all the things he's "had and needed, college, security and all that social stuff, they don't seem to mean a thing anymore."

Griswold looks at his son with admiration as he's taken out the door to the investigator's office. The last scene no longer includes a former-tycoon-turned-bum; instead we return to the Joylane Dance Hall, where viewers see Lana listening to her roommate read a news story. Mr. Griswold has confessed to fraud and will go to prison as soon as he helps the lawyers clear up the huge network of financial entanglements that plague his company. Lana gives up hope of seeing Phil again, until he surprises her at the dance hall. The couple reunites where they met, laughing together as they start to dance and realize they are on the road to a bright and happy future together.

JANE FELT GOOD ABOUT THE new script when they turned it in on January 24. But she was "worn to a frazzle" and couldn't wait to escape to the desert in Palm Springs, a favorite place for Hollywood artists and stars to relax in the late 1930s. She left for the twelve-year-old luxurious El Mirador Hotel on Saturday, January 28, with her collaborator Marion Parsonnet, plus illustrator Jon Whitcomb and his cousin Cynthia. She told Dick several other screenwriters were there, too. Although it was too chilly to swim, Jane welcomed the chance to get some real exercise on horseback for the first time in weeks. Her break was a short one, though, as Sam Zimbalist expected to have his writers "caged in their offices at all times, idle or not." On Monday, the studio phoned to tell her "to come back at once." After only two days, she returned to West Hollywood, reporting that Hi Toots "made 115 miles in two hours to the minute."

"*Everybody* who has read the script so far likes it very much—which is unusually favorable," she also bragged. "Surely I will be able to come home very soon." Jane had not planned to spend the winter in

Hollywood. Alas, another trip east was not in the cards for almost three more months: That week, L. B. Mayer heard quite a bit about what should and should not be in *These Glamour Girls* from the Production Code Administration's powerful guardian of American values, Joseph I. Breen.

Mayer was used to input from Breen on every picture his studio tried to make. The Catholic former newspaperman was in charge of enforcing the Motion Picture Production Code, a lengthy document adopted in 1930 by the Motion Picture Producers and Distributors of America "and those speaking with the voices of cultural authority." According to film historian Richard Maltby, throughout the 1930s the Code "contributed significantly to Hollywood's avoidance of contentious subject matter, but it did so as the instrument of an agreed industry-wide policy. On the other hand, it was a determining force on the construction of narrative and the delineation of character in every studio-produced film after 1931."

Joe Breen had replaced Will Hays as head of the Production Code Administration (PCA) and chief enforcer of the Code in 1934; his job was to ensure that municipal, state, and foreign censorship boards would not find anything offensive in the material that came out of Hollywood. Breen was someone L. B. Mayer thought he could manage, even though the Hays Office had been dissecting MGM scripts for years. An anecdote told by a producer goes as follows: " 'Mr. Breen goes to the bathroom every morning. He does not deny that he does so or that there is such a place as the bathroom, but he feels that neither his actions nor the bathroom are fit subjects for screen entertainment. This is the essence of the Hays office attitude . . . At least as Joe told it to me in somewhat cruder language.' " Breen biographer Thomas Doherty notes that the PCA office would not hire women: "The hyper-masculinity of the PCA chief and the rough language bandied about the office during negotiations with foul-mouthed producers made the men squeamish about having a woman within earshot. Likely too, Breen avoided hiring a woman because female censors were associated in the popular mind with bluenose spinsters and prune-faced harpies."

Persuading "roughneck moguls" to "submit to self-regulation" was a complex process. A large team of men acting as Breen's eyes and ears sifted through screen treatments, best-selling novels, magazine stories, and original screenplays. Breen used an assembly-line system that he supervised meticulously. He stayed on top of his staff, "poring over some one thousand scripts per year," and frequently taking work home. A memo about Breen's psychological state by a Jesuit priest, Rev. Gerard B. Donnelly, SJ, underscores how much the Catholic watchdog thought he was on a moral mission: "Again and again he told me how he was sitting at the top of regulating the entertainment and moral thinking of 200 million people. He had stopped dirt and filth and outrageous ideas from getting to millions of impressionable young people."

The first PCA response to Jane's and Marion's script came within the requisite seventy-two hours after Breen and his team saw it. They were not pleased. On January 28, Breen sent L. B. Mayer eight pages of comments. "THESE GLAMOUR GIRLS," he informed the studio chief, "in its present form is not acceptable under the provisions of the Production Code." He continued: "As we read this story, it is concerned largely with the activities of a group of young people who spend most of their time carousing and in its present form it seems to violate that part of the Production Code which says: 'No picture shall be produced which will lower the moral standards of those who see it.'" Breen went through every page of the script, pointing out words or scenes that needed to be adjusted. His chief complaint was the "many scenes of drinking and drunkenness which violate quite clearly the regulations regarding drinking in pictures."

Discouraged after she saw "the stupid letter from the censors," Jane stated, "People can get wrecked by details." A week later, when her virus had returned and her ears were "ringing like the bells of St. Mary's," she elaborated further on Breen's letter to Louis B. Mayer: "Our picture was censored for just one reason—alcohol! Movie laws are getting stricter all the time about showing any drinking on the screen, and in the case of young people, the surveillance is trebled. Even lines like the bromidic 'it's not so drunk out here' are censorable." Breen had flagged each scene in which the glamour boys appeared "disgustingly drunk," or even just heavily under the influence of alcohol. Homer's perpetually inebriated state would not work for the PCA at all. Breen took the position that if bad behavior is essential to the plot of a film, it must be condemned by a character the audience admires. (This explains why in the movie version of the story, Phil goes out of his way to express his scorn for the debauched behavior of his Kingsford compatriots.)

It's hard to know who added this gag to the script, but the story included a thoroughly drunk, elderly Harvard alumnus who pops up when he is least expected. Breen found this screwball device both unnecessary and offensive. Nevertheless, those scenes remained in the film despite Breen's warning that "all of these references to 'Harvard' will undoubtedly give great offense." After all, "Princeton" had been replaced by "Kingsford" early on in the scripting process—perhaps lampooning Harvard by name was too hard for Mayer or producer Sam Zimbalist to resist. This was the first time Jane's work had been subject to such scrutiny; she could understand now why Viña Delmar thought writing under the restrictions of the censors "takes the fun away."

But alcohol abuse was not Breen's only concern. The PCA's mission was to oversee the "impact of entertainment on children specifically on the criminal behavior of adolescent males and the sexual behavior of adolescent females." Most of the glamour girls were still adolescents, and their beaux were in their early twenties. So Breen insisted that they all be modestly clothed at all times. He marked several scenes in which "young men and women are shown in various stages of undress. The greatest care would have to be exercised that there is no undue exposure of the persons of either the men or women, at any time in the picture." No negligées, no alluring nightgowns but rather robes or pajamas were in order, and that is how the girls appear in the movie. Specifically, Breen flagged Scene 106—"This feminine underwear should not include intimate garments"—and Scene 158—"It, of course, will not be satisfactory to show Daphne in her 'undies.'" Nor should Betty appear in a "very tight revealing sweater." Overexposed young men were just as unacceptable; Breen urged caution in scenes that included a "partially dressed boy." Local political censor boards would surely object to seeing Homer in his shorts.

Enforcers of the Production Code saw it as their duty to protect young audiences from exposure to loose morals or untoward sexual behavior outside of marriage. The least suggestion of homosexual be-havior, such as the description of a boy as a "peach-cheeked Casanova" (Scene 24) raised hackles: "We presume there will be nothing of a 'pansy' flavor about this boy which would, of course, be utterly unac-ceptable," Breen warned Mayer. In Scene 29, "Greg's line, 'Can I fall in with you tonight?' should not have anything of a 'pansy' flavor." Public perception was what mattered; at no point should the film condone il-licit sex. No dialogue should suggest there had been a "sex affair" be-tween Carol and Joe the previous summer, and all dance scenes should be restrained rather than erotic. Marion and Jane had come up with a racy new plot twist to explain Betty's desperation to marry the perpet-ually intoxicated Homer, and Breen balked at that as well: "There is also the sex affair between Homer and Betty, which causes Betty to commit suicide. There are no proper compensating moral values present and there is no indication that Homer suffers in any way as a result of his participation in this affair."

As a hybrid comedy-drama, *These Glamour Girls* combines elements of sophisticated comedy, such as ridicule and satire, with more sentimental elements that appeal to the heart; the latter gave the writers a way to incorporate messages about honest and decent behavior into the story in answer to Breen's concerns. As for the details of Betty's tragic death, Breen wrote: "Please avoid gruesomeness as to the suicide of Betty and your attention is invited to the fact that suicide is regarded generally as bad theater and should be discouraged whenever possible." The movie would handle this delicate matter by having Betty drive onto railroad tracks in the face of an oncoming train; the audience would not see her die (as she had in the novel and original film treatment) by collapsing from a self-inflicted gunshot wound in one of the eating clubs.

Two other foci of Breen's criticism are intriguing. When the scuffle breaks out at the dance hall between Phil and an amorous sailor, Breen's hackles went up at the mention of the word "gob": "We presume you intend to show a United States Sailor. You will have in mind the laws against the misuse of the naval uniform and the naval authorities object particularly to sailors being shown in fights and brawls. At scene 43, you introduce three more gobs, who apparently participate in the free-for-

all brawl. We believe this should be modified." Additionally, in an early
script, Betty snaps at the other girls: "Who do you think I am Joan of
Arc?" This "flippant reference to Joan of Arc is objectionable," Breen
noted, perhaps thinking of the vocal Catholic Legion of Decency. "Your
attention is invited to the fact that Joan of Arc is the patron Saint of
France and revered by millions of deeply religious people, who will be
offended by this reference." Jane changed the line to read "Who do you
think I am Scarlett O'Hara?"

Inappropriate vocabulary was another target of Breen's caveats.
Again fearing that "political censor boards" might object, Breen flagged
dialogue that was disrespectful of women: Phrases like "strip tease,"
"babes," "filly," "wench," "twitch," "hag," and "witch" he thought had
to go. He also went after one of his least favorite words, "lousy." And
Breen warned against using the names of products such as Oldsmobile,
Cadillac, Duesenberg, and Vitalis, which might be construed as advertising; hence Charley Torgler's magnificent "yellow car" is referred to as
a "dream-sled" rather than a Cadillac.

Jane bristled at what seemed to be excessive nitpicking, and her colleagues surely did as well. But it was her job to produce a more acceptable script while not destroying the premise of These Glamour Girls or
its entertainment value. She and Marion found it would not be easy to
satisfy the PCA. However, it was common practice for producers and
writers to test Joe Breen by leaving in some offensive material "in hopes
of negotiating something else through." No matter how stern his repri-
mands, Breen's authority was primarily advisory unless the PCA refused
outright to approve the release print. But he was not done yet and would
stick with the project through post-production.

OVER THE WINTER OF 1939, as they labored to satisfy Joe Breen, Jane
led a more balanced life of work and play while Sam remained impatient
to start shooting the film he had hoped to produce the previous fall.
He'd interviewed veteran director King Vidor for several hours at the
beginning of February, but Vidor was about to take over the last several
weeks of production for The Wizard of Oz. Jane thought Sam might also
be waiting to see if Robert Taylor would play the male lead. She felt

frustrated in February and March because there were such long gaps of time between script revisions; she was never sure from day to day why production was still "suspended in midair," though Sam had talked with her about the casting.

So Jane was happy to make it to Palm Springs again for a week in mid-February. She sent Dick an amusing description of her encounters at El Mirador with John Jakob Raskob, the fifty-nine-year-old tycoon who had built the Empire State Building. "He is a charming old man—probably never relaxed during the first 40 years of his life but boy is he relaxing now . . . He sat at the bar at the Racquet Club beaming while all the younger marrieds filed past and planted gin-flavored kisses on his up-thrust chin. He's only about 5'3" but claims 5'7". Vanity, vanity." At the end of the month, Jane and Kate were back in Palm Springs—she played tennis with the pro and bowled a 67 against Mr. Raskob.

Now quite at ease in Hollywood, Jane enjoyed regular lunches with MGM's recording director, Doug Shearer, who often spoke about his three-year-old son, Greg. "This child has an imaginary friend that lives in the mountains and comes down to play with him every day. Did you ever hear of anything like that?" she asked Dick. "I know I didn't." She also found time for fun with the "very social" Dolly de Milhau, columnist and future war correspondent, who now had the office next to hers thanks to some pull from two of MGM's most respected screenwriters, Ben Hecht and Charles MacArthur. "Dolly is swell," Jane reported. At the Brown Derby, she'd introduced Jane to Alfred Gwynne Vanderbilt II, and Albert R. "Cubby" Broccoli (future producer of the James Bond films). Jane thought Al Vanderbilt was much more attractive than the overweight Broccoli, with his "high pitched voice and frightened smile. He is charming, Dick—really nice. He had a baby (or rather his wife did) last week—a girl. I hear she [Vanderbilt's first wife, Manuela Hudson] is wonderful. Half-Spanish." And then, between last-minute rewrite conferences, Jane took on a new project that was far more interesting than socializing or trying to please the censors.

Your favorite storybook characters are at last on the screen. And the making of the film is almost a fairy-tale itself

The

WIZARD OF OZ

by Jane Hall

WE'RE pretty much wrought up, around the Factory here. Especially in the Thalberg Building, which is where they keep Womenwriters. It began a year ago. Along about July a few tall, furtive figures began to sneak along the alleys near the Wardrobe, every twilight. They didn't look quite Human, and their coiffures were something not even a Crawford would wear. Diplomacy is the A-1 virtue, in this light-and-shadow business. Nobody said anything; but best friends began avoiding each other's penetrating eyes. The whole morale of Metro was unnerved until the news got out—and just in time: Mervyn Leroy was starting the wheels for *The Wizard of Oz!*

I hate to stress such sordid monetary values, being the Spiritual type myself; but it just happens that this is no "B"-budget Quickie. When a movie costs three million dollars—Ladies and Gentlemen, it better be

good. Incidentally, I think that's the reason this picture hasn't been produced before. Nobody with Leroy's imagination has also known the password to the Mint.

Mervyn Leroy being entirely responsible for the making of *The Wizard*, the first thing to do in preparation for this piece was see him. After checking the legality of Work (you're not supposed to do any when you're under contract), I clapped on an old Wimple and trucked up to the Luxury Wing.

He seemed to have two secretaries, one of each kind. I chose the boy. I said, Could I get into the Presence? Sooner then it takes to type it—I was In. In the inner sanctum, where there was a couch and a tobacco jar, Mervyn sprawled cross-legged, comfortably, and after a few polite triteries (such as Who was I, by the way? He'd never heard of me before!), we got around to the subject of Oz.

I lit a cigarette, for poise. "Well,

Mr. Leroy—" (in a businesslike alto) "how'd you happen to attempt *The Wizard,* anyhow?"

He said quietly, producing his pipe, "Because I've wanted to do this story since I was fifteen years old. It just happens"—he eyed me keenly—"that *The Wizard of Oz* was written in the same year I was born!"

I FELT strangely hushed. Mervyn and the Wizard—zodiacal twins! Only in Hollywood could such a thing happen. But ... so long ago? I checked quickly in one of the three or four hundred copies of *Oz* that were lying around. 1900. That makes him 39! For heaven's sake! He doesn't look it.

I said, "Has the book ever been done before?"

"As a play, yes. In 1902. Very successfully. But movies weren't equipped to make such fantasies till recent years."

Knowing what time and effort he had put into it (and also because I

40

ELEVEN

Off to See the Wizard

At the end of February, Metro's publicity department informed Jane that William Bigelow needed an article on *The Wizard of Oz* for the August issue of *Good Housekeeping*. Bigelow loved Jane's buoyant voice, and the blockbuster Technicolor production—with an oversized budget of nearly three million dollars—was highly anticipated. Production on *Oz* had started on October 13, 1938; the picture would wrap on March 16, so she had little time to lose.

The first thing Jane did was reread L. Frank Baum's book: "While the wind whistles through the hollow scripts in the Thalberg building and writers in their air-conditioned crypts die off like flies, I, Jane, sit reading *The Wizard of Oz* [sic]." She liked it even better in 1939 than she had as a schoolgirl in Manhattan Beach. "Now, like Alice in Wonderland, it has a Meaning. It is timely. You just think of the Wizard as a Dictator (a nice one but—oh! what a phony!)" Jane recalled the time when *The Wonderful Wizard of Oz* ran as a Sunday serial and she and her brother lay on the floor to watercolor the illustrations. Ever since then, she'd been fascinated by the colorful characters in the book.

More than a decade later, the atmosphere at MGM surrounding the film was electric. "We're pretty much wrought up around the Factory here," Jane explained to her readers, "especially in the Thalberg Building which is where they keep Womenwriters. It began a year ago. Along

about July a few tall, furtive figures began to sneak along the alleys near
the Wardrobe, every twilight. They didn't look quite Human, and their
coiffures were something not even a Crawford would wear. Diplomacy
is the A-1 virtue in this light-and-shadow business. Nobody said anything; but best friends began avoiding each other's penetrating eyes. The
whole morale of Metro was unnerved until the news got out—and just
in time; Mervyn LeRoy was starting the wheels for *The Wizard of Oz*."

So Jane's next step was to seek out the man she described as "entirely responsible for the making of *The Wizard*." She headed up to the
exclusive third floor of the Thalberg Building to interview the versatile
producer whom Mayer had hired away from Warner Bros. early in 1938.
LeRoy earned an almost unheard-of six thousand dollars a week, working out of one of the corner executive suites that had its own private
bathroom. *The Wizard of Oz* took twenty-two weeks to produce with
input from four different directors and ten screenwriters. (In 1938, the
average feature took twenty-two days.) Sam Zimbalist had wanted *These
Glamour Girls* to be an important film, but there was no way it could
match production No. 1060.

When she reached MGM's "Luxury Wing," Jane noticed that LeRoy
seemed to have a male and a female secretary. To announce her arrival,
she "chose the boy." She found LeRoy in "the inner sanctum, where
there was a couch and a tobacco jar, and Mervyn sprawled cross-legged,
comfortably, and after a few polite triteries" she was in. Of course he'd
never heard of her. She "lit a cigarette, for poise."

"Well, Mr. LeRoy—" (in a businesslike alto), "how'd you happen
to attempt *The Wizard* anyhow?"

He said quietly, producing his pipe, "because I've wanted to
do this story since I was fifteen years old. It just happens"—he
eyed me keenly—"that *The Wizard of Oz* was written in the same
year I was born!"

I felt strangely hushed. "Mervyn and the Wizard—zodiacal
twins! Only in Hollywood could such a thing happen. But . . . So
long ago? I checked quickly in one of the three or four hundred

copies of Oz that were lying around. 1900. That makes him 39! For heaven sakes! He doesn't look it.

I said, "Has the book ever been done before?"

"As a *play*, yes. In 1902. Very successfully. But movies weren't equipped to make such fantasies till recent years."

Knowing what time and effort he had put into it (and also because I hope so), I said that I thought The Wizard would be better than Snow White. My victim looked charmingly modest. Snow White was terrific, he said. We eyed each other steadily in mute but friendly fashion—not like two geniuses at all.

Before leaving Mervyn LeRoy, sitting cross-legged in his late thirties, I would like to remark (and I have NOT got my eye on my Option) that he is one of the most interesting producers in the business. He has been actor, director, writer—and not only that—he has a most appealing attitude toward Work. He believes in letting Writers write themselves to death, for, say, four weeks—and then take two at Sun Valley. That is, if they've turned out a likely script. Studying Mr. L. detachedly, I decided I'd hate to be on the LeRoy payroll four weeks *without* a likely script.

After the interview, Jane began to do more research. The MGM publicity department inundated her with "great sheafs of statistics about how many million-watt lights and how many thousand magicians and how many dozen make up experts went into this whole creation; but I would rather just tell you that you haven't even dreamed of Fairyland until you've seen The Wizard of Oz." It was, Jane wrote, "the most spectacular motion picture ever attempted," adding "That sounds like a blurb!" However, it was beyond the scope of her work to bring up the differences between Baum's book and the MGM production.

Jane had heard how tough it was to get on the set: "Even Mr. LeRoy had to write himself a pass, they said. No executives, no nothing. But being the goaded-by-adversity type, after lunch one day I wandered down with Douglas Shearer, who is a Big Shot (he is also Norma's brother), and M. Rykoff Parsonnet, who is a Wolf." Shearer was in charge of the sound on this and the other films of 1939, including Jane's.

They wandered past electricians, makeup men, and a few old rubber hoses and right into Munchkinland: "It's the place where everything is in bloom, and everything looks new, and nobody else's Unattractive Friends are wandering around." The entire film was shot indoors and on this day the team—under the direction of King Vidor—focused on Dorothy's arrival from Kansas. Jane's two male colleagues became unnerved by the sight of the Wicked Witch (or so she told her readers), so she "sent them back to their offices with a couple of studio cops." Doug and Parso (in the article she calls Marion "Parso") had clearly been her entrée, but now Jane was on her own.

At first she thought the Munchkins were "dressed up children." But in fact they were "the largest collection of Midgets in the world—especially gathered for *The Wizard*. And what a collection! . . . The younger Munchkins have transparent ears and long green feet, which curl in corkscrews almost to their knees. They are uncommonly attractive as to faces—with sly wrinkled smiles and luminous dark eyes." She was surprised to learn that most of the little people ("midget" is now considered to be a pejorative term) came from "very ordinary walks of life." The mayor of Munchkinland, Charles Becker [born Karl Becker, in Germany], had graduated from an engineering school. "He looked rather weary, discussing it. 'But nobody takes an engineer seriously, these days,' he said sadly. 'I mean, if he is also a Midget.'"

Jane explained that the small performers lived just the way ordinary folks lived. But when MGM needed to supplement their 124 Munchkins, the studio hired children "to pad out the ranks." She continued:

> There is a California law that children, even working part-time, must still go to school in proper sessions. So, the first day MGM established a school on the lot, and, at the required time, tolled out the school bell. Nothing happened. In their unrecognizable garb, three hundred Munchkins wandered off the set in happy groups—but not toward the classroom. Their teacher, only briefly baffled, laughed and swooped into the crowd.

"Here, come on, you!" she cried chastisingly to one weird, green-and-purple figure. "You don't escape arithmetic that way!"

A tiny shoulder wrenched itself from under her hand with dignified annoyance. The Munchkin frowned. "Madam! You apparently are not aware that I have been awarded two degrees from Iowa State!" All the Munchkins laughed and laughed.

Naturally Jane was fascinated by Toto, the five-year-old female Cairn terrier that had been carefully schooled by her enterprising trainer, Carl Spitz, before casting began. (The dog's real name was Terry.) Spitz had gone through Baum's book page by page, "picking out whatever tricks or mannerisms Toto was supposed to have"; he then taught the little dog "every mood and gesture of the book dog." Of course, his dog got the part. "Spitz trains many dogs, not only for the movies," Jane explained. "Local Glamour Girls all go for dogs (they look so *chic* in outdoor shots); but naturally, you can't housebreak a puppy and still get beauty sleep. So Carl does that." Judy Garland later told Jane that Spitz had refused to sell her the little dog.

As for Judy, Jane thought she was "the nicest little girl in Holly-wood and one of the best actresses." But, even corseted, her character in the movie appears to be twelve or fourteen, much older than the little girl in Baum's book. The official seventy-fifth anniversary guide to the movie notes that Judy, who would turn seventeen in June, had not been completely happy playing "a much younger, simpler girl" than she was—it meant that she "had to forgo the debutante parties she aspired to." In private, she "mortified her mother with her desire to emulate the essential sophistication of teenage contemporary Lana Turner." On the set Judy worked four hours each day, went to school for three—during which time production would often be stopped—and had one hour of recreation. She told Jane little about the production when they spoke on the phone except that the role of Dorothy was her "Most Thrilling Part." But it's clear that she was genuinely fond of Victor Fleming, who called her "Judalein"; he presented her with a motorbike at the end of the shoot. And, Jane noticed, the wardrobe department had an easier time with Dorothy, who wore the same blue-and-white-checked farm dress throughout the picture, than with any other character in the story.

For example, Jane recounted that Bert Lahr, the Cowardly Lion, carried a fifty-pound costume "borrowed from an old dead lion"; his expressive tail "was animated by an Automatic Tail Wagger, 'with an electric motor equipped with gear, lever, and fish line thus creating Wags of all characters,'" according to the MGM publicity desk. Jane didn't meet Jack Haley but said his Tin Man costume weighed "hundreds of pounds"; "he faints regularly with the pain of it." She also stated (erroneously) that his face was "made up with silver [it was aluminum] . . . and it costs fifty cents a day to put on."

Jane found the loose-limbed Ray Bolger, who always smiled at her in the commissary, "terrific" as the Scarecrow. "He is also one of the finest dancers of our time, and he has never gotten half the chances that he should in Flickersville." As for the Wicked Witch of the West, Jane thought she was the most picturesque character in Baum's book. In person, Margaret Hamilton seemed a "mild, though rather greenish, little woman." Hamilton was actually a former kindergarten teacher and the single mother of a small boy. But Jane claimed to be scared to death when she had a look at the witch on film. She warned her readers to "take a bodyguard" to the movie, "if you frighten easy." In fact, the Wicked Witch of the West was far more terrifying in the movie than as a character in Baum's novel; in the end some of her scenes were cut so that children would not end up with nightmares. Jane preferred watching Billie Burke as Glinda, a perfect version of that "small Woman-with-the-Wand that every child has tried to corner in the moss." Then her sassiness came out as she quipped: "What more can one glamorous creature say about another?"

"The sad little human interest story" of a man who had been desperate for years to get a break in Hollywood made a big impression on Jane. Ecstatic upon hearing he could report to work on *The Wizard*, "he was sure his chance had come." The job? To stand inside a hollow apple tree and call out one line: "You've got a nerve, picking my apples!" And that was it. She was happy to learn, though, that the ASPCA insisted the makeup department use lemon and raspberry gelatin and no toxic dyes on the animals that played the Horse of a Different Color. Actually, two white horses, Jake and William, "were colored with the same vegetable-dye pigments found in Jell-O" but not with the product itself. Jane's readers may also have been surprised to learn the "Field of Poison Poppies has 40,000 silken flowers in it—all made by hand."

Recounting facts did not interest Jane nearly as much as meeting people, so Mervyn LeRoy suggested she interview Victor Fleming, who had recently left *Oz* to direct *Gone with the Wind*. "If a person fancies Older Men (and she does!), it just happens that Director Fleming is one of the best looking men on the Metro campus—if not in the West. I hesitated for the right amount of languor, then I said—'well alright.' VF was over at Selznick's, so, not wanting to hurry things too much, ten minutes later I was there."

Fleming had not been eager to take on either production, but he was devoted to his two daughters and some feel he had agreed to do *Oz* for that reason. Known for his "no-nonsense directing style and a penchant for manly outdoor activities after hours," to Jane he'd seemed an unusual choice as director of *The Wizard of Oz*. He had a strong ally and close friend in Clark Gable, who much preferred to work with him than with George Cukor (Cukor had been fired from *Gone with the Wind* by David O. Selznick). For his part, Selznick thought Fleming was the "most attractive man, in my opinion, who ever came to Hollywood." "Six-foot-one and ruggedly handsome with piercing gray eyes," Fleming "came in like a lion on the first day of March and started directing the picture's first scene." Fellow director King Vidor described him as gruff, "like a big dog can be gruff or something." When she first arrived at Selznick International, though, Jane found not Fleming but Clark Gable and Vivien Leigh doing a scene together:

> I forgot all about *The Wizard of Oz* and my tea date and my new sore throat and—well, whatever else there was to remember. It came over me in a sort of Grim Wave that *that's* what is thrilling about Hollywood—that Mister Clark Gable. He was rigged out in a flowing white shirt and tight britches and the cynical grey eyes of the Georgia love-pirate, and I—I was collapsed under

an arc light." When they finished the scene, "Clark yawned, and then he and Victor Fleming came over to sit on the Prop box, near which I was cowering. Mr. Fleming got there first, and Clark said, 'Well, Jane—(he calls me Jane!) You're in pretty bad comp'ny!'

Falling over my feet and quite Choked with emotion, I replied in a similar vein. What was I doing over here? Mr. Fleming said grimly. Why wasn't I home?

Not wanting him to guess my true motives, I said mildly that I was working for Mervyn LeRoy—on *The Wizard of Oz*. How come he had directed it, by the way, since it wasn't his Type?

He sighed moodily. "They made me. You don't think I wanted to, for Gossakes?" His Roman mouth drooped wistfully. "I want a vacation."

I said I had heard he'd done a magnificent job. He pierced me with a gimlet eye.

"How could you hear that? Picture isn't even put together yet."

(That's what happens to my Tact.)

Gable interrupted just in time, his hazel eyes bespeaking all the lure of Arctic Nights. I answered quite detachedly. But in the back of my mind (which is generally not open to the Public) I was thinking: it's a funny thing, how much less Potential this Metro factory has since Clark and Lombard—(not that anybody ever *thought*—)

Just then something happened, or somebody yelled. Anyway these two Best-looking men in Hollywood sprang to their glamorous arches and went to do the scene again, Mr. F. telling, Mr. G. doing.

They came back twice after that, between shootings. Once to talk about John Steinbeck's new book [*The Grapes of Wrath*]; the next time to groan happily about how everybody Else got to take a Vacation. Mr. Fleming said, well, next time he gets one he's going to Africa to hunt lions again. Mr. Gable said, well, he's going with him. I was thinking that either of them would do all right in a Sidewalk Café . . . But of course that type always prefers to hunt lions.

"Oh! But what about *The Wizard of Oz?*" I pleaded, white faced, suddenly remembering what happens to those Luckless ones who double-cross the House of Mervyn. "Say something about *The Wizard of Oz!*"

"Most interesting picture I ever directed," Mr. F. said obligingly. "Finest thing's ever been done," said Mr. G.

Which was all I wanted to know.

Jane's account would not have been complete without mention of the writers; after all, she told her readers, "everybody hates" writers—they never get a break. So she persuaded William Bigelow to use all uppercase letters for the names of the three who received credit on the film: Florence Ryerson, Noel Langley, and Edgar Allan Woolf. Jane declared they had done a great job in adapting the book as a movie and creating an effective transition between Kansas and the Technicolor world of Oz.

She ended her article with an appealing anecdote that has been retold, with some of the facts changed, a few times since 1939. Frank Baum had lived in Hollywood between 1911 and his death in 1919; twenty years later his widow still lived in the same gray house. As production started, the wardrobe department sent a messenger to scout old pawnshops for a ragged old topcoat to be worn by the Scarecrow. He found one and once he got it back to the studio he discovered the initials in the topcoat were "L. F. B." Baum's widow confirmed that it was the coat that Frank Baum had worn in the days when he was writing *The Wonderful Wizard of Oz*. Jane's interest in the supernatural kicked in: "I think, of course, that Frank Baum, as a Ghost, arranged the whole coincidence. He wanted to insure that there'd be *something* in the picture that was altogether his." In fact, like Jane and her grandmother Rosa (whose psychic abilities and ghost sightings created a national sensation in 1909), Baum believed in spirits. He and his wife Maud, the daughter of suffragist Matilda Gage, even hosted séances at home. Whether Jane was right about the input of Baum's ghost on this fortuitous event must be left to the reader's imagination. Who's to say the anecdote is not true?

Jane then put in a pitch that would obviously please her employers. "But Mr. and Mrs. Little America—all psychics aside—I think that you are going to like the way my studio has brought your favorite fairy tale to life. It has been done expertly, lavishly, and sincerely—by the most Magical industry in the world."

The cover of the August issue of *Good Housekeeping*, which ran this special feature, depicts a little boy in a sailor hat; ads for Kellogg's All-Bran, Campbell's tomato soup, and Coca-Cola affirm that this is a family magazine; it is devoid of the cigarette and liquor ads that were often scattered throughout *Cosmopolitan*. On the "Fact & Fiction" page put together by "The Staff," readers learned a bit about Jane:

> Jane flew East from Hollywood a few days ago, bringing us her article "The Wizard of Oz" (page 40), which we readily concede to be a honey. But shortly thereafter, lunching with Jane, and Jon Whitcomb (who illustrates most of her stories), we were introduced to an engaging little wire-haired terrier named Kate.
>
> 'Kate,' said Jane, 'is the most thoughtful animal I've ever known. She was listening when the airline people told me that pets could be transported at so much per pound. Guess where I found her next? On the bathroom scales, weighing herself!'
>
> 'Oh,' we said feebly.
>
> 'And for three days,' Jane continued triumphantly, 'she went on a diet. Wouldn't eat a thing but milk and bananas.'
>
> So now you know why we feel the way we do about Jane Hall.

Editor William Bigelow proclaimed at the top of the two-page spread that began Jane's article: "Your favorite storybook characters are at last on the screen. And the making of the film is almost a fairy-tale itself." The pages are sprinkled with photographs of the five principals in *The Wizard of Oz* plus Toto.

Jane enjoyed the assignment, though it's hard to tell if she knew how dangerous it had been to be part of the cast of this difficult and at times chaotic production. Even Victor Fleming became exhausted by the spring, throughout which he juggled two movies at once. "As Fleming pulled together Selznick's monster production during the day, he supervised the editing of 'The Wizard of Oz' at night. He may have been an artist after all," according to David Denby. Fleming finally took a break from *Gone with the Wind* in April: "All through the shoot, Fleming took vitamin shots to keep up his energy, and downers at the end of the day, and he became so jangled and tired and so enraged by Selznick's daily memos about virtually every shot, that he retreated, under doctor's orders, to his beach house, in Balboa" for eighteen days.

But Jane's employer expected upbeat accounts of its productions and its personnel, not exposés. She could not touch on subjects such as the many challenges faced by the actors who played the Munchkins, most of whom stayed at the Culver Hotel, where rumors of depravity and ribald behavior could not be quelled. Aljean Harmetz found the small people were often plied with liquor by those who frequented the many bars at the studio complex. Fleming's biographer, Michael Sragow, discovered that many of the diminutive performers, "veterans of the gritty road life of circuses and carnivals," got a bad reputation after Jack Paar grilled Judy Garland in a 1967 television special. Clearly some of them were prone to wild behavior that may have been exaggerated in the press. But Fleming handled them carefully and "never raised his voice."

A tight lid was kept on accidents, and that may explain why the set was so well guarded. Buddy Ebsen had a severe allergic reaction to the aluminum powder used as facial makeup for the Tin Man. After Ebsen was hospitalized, Jack Haley was told to replace him, with no choice as to whether he wanted "the most horrendous job in the world" because he was under contract. (The assumption on the set was that Ebsen had been fired.) Haley's facial makeup was applied as aluminum paste rather than a powder. He fared better than his former colleague—he only contracted an infection in his right eye that lasted for four days.

Nor could Jane report that Margaret Hamilton had been severely burned in December when a fire got out of hand and flames "jumped from the broom straw, scalding her chin, the bridge of her nose, her right cheek, and the right side of her forehead." Only then did she realize that "from the wrist to the fingernails, there was no skin" on her right hand. At the end of February, her double, Betty Danko, also had a hard time; a pipe exploded and blew her off a broomstick, landing her in the hospital for eleven days. Years later, she still blamed Victor Fleming. Even Toto—as played by Terry—was injured: A soldier jumped on her foot, and Carl Spitz had to find a temporary double, eventually locating one in San Francisco for $350. Terry recovered in a few weeks, but Spitz came to regret his enthusiasm about putting the little dog through so many traumas.

However, the film did have a much easier time with the PCA than *These Glamour Girls*. Joe Breen had only a few minor complaints about *The Wizard of Oz*. He warned that "care should be taken to avoid an effect which is too frightening to children"; censors in Great Britain, Denmark, and Sweden had additional reservations about segments that would scare children. In June 1939, Breen wrote that "the picture is a superb musical extravaganza, with much of the flavor of 'Snow White,' and a special musical score."

The huge success of Disney's *Snow White and the Seven Dwarfs*, with its popular song "Someday My Prince Will Come," had spurred MGM's enthusiasm for Mervyn LeRoy's *Wizard of Oz*. LeRoy, a great admirer of Walt Disney, had screened *Snow White* at MGM for his production team. Once *Oz* was released, Disney sent him a congratulatory letter. It is interesting that "early drafts of the script . . . featured Auntie Em as a coldhearted woman who doesn't believe in kissing children and Dorothy as longing for a prince" like Snow White.

Many of Jane's letters indicate that—like Dorothy—she felt there was no place like home. For L. Frank Baum, Oz was real, not a place Dorothy conjured up in a dream as a result of a head injury. There are parallels between Jane's transformative odyssey to Hollywood and Dorothy's quest for identity. Jane, too, was an orphan (and a dog lover) who lived with her much older aunt and uncle. At the end of 1937, she'd been eager to leave a gray, chilled, and stress-ridden city for a place where "dreams that you dare to dream really do come true." Hollywood was her Technicolor world, filled with sunshine, populated by real and imaginary characters—including many phony ones—and rife with the prospect of adventures that would both fascinate and disappoint. Dorothy likewise craved new experiences; in the movie, she asks the imposter, Professor Marvel, "Why can't we go with you to see all the crowned heads of Europe?"

But then Dorothy faces a critical choice. Marvel knows just how to manipulate the young girl—by suggesting that careworn Auntie Em, who has done so much for her, may be having a heart attack. This symbolic scene, in which Dorothy's sense of obligation must override her aspirations, concludes with her instantly opting to return home, just as Jane would do should her family need her. Sragow addresses this issue in terms that handily apply to Jane: Oz, he finds, is "a place for all the characters to become what they want to be, including Dorothy. The paradox is that she wants to be a loving, appreciative niece to Auntie Em. *The Wizard of Oz* is the movies' most enduring transformation fantasy because it speaks at once to wanderlust and to the nesting instinct, to a yen for license and make-believe, and to a hankering for roots." It's likely that Jane's decision to give the protagonist of *These Glamour Girls* Kansas roots was a deliberate choice inspired by Baum's book. In fact, that story's heroine, a small-town girl who speaks with Jane's voice in several scenes, also finds a fascinating if flawed new world that she wants to experience but not be part of on the magnificent Ivy League campus that is the locale for most of the novel and the movie.

THESE GLAMOUR GIRLS

SEE...youth on a spree-dancing in stocking feet-because it's more fun with your shoes off!!

SENSATIONAL ROMANCE OF A DANCE-HALL BEAUTY CRASHING SOCIETY'S PLAYGROUNDS!

Meet the girls who have everything! Rich, beautiful, carefree, dazzling diamond studded debutantes! Pampered darlings of fortune who have only to wish and it is handed them! Platinum-plated playgirls peddling their glamour where it is bid for in millions! Spoiled darlings of the Smart Set...and the prize male catches of Park Avenue...off on a week-end of exciting pleasure that will leave you gasping with excitement ...thrilled with its entertainment.

with

LEW AYRES • LANA TURNER

TOM BROWN • RICHARD CARLSON • JANE BRYAN • ANITA LOUISE

MARSHA HUNT • ANN RUTHERFORD • MARY BETH HUGHES • OWEN DAVIS, Jr.

Directed by S. SYLVAN SIMON • *Produced by* SAM ZIMBALIST

JUST AS DARING AS IT APPEARED IN COSMOPOLITAN MAGAZINE!

Movie poster in the author's collection.

TWELVE

"Just Another Dame Who Wanted a Career"

ON THE THIRD WEEKEND IN MARCH 1939, MGM'S ENTHUSIASTIC
sales staff braved the Midwestern chill to network amid the opulent cor-
ridors and conference rooms of Chicago's famed Palmer House. There,
more than two thousand rooms stretched twenty-five stories up into
the clouds, making it one of the world's tallest and most elegant hotels.
Metro's annual three-day sales convention had brought them east, where
reporters waited eagerly to hear what they had to offer. "M-G-M Schedules 52 New Pictures," the *New York Times* declared on March 21. The
sub-headline read: "Wizard of Oz' In Color."

Movies planned for the exceptional 1939–1940 season included an
adaptation of Sinclair Lewis's *It Can't Happen Here*; *Northwest Passage*, from
the Kenneth Roberts novel; *The Women*, adapted from Clare Boothe's
play and starring Norma Shearer; and musicals such as *New Moon*, with
Jeanette MacDonald and Nelson Eddy, and *Babes in Arms*, the Rodgers
and Hart comedy featuring Mickey Rooney and Judy Garland. MGM
was also the proud distributor of David O. Selznick's *Gone with the Wind*.

Among the other book and play adaptations on the roster was *These
Glamour Girls*, by Jane Hall and Marion Parsonnet, "with an all-star cast."
But in March, that cast had yet to be determined. Six weeks later, on
May 8, in a sixteen-page insert in *Daily Variety*, MGM would again adver-
tise its expected releases; by then many listings had their stars on board.
"For selected young female players," was all that the studio revealed

about the performers who would bring Lana Peters and Daphne Graves
to life on the screen. And who would direct the picture? These questions plagued Sam Zimbalist while Jane and Marion kept refining the
script. During a hiatus, after she'd finished her article about *The Wizard
of Oz,* Sam gave Jane another new project. As usual, he needed the work
done quickly.

Jane was to "tear off an original" story about a girl, a boy, and a dog,
focusing on just one day in their lives. On March 25, under the headline
"Screen News Here and in Hollywood," the *New York Times* broadcast
this "New Stewart Vehicle" with considerable flourish—"Jane Hall is
preparing a scenario at Metro under the title, 'Two People,' as a prob-
able vehicle for stars James Stewart and Margaret Sullavan. The action
will be confined to one day, and the story will deal with a picnic party."
Variety confirmed the unusual project for the popular Sullavan-Stewart
combo on the same day with "Zimbalist Plans 2 People, Dog Pic," and
again in a small blurb on March 29: "Just We Two" repeated that Jane
Hall was developing the feature-length story for a cast of two people
"supported by a pooch."

At first, Jane felt bewildered. "To work on such a thing is appalling—I
am stymied as to where to begin but I have begun and what I think of is
the days we have spent together . . . It's all a great gamble whether or
not it pans out and surely problematical," she confided to Dick Clarke.
After weeks of dealing with endless conferences and Breen's complaints
about her misbehaving glamour boys and glamour girls, Jane spent the
next ten days on a more introspective narrative filled with lyrical descriptions of pristine natural settings and the interior dialogue of her
heroine, Georgia Clarke. I discovered Jane's forty-five page treatment
for this film in a small "Archive of Jane Hall's work" available for sale
online by a used bookshop in Virginia. (It may no longer exist anywhere
else.) Her story reads like a romantic novella set in a Thoreauvian landscape; perhaps even more significant, "Two People" reflects many of the
dilemmas that Jane had experienced in her own life.

Attractive Georgia Clarke, from fictional Wickleysburg,
Pennsylvania, works high up in Rockefeller Center for an advertising

agency, T. Abbott Company. Georgia had hoped to write ad copy, but has settled for a job as Townsend Abbott's secretary. She's been in New York for two years and has learned how to look and act like a New Yorker, though she doesn't feel like one. Her boyfriend, Pete Curran, is a fine-looking young photographer whose best friend is his large, brown-eyed dog, Bob. Georgia's dates with Pete have become predictable, though, and her suave, wealthy, forty-five-year-old boss intrigues her. One spring afternoon, Mr. Abbott's "stone man" image cracks; he invites Georgia to dinner. At that moment she "stopped being one of New York's two hundred thousand secretaries."

Despite the photograph of Mr. Abbott's wife and daughter positioned prominently on his desk, Georgia breaks her date to go to the planetarium with Pete. The evening is exhilarating: drinks at the Ritz, dinner at a small, smart restaurant followed by *The Philadelphia Story* at the Music Box Theatre. And then it's on to the Stork Club, where "T. A." has a lot of pull. Champagne appears with a "mammoth size Gardenia." Then "Georgia looks around—upon the stamp size dance floor was a debutante (immortalized in half a hundred pictures), doing some sort of a double-jointed rhumba . . . And two of Bauer's best-known models . . . And oh, gosh—there was Franchot Tone . . . *He smiled and nodded at T. A.!*" Before they head for the nightclub El Morocco, T.A. confesses, "I'm afraid that I'm in love with you, Miss Georgia Clarke." It's a well-worn tale, and Georgia is vulnerable to it: her boss assures her that Mrs. Abbott has agreed to give him a divorce. He only feels half-alive in his marriage and wants a more exciting future. His wife understands him all too well, but now there is "no interest—mystery—nothing."

Townsend Abbot and Georgia Clarke are not the two people at the center of this would-be film. Their evening out provides the story's central dilemma for Georgia, who must choose between T. A. and her modest, authentic, long-legged boyfriend—her Jimmy Stewart—with his fetching, floppy-eared dog. Pete cannot offer expensive evenings out, designer clothes, or luxury travel. Besides, she reasons, he has not asked her to marry him. After T. A. invites Georgia to spend Sunday on his boat, she "stared into his quiet handsome face . . . Feeling almost dizzy. *This is the way the Bronte women felt*—Not *me!*—Not an American secretary—1939!"

Georgia has promised Sunday to Pete, and she will not break this date. Instead, she decides she'll try to make him understand before the end of the day why she has chosen Townsend Abbot. As a surprise, Pete drives her up the Henry Hudson Parkway for a picnic near the cabin of one of his friends. While Georgia wrestles with how to bring up the bad news, her confusion grows. Although she loves streaking north past the city in the secondhand convertible Pete has just bought, Georgia winces each time he refers to their future together. Yet she feels a rush of childhood memories as they reach their destination in the woods near "a perfect little lake! . . . A piece of fallen sky that stretched for several miles" hugged by a sandy beach; there was even a "sagging toy-size pier."

This is the first time in two years that Georgia has ventured outside the city into a landscape that brings back "the nostalgic ache of spring," and she yearns for the times when she and her sisters roamed the woods and marshes near their aunt's farm. Georgia and Pete have never spent a full day alone together—just *two people* and a dog, with no distractions. It's so different from their dates in New York City, Pete comments, "when we're all messed up with the unimportant things—like where we can afford to go or what we have to wear . . . Out here, alone like this—the only bill of goods we have to sell is—us."

Before long, Georgia begins to have second thoughts about her impetuous decision to leave Pete. They establish an even stronger bond amidst the "breathless, unexpected beauty" of the pristine setting. She reminds Pete that "there were Indians . . . all over New York and Massachusetts . . . camping here in places just like this . . . using up our lake before we even thought of being born!"

Pete has brought a scrumptious picnic and adds to it by grilling two trout that he's caught over a fire. They swim, eat themselves "into a stupor," and take a long walk. Pete soon reveals that he, too, is in love with Georgia. Their banter turns into friendly sparring, though, after Pete suggests that women are governed by impulses rather than by brains:

Georgia could feel ridiculous rage sending blood to her cheeks . . . At this idle, silly creature who lay on his back in the grass, taunting her.

"All right, wise guy! How about Dorothy Thompson? I suppose you think she's an intellectual *midget?* Sure! Compared to you and your friends!"

"That's very easy to explain." Pete crossed his long, sprawled legs. . . . He swung a languid ankle. "Dorothy Thompson has the mind of a man."

Celebrated journalist Dorothy Thompson—whom Jane admired—was "out of sync" with her times and struggled with her femininity, or perceived lack of it, throughout her life. Pete's comment, typical of many males' response to intelligent, ambitious women in 1939, makes Georgia furious. She takes off on her own, but he follows her to apologize. They embrace in a spectacular field of daisies. Later that afternoon, the two set off in a canoe just as the lake changes to "liquid silver." Georgia realizes how awkward Townsend Abbott would seem in a setting filled with the "wonderment of twilight on a lake." As Georgia gazes at her fingers trailing just below the surface of the lake, silver lines appearing along her knuckles "etched in minute bubbles," she decides that T.A. "wasn't growing; he was made."

To Georgia's surprise, Pete admits that he's been out with lots of girls, including *Vogue* models. At the 21 Club he found "guys too busy getting drunk to listen to the cracks their babes are making. . . . And the babes afraid to drink for fear they'll lose their guys!" On one evening, Pete's date had fretted that she'd be seen staying at the Stork Club for too long and that they wouldn't get to El Morocco soon enough. Pete prefers spending time with his dog, Bob, rather than with dates who "do the same thing every night just hoping somehow, they'll find something real."

In a sudden amorous move, Pete reaches out for Georgia, causing their canoe to capsize; they make it to shore and quickly change into dry clothes. Pete stokes the fire and the shivering couple marvels at a huge red moon as it rises over a rim of pine trees. As night descends, Townsend Abbott seems far away, wrapped up in an artificial, materialistic world. Georgia remarks that her boss would probably see the surface of the moon as a space for advertising. " 'That was a cartoon in *Esquire*,' Pete said, gently." The "long, lonesome whistle" of a train cuts into "the music of the night." A transport plane heading north breaks into their reverie, its tiny lights twinkling in the sky "like misplaced stars." "Small warnings that there was a world, so near . . . where people and jobs and poverty were important. Life without lakes . . ." Jane's story treatment leaves us knowing that Georgia Clarke has finally found her true home.

Jane's account of the hours Pete and Georgia (and Bob) spend together evokes the poems and stories that she wrote before she was fifteen, as well as the many descriptions in her letters to Dick Clarke of the sights and sounds of the natural world near Poplar Springs. Georgia's initial infatuation with Townsend Abbott echoes the fictional Fauquier County teenager Liz McKelvey's fondness for much older men, and Carol Cameron's misplaced affection for the married Hyatt Rhodes in "Sunrise over Newark." These men seem exciting and sophisticated, but they are inappropriate choices. Georgia choses the authentic, savvy but modest man who can really be her soul mate, just as Veronica Alcott does by admitting her love for composer Gordon Kelva in "Such Mad, Mad Fun." Jane's graceful prose in the treatment for "Two People" suggests that she was eager to engage in another type of writing again.

In spite of the initial publicity, "Two People" never became a film. It was one of countless stories, treatments, and screenplays that writers turned out on a producer's whim as a possible vehicle for particular stars. Margaret Sullavan and/or Jimmy Stewart, who worked on at least four movies released in 1939, may have turned it down for other projects. The two stars, with their great screen chemistry, did film *The Shop Around the Corner* that November. For Jane, this would not be the only time that she put a great deal of effort into a project that came to naught—unproduced work was time wasted, and could be debilitating to screenwriters' morale.

AT THE END OF APRIL, Jane finally returned home to Virginia for a much-needed break. She wasn't sure what her next assignment would be and left her Chrysler in California rather than pay the cost of sending Hi Toots back across the country. She'd acknowledged to Dick: "I had to pay my income tax and can only pay a fourth of it and got a notice yesterday that I'm overdrawn $18.65. This Hollywood money angle is a joke—I shall write a treatise on it. I am in the worst bracket of all— single, with no dependents, and just high enough to really get socked."

Even without her own car, Jane loved being in the east while the dogwoods, azaleas, and multicolored bulbs burst into bloom. But spring also meant that her aunt and uncle would be apart again. After a winter of managing Poplar Springs from Manhattan through correspondence with her farm manager, Rose returned to oversee the property in person on April 2—an event duly noted in *The New York Herald Tribune*. Her husband continued to put in long hours at his law firm, still hoping to rebuild his lost savings. To Jane it seemed a shame that Randolph, who would be sixty-nine in July, still had to fend for himself as a bachelor for much of the year at their Berkshire Hotel apartment. So while she was in the east, Jane split her time between the two locations. In Casanova, she rode the horses that she had helped train, caught up with her friends, and introduced Kate to the dogs that had kept her company during the many summers she'd spent at Poplar Springs. With unexpected good timing, "Elizabeth, Femme Fatale," Jane's third *Cosmopolitan* story about Virginia teenager Liz McKelvey, who in this episode falls for a magazine illustrator, came out in June. (She'd written it at the end of 1937.)

She also heard good news from Swanie, who'd made sure that "Jane Hall" was a familiar name in the trades. He'd secured a contract for her at Universal Pictures for $750 per week ($250 a week more than MGM had been paying her) with a start date of Monday, June 26. The new position "was an opportunity which no one should refuse," Randolph explained to Rose, noting that MGM had hoped to get Jane back on a longer contract for less money, but Universal was willing to let her work on a short-term, project-to-project basis, which she much preferred. Randolph had cautioned his niece "never to sign another long-term agreement as such agreements are devices for tying up . . . employees."

In her Voice of Broadway column, Dorothy Kilgallen informed her *New York Journal and American* readers that "authoress Jane Hall" had dropped into 21 with her "fascinating dog, Katie Scarlett O'Hara, for a final lemonade before taking the plane to the Coast to write the new Deanna Durbin picture. She explains the origin of Katie's name. 'She wandered up to me during the California flood,' Jane relates. 'Everyone was searching for a Scarlett O'Hara—and I found Katie.'" On Saturday, June 24, Jon Whitcomb and her uncle Randy saw Jane and Kate off at the airport. Jane wired her aunt that she would take her advice about Hollywood and turn her days "to work and thrift."

Once their plane landed, Jane and Kate focused on finding a place to live. No dogs were allowed in the Sunset Tower, where Jane had hoped to lodge, so "in desperation," she headed back "to that DEN the G of A [Garden of Allah]. Well, this time I got a small villa instead of a room in the main building, and this time it is June instead of January, and Dick," she exclaimed, "it's wonderful! Monday I got up at 6 o'clock and went swimming [before work] in their gigantic sky blue pool with the early birds heckling me from the palm trees. Yesty morn up at 7, same performance, this morning up at 8—ditto. I hope that doesn't mean by Friday I won't get to work at all! Mentally I am still on NY time so guess that is why I wake so early. This is the first time in the last ten years that I have gotten to bed before eleven three nights in succession and I look awfully nice as a result!"

Rose sent a long, gossipy letter to Jane that closed with words of encouragement: "Now, my darling, I've always found it wise to be in hand to attend to one's own business; so much as I regret your being there, I think it best you are. Hope you'll treasure your $750 [per week] and you will see your Glamour Girls presented to the public . . . Have you seen Marion?" That was a good question. It's not clear whether Jane had had much contact with her former colleagues at MGM while she'd been at home, but she was eager to learn about the progress of *These Glamour Girls* when she returned to Hollywood.

Much had happened in her absence. In April and May, Sam had chosen his production team and the cast. For the part of the film's heroine, he settled on a beautiful, shy small-town girl from Wallace, Idaho, who had come to MGM from Warner Bros. as a protégé of Mervyn LeRoy. Julia "Judy" Jean Turner began her Hollywood career at fifteen; an aspiring fashion designer, she'd been discovered in January 1937 by *Hollywood Reporter* publisher Billy Wilkerson at a small café near Hollywood High School (where she had been for only three months). At five foot four inches tall, "Lana" Turner—she and LeRoy picked the new stage name—had an ideal figure, hazel eyes, and titian hair; she seemed older than her years.

In 1939, Lana Turner worked under the strict supervision of L. B. Mayer instead of LeRoy. By then, she'd had small roles in ten pictures and become popular among the crowd of young actors and actresses at Metro, many of whom Jane knew. *These Glamour Girls* was the first movie in which "Lana took center stage for an entire film." Loaded with personality and a great sense of humor, and a fabulous dancer as well (her father was a professional), she seemed perfect for the part. But it would never do to have her play a character with the same name, so "Lana Peters" (as she was known in all the scripts) now became "Jane Thomas" in the movie; the choice of "Jane" for the film's protagonist was surely not a coincidence.

Lew Ayres, a thirty-year-old musician, actor, and director from Minnesota, won the part of Phil Griswold. During the filming of *These Glamour Girls*, Ayres was separated from his second wife, Ginger Rogers. (The two were legally divorced in 1941.) He'd been in fifteen films, most notably *All Quiet on the Western Front* (1930), *Holiday* (1938), and *Young Dr. Kildare* (1938), his first of seven Kildare films. He and Lana were supported by several talented young actors who played the glamour girls and glamour boys.

Sam's choice of a director was twenty-eight-year-old S. Sylvan Simon, who had also been hand-picked by LeRoy to come to Metro after his contract at Universal expired in 1938. Exceptionally bright and well-educated, Simon was one of the youngest directors at MGM. A Phi Beta Kappa graduate of the University of Michigan, he'd earned a Master of Arts degree and spent time at Columbia Law School. He worked on six other films in 1938 and early 1939. The rest of the team included Jane's close friend, the "brilliant but slightly pedantic" recording director Douglas Shearer, who had already won three Academy Awards by 1939; well-known fashion designer Dolly Tree, who produced the elegant costumes; and "the most powerful arbiter of style at the studio," veteran art director Cedric Gibbons, who oversaw the production design of more than thirty other films in 1939 alone including *The Women, The Wizard Of*

Oz, *Babes in Arms*, and *Another Thin Man*. (Over the course of a brilliant career, Gibbons won eleven Academy Awards and designed the Oscar statue.)

Everything needed to bring the story to life could be found at the vast MGM complex in Culver City and on its back lots, where a "Small Town Railroad Depot" set became Princeton Junction, aka Kingsford. An unspecified location in New York where Jane Thomas lived with a fellow dance-hall hostess, Mavis, would be filmed on the "Brownstone Street" set. On Lot Two you could find Fifth Avenue and Park Avenue, "Waterfront Street" and "Eastside Street," plus every conceivable setting from a Southern mansion to Grand Central Terminal. "Whatever you wanted, whatever you needed, it was there. And if it wasn't already there, someone would make it for you," Aljean Harmetz noted. Principal photography on *These Glamour Girls* would begin on June 5 and last until July 6—but not until Joe Breen came up with a few more objections to the script after Jane left town.

Breen's reservations about the revised "temporary complete script" of "THESE GLAMOUR GIRLS" (dated May 16, 1939), exposed his resolve. Some material still remained "quite definitely in violation of the Production Code and, as such, cannot be approved," he told Mayer on May 18. He had two objections: The writers still suggested that Homer and Betty had slept together without having another character chastise them for it; plus many "scenes of drinking and drunkenness" remained. The boys could be a little "high," but "they must *not* be shown as offensively drunk." Breen remained unconvinced as well that the audience would not be exposed to any female nudity—"more particularly, to the breasts." And it irked him to find that the scene in which sailors engaged in a brawl at the Joylane Dance Hall had not been eliminated:

> Please have in mind that the Navy Department in Washington will surely object vehemently to any such portrayal of American sailors. Have in mind, also, the special act of Congress, of June 3, 1916, which forbids the use 'in theatrical entertainment, or in motion pictures' of the uniform of the Army, Navy, or Marine Corps in such a way as may tend 'to bring discredit or reproach

upon the United States Army, Navy, Marine Corps, or Coast Guard', and that any person who offends against this provision shall upon conviction 'be punished . . . '. In the face of this, you will, of course, be careful not to show persons, wearing the garb of a sailor, engaged in any brawl.

Breen again made comments such as "Scene 154: It will not be acceptable to show Homer lying on the floor without his trousers" or "merely dressed in a pair of shorts," and "Scene 96: We presume there will be no showing of a toilet in the scene in the bathroom." He now seemed resigned to the gag of the drunken Harvard alumnus, but he insisted the man should not appear offensively drunk—just a little "tipsy." And in one scene where the dancers are described as "going African," he again cautioned that this dance must not be offensive.

By this time, L. B. Mayer must have been exasperated as well. Production had already gotten way behind schedule. On Friday, May 26, Breen had met with three men—producer Sam Zimbalist; Al Block, Mayer's point man for the PCA; and "good-natured, quiet and reserved" Bernard ("Bernie") Hyman, who had come to MGM with his mentor, Irving Thalberg. With Jane away and no writers present at the meeting, the four dissected the story "at considerable length." (Writers had little clout or respect from L. B. Mayer.) The men finally agreed that the illicit affair between Homer and Betty could remain if it was "specifically and definitely" condemned by Phil. "The scene will be rewritten definitely to condemn the act and to make certain that there be no condonation anywhere, of it. This we believed to be acceptable, in the face of the fact the Betty's life will end tragically." Scenes where excessive drinking remained would be toned down or deleted entirely; United States Navy sailors in the brawl scene would "be either truck drivers, or sailors of the American Merchant Marine." (Sam chose the latter.) Breen left the meeting reassured that any minor quibbles would be taken care of in the final rewrite. For the most part, he was correct, although the PCA would still monitor the film during production in June and July.

Zimbalist had approved the "OK Script" on June 8, and on the twelfth Breen wrote: "The material is technically within the provisions of the Production Code, and reasonably free from suggested difficulty at the hands of political censor boards." The continued vigilance of the PCA during the shoot may be why George Oppenheimer, a well-known MGM screenwriter (and the future *Newsday* drama critic and co-founder of Viking Press), was brought on to help Marion handle last-minute revisions. (Oppenheimer did not receive credit.) After Al Block sent Breen twenty-five pages of retakes on July 27, Breen found only two scenes objectionable; but, he warned Mayer one last time, "our final judgment will be based upon the finished picture." (Ultimately, the picture would pass muster with the PCA.)

WHILE POST-PRODUCTION CONTINUED IN CULVER City, Jane was ensconced in an office "with a desk and a secty and an electric fan" about twenty miles away "in the hottest place in California." Universal City lay nestled in the San Fernando Valley, about a seven-mile drive from the Garden of Allah. Founded by Carl Laemmle in 1912, the studio was the oldest in Hollywood, but it had barely squeaked through the Depression; the first year during the 1930s in which Universal showed a profit was 1939. Swanie knew the studio was a step down for Jane, though she now had a more flexible schedule. Universal was not one of the big five (MGM, Paramount, Warner Bros., Twentieth Century Fox, and RKO); at the end of the decade it had no theater chain as a distribution arm. Comedies, inexpensive Westerns, horror films, and serials were its forte, and Universal had pledged its "commitment to 'clean' pictures" in the face of pressure from Joe Breen and his PCA.

Producer Joseph Pasternak may have encouraged the studio to hire Jane. A 1938 Universal ad in the *Hollywood Reporter* promoted Pasternak as "the producer who has never failed to make a big-money hit." His primary vehicle was teenage singing star Deanna Durbin; the two of them deserve much of the credit for improving Universal's bottom line. Pasternak's first film with Durbin, *Three Smart Girls* (1936)—one that Jane loved—had been a big success. Jane had been hired to work on Pasternak's seventh film collaboration with Durbin, *It's a Date.* However, once she arrived, he assigned her to help another writer on *First Love,* a modernized version of Charles Perrault's fairy tale "Cendrillon, ou la petite pantoufle de verre" (Cinderella), which also starred Durbin.

"In the mines," Jane quipped at the top of her letter to Dick on Universal Pictures Company, Inc. stationery on July 10. Already she was exhausted by the schedule: "It is very sad to have to stay in a place you do not like to earn the dough that almost makes it obligatory. On this job I am at work in Universal City at 8 a.m. (up at 6:30). Off at 6 p.m. if I'm lucky—and Sunday is a weekday as far as shooting this film is concerned. I'm doing "First Love" an original screenplay with Stephen Morehouse Avery—from scratch. They started into production last Monday with no screenplay so now we are writing one jump ahead of the cameras. Avery is a nice fellow—about 50—and pretty much caught in the Hollywood hack web. He has a daughter 17 and his wife is tetched . . . Very much like the Fitzgerald set up. Why do writers' wives go batty? (Maybe the same reason as their husbands do!)"

First Love would credit five different writers, but Jane wasn't one of them. On July 10, she explained the reason to Dick:

> *I had a feud with the associate producer and director [Henry] Koster apropos of working seven days a week and all night too so I walked out on Saturday morn two weeks ago with the declaration that I was at least going to have a half a day off out of seven. (They work all day Sunday.) Monday morning found me no longer working for Koster. Joe Pasternak (the real head) was so swell—he told me to write a screenplay by myself because he liked my work so much, to work at home or wherever I wanted to and 'let my conscience be my guide.' I don't know whether they'll like what I've done so far or not. I'm week to weeking it now so I may be home almost any time in the next month. Don't scold because I can't help it any more than you can help the exigencies of the insurance business.*

Jane was relieved to finally tackle *It's a Date*. "They are letting me do my own screenplay now and I work at *home* and I go *swimming* and I'm 'discovering' California health." She'd been put on the project officially on July 17 and would stick with it through at least eight drafts of a treatment until she again returned to New York in the third week of September. Three others shared in the final credit on the film: Frederick

Kohner and Ralph Block for the "original story" with Jane, and Norman Krasna for the screenplay. The first treatments appear to have been Jane's, though numerous changes would be made in the narrative before production began in December. At the film's center is the tension between a mother and daughter who each think they have the same lead in a play, and who both have their eyes on the same man. Pamela Drake is just seventeen; her mother, Georgia, is a seasoned actress of thirty-nine. Jane suggests the nature of their relationship in her description of one scene: "I think we should get a feeling of real feminine conflict underneath all the mother-daughter affection."

The characters face several quandaries. Georgia Drake (played by Kay Francis) worries about how her age will affect her brilliant acting career. Having just completed a three-hundred-performance run to great acclaim, she takes off for a six-week break in Honolulu to rest and prepare for the lead in a new play. It's a superb role, but one meant for a youngster closer to her daughter's age, and Pamela wants to be an actress as well. A crisis ensues once the director and the playwright see Pam perform part of their play at her summer stock school. She seems perfect for the role. Pam heads for Hawaii to explain the awkward situation to her mother but can't bring herself to do so.

On the ocean liner, Pam develops a crush on a handsome plantation owner more than twice her age. The film makes it much clearer than Jane's original treatments that wealthy John Arlen (played by Walter Pidgeon) is not interested in Pam romantically despite her fantasies to the contrary. Instead, and more appropriately, John and Georgia fall in love. Their romance and engagement helps Georgia cope with the upsetting news that she has lost the part she wanted, although she is happy for her daughter. A decade later, Pasternak liked the story enough to produce *Nancy Goes to Rio* (1950), a remake of the same plot set in Brazil instead of Hawaii (screenplay by Sidney Sheldon; story credits again went to Jane Hall, Frederick Kohner, and Ralph Block).

After she finished her work on Georgia and Pam's Hawaiian adventure—the movie would not be released until March 1940—Jane had her fourth stint as a Hollywood reporter. In September 1939, *Cosmopolitan* asked for a short piece about Bette Davis's new picture, *The Private*

Lives of Elizabeth and Essex. Production on the Warner Bros. period drama had begun in June; by early September the film was almost ready for its Beverly Hills premiere. Jane begins her article, "Good Queen Bette," (*Cosmopolitan*, January 1940) by giving her readers further glimpses of her own life at the Garden of Allah:

> It isn't that we don't Face Things out here; sooner or later even a Hollywood Hedonist has to crawl out of her swimming pool and snag a Deadline. The lawn in front of my villa (that's what I live in—a *villa*) was strewn with orange peels, OLD? bottles, and Nunnally Johnson. [Documentary filmmaker] Pare Lorentz was quietly dozing in his Early Thirties; from the pool came happy cries of Mr. and Mrs. Charles Laughton. Beyond the pool were [playwright] Mark [*sic*] Connelly and Franchot Tone. Can you imagine *working*? We will leave these Big Shots and get over to Warner Brothers.

Jane's target at the Burbank studio was publicity head Robert Taplinger. She asked Bob to run the picture for her. "No soap," he replied, adding that "Jack Warner Himself had ordered that no one was to see 'Elizabeth and Essex' run until the previews."

They lunched in the Green Room (the fine-dining portion of the Warner Bros. commissary), where Jane noticed that she was surrounded by "grim, poignant, harassed" portraits of Bette Davis; she learned that Miss Davis had insisted the studio portray the aging queen accurately. Once Bette found out that "Good Queen Bess in later years had cached her hairless pate beneath a huge red wig," she "demanded that she be photographed in one scene with her wig slipped off—completely bald!"

Of course Jane also inquired about Davis's costar: "I ought to meet Errol Flynn if I want to write about him," she commented. Bob "stared into space, deadpan. 'Oh, yes, Errol,' he said. Well, it's like this. Nobody knows where he is. He's gone." Jane had met Flynn briefly at a Saturday night craps game and remarked that he was "just as pretty 'Off' as he is 'On,' if you like that Oomph-Boy type." According to the AFI Catalog, Flynn had wanted the original movie title, "Elizabeth the Queen," changed so that the presence of Essex in the film would be acknowledged prominently. But Bette Davis "threatened to walk out of the picture" after they tried to name it "The Knight and the Lady."

A few days later, Jane tried once more to get a look at the movie—her editor saw to it that this time she was successful. But who wants to see a film alone? Jane's canine sidekick tagged along with her to the projection room. She told her *Cosmo* readers the story of how she found Kate, adding: "She is a lively, tolerant, ironical little creature from the Spirit Realm, occupying the body of a wire haired Fox Terrier."

There they sat with the lights dimmed as the projectionist moved behind the wall. Jane urged her readers to see the film—she merely touched on some of the highlights: "Bette's makeup for Queen Elizabeth is magnificent. So is Bette. She has wanted to do this characterization all her life. So sincerely that when the time came she was ready to postpone it for another five years—for fear she wasn't yet quite good enough." And then Jane gave a plug to the studio that had finally let her preview Davis's first Technicolor film: "The entire handling of the picture is as expert as you would expect from a studio like Warner Brothers, whose ever-mounting total of successes is not an accident."

Jane loved the scene in which "Essex whaps Elizabeth on her majestic bustle"; Kate preferred the battle scene in the bogs of Ireland and ran down the aisle at the sight of Robert, Earl of Essex, being "badly bested by [the Earl of] Tyrone." They were both mortified that Essex lost his head. Jane glanced at Kate: "The rain was dripping down her beard." She tried to elicit a response from her teary-eyed pooch as they left the theater, but Kate "pretended to be watching the other side of the street. 'So what?' Kate shrugged. 'Just another dame who wanted a career.'" And then she turned to look at Jane "with great intentness."

THIRTEEN

Glamour Girl

WHILE JANE TOILED AWAY ON *It's a Date* AT UNIVERSAL, *These Glamour Girls* went out to previews in local theaters for an audience response before its official release. On August 2, Jane mailed the results and her reaction to Dick:

> *They sneak previewed Glamour Girls again last night—and the cards were* rapturous. *400 of them—and only three bad in the whole lot. They were like this: 'best-good-perfect,' 'best preview I ever saw,' 'should be released as is,' and 'best picture of the year,' 'terrific,' 'why can't we have more like this?' etc. etc. etc. It is heart breaking; L. B. Mayer himself went to the preview last night and said, grimly: 'that could have been a great picture.' You see—because it took so long—they gave it cheap production, the worst! director on the lot, and a no-name cast. And a 26-day shooting schedule (instead of 45 to 50). It is so fury making—to see, from two different previews, supposedly in the 'toughest' houses on the Coast (Long Beach and Inglewood) such 98% enthusiasm for a BAD JOB. Now they all think they missed the best bet of the year! I'm pouring my heart out to you about this—I guess you will know how disappointed I am without further tears.*

Jane followed this premature outburst with an exuberant exclamation about how suntanned she was (though not on her face, which she always protected). She hoped that Dick would keep his suntan until she returned home, "on account of that is how you look Elegante." As it turned out, she'd been way too quick to denounce the film—most critics appreciated the seventy-nine-minute black-and-white comedy-drama on its own terms.

The movie's trailer, created a few days after the previews, highlights Jane's role. As the music comes up under close-ups of various glamour girls or brief clips from the film, we see superimposed titles laced with satire: WE THE BETTER PEOPLE—THE PLATINUM-PLATED DARLINGS OF THE SMART SET—THE GLAMOROUS!—THE DAZZLING!—THE SOUL-FREE!—"THESE GLAMOUR GIRLS"—THE INSIDE STORY OF THE DEBUTANTES . . . AND HOW A DIME-A-DANCE BEAUTY . . . BEAT THEM AT THEIR OWN GAME!—JANE HALL'S BLISTERING EXPOSÉ—BLAZES ACROSS THE SCREEN WITH ALL OF ITS FLAMING TRUTH. The writing credits read "Screen Play by Jane Hall and Marion Parsonnet from the Cosmopolitan Magazine story by Jane Hall." Few knew that the *Cosmo* version had actually originated as a film treatment.

Although the picture's official release date was August 18—a day after the *Wizard of Oz* opened in New York City—reviews in the trades had come out three days earlier. Given her skepticism, Jane must have been surprised that the director and the cast received so much praise. *Variety* found both Lana Turner and Lew Ayres "splendid," adding that the "screen play, direction, characterizations, musical score, and last but by no means least, production mounting, combine to make 'These Glamour Girls' an excellent programmer. It is a type of thing that will unanimously win the *femme* vote, while claiming far more than a passing interest from males." Jane and Marion had created a script that "carries romantic suspense throughout, the whole well-seasoned with laugh provoking situations." And Simon, far from being the "worst director on the lot," as Jane had declared, handled a "big thespian roster with expert touch, ably blending his many elements, and at times maintaining an ideal pacing."

The Hollywood Reporter agreed the film was good entertainment, "fast and smartly paced"—"the production values throughout are generally a very noticeable shade over the average in this budget class. . . . a fresh treatment with some fine dialogue, which at times sparkles. Elements in the story range from out and out zany situations to stark tragedy." The *Reporter* focused primarily on the comedic rather than the dramatic strength of the movie: "Liberally spiked with so-called 'good audience stuff' the picture evokes numerous hearty laughs with its amusing comedy that at times reaches over on the zany side, but which should give ample satisfaction on any bill." Again Simon is praised for his "unusually good job of directing," and Lew Ayres and Lana Turner (as well as Jane Bryan) for "outstanding performances." Most reviews do not name Sam Zimbalist, but this one refers to the fine production values he gave the film.

Hedda Hopper's Hollywood column in the *Los Angeles Times* reported that the film was good comedy that "will probably satisfy if you're just looking for light, hot weather entertainment." She found it a "trifle better" than the 1939 college film *Winter Carnival,* a project that had been a disaster for Scott Fitzgerald, who went on a drinking spree at Dartmouth after he and Budd Schulberg had been assigned the script. *Motion Picture Daily* (August 17) thought Jane's film timely, given the "columns of newspaper space being accorded to 'glamour girls' self-made or otherwise." The October *Photoplay* would list it as one of the ten best pictures of the month—noting (inaccurately) that the "fun making picture . . . doesn't deviate from Jane Hall's magazine story by so much as an adverb."

As these reviews came in, Jane, still focused on her work at Universal, was heartened by a congratulatory telegram sent from Washington, DC, on August 22 from her aunt and uncle; her brother Dickie, who was about to start teaching at Brown University; Randy Carter and his wife, Nikki; and three other friends who had all seen the "fine" film together.

And then, on August 31, East Coast critics reacted to the New York City premiere at Loew's Criterion, a Broadway theater with 1657 seats. Three of the reviews were brief and lukewarm. The *Daily News*'s Wanda Hale judged it "a picture that flounders around in a futile effort to show snobbishness to be one of the major sins," and yet she also said: "If *These*

Glamour Girls had been less hysterical it would have been a good preach-ment against snobs." Hale found Lew Ayres far too old to be cast as a college boy. Rose Pelswick (*New York Journal and American*) pegged it as "a slim, rather diffuse yarn set against a campus background." Bland Johansson (*Daily Mirror*) had a mixed reaction to the "very light and very summery . . . harmless little daydream for the teens," that, on the other hand, was "well-directed, ably acted and timely in its discussion of just what constitutes this 'glamour.'" More enthusiasm came from New York's *Herald Tribune*, which remarked on the "excellent dialogue," before concluding the movie was a "lot of fun."

But the most comprehensive East Coast review appeared in Frank S. Nugent's The Screen column in the *New York Times*. Nugent was an im-portant critic who would one day turn to screenwriting himself. On the last day of August, he and a colleague, Benjamin R. Crisler, weighed in on a new Bing Crosby film, *The Star Maker,* as well as *These Glamour Girls*:

> The movies are a curious phenomenon. We go on for years living with them, expecting nothing better than the obvious, and then, unpredictably, they sprout out, like a forgotten box of seeds left in a hothouse, with a picture like "These Glamour Girls," at Loews Criterion. We don't know whether it is the confusion of the age or just the confusion at Metro-Goldwyn-Mayer, but it strikes us that "These Glamour Girls" is not only the best college comedy of the year but the best social comedy of the year. Correct us with indignant letters if we seem to be wrong.

Nugent applauded the performances of key cast members "because they all admirably serve the very high and rare cinematic purposes of social satire, deliberately rigged from the underprivileged viewpoint, and—even in its affected callowness—more brutally assiduous than Clare Luce [Clare Boothe Luce] ever dreamed of being." Unsure who to credit for the clever story, as he was not familiar with Jane's work, Nugent concluded that *These Glamour Girls* "affords a rare insight into what we hope to be pardoned for referring to as a vacant room."

This assessment elicited encouragement from Marguerite ("Peggy") and Howard S. Cullman, two influential investors in the American theater who knew Jane. (The Cullmans backed numerous Broadway hits including *Oklahoma!*, *South Pacific*, *Annie Get Your Gun*, and *Fiddler on the Roof.*) Jane received their wire at Universal: CONGRATULATIONS ON THIS MORNING'S NEW YORK TIMES REVIEW OF THESE GLAMOUR GIRLS STOP CAN WE SIGN YOU UP FOR PLAYWRIGHTS PRODUCING COMPANY LOVE AND ALL GOOD WISHES.

Jane had now proven that she could support herself reasonably well by writing screenplays as well as fiction and nonfiction for magazines. Yet, like many of her colleagues who had come from the east, she never felt completely at home in Hollywood. Working on the assembly line of the dream factory did not foster progress toward her childhood goal of becoming a serious novelist; she'd had more creative freedom and flexibility in choosing her subject matter while a juvenile author in the late 1920s. Five years later, though magazine editors expected her to submit a specific type of young adult romance and made changes she did not always like, at least the stories remained her own. But late in 1939, as she tried to sort out whom she was meant to be, two other priorities began to compete with Jane's literary aspirations.

The "glamor girl is today an occupation, sponsored by press agents of such eating joints as Coq Rouge, Stork Club, 21 and publicized by columny," *Time* magazine would observe on January 1, 1940. By then "the voodoo of Glamour," a phrase coined by John Lahr a half century later in the *New Yorker,* had cast its spell on Jane. Glamour, Lahr wrote, is "a syntax of seeming and enchantment, and, like all enchantments, it never quite reveals its mysteries. It thrives on detachment and elusiveness." Quoting director Mike Nichols, Lahr added, it is "a series of decisions. Things done and worn and said that add to someone's natural gifts." He notes that Louis B. Mayer was so enthralled by the seductive power of glamour and female beauty that he told Joan Crawford she should never appear in public "looking the way 'just any woman' would."

In fact, well before Jane arrived in Hollywood, MGM had "turned glamour into a corporate product"; and the message from Metro and other studios was one that Jane, like millions of her contemporaries, bought into. Jeanine Basinger defines it by saying the movies of this era "make a plain statement: women should be physically beautiful in order for men to love them." Moreover, a woman needs to be "properly turned out" to succeed in her "natural career of love." Both fashion and glamour were "fundamental to a woman's definition of herself . . . a woman *is* what she wears so it had better be right. . . . When the prince comes to town, she's got to have a glass slipper." And these priorities were not just emphasized in the movies. "Women's history, if they had any, consisted in their being beautiful enough to become events in male lives"; magazine role models were "all beautiful, thin, young, and exquisitely made up. What else was there?" historian Carolyn Heilbrun asked in a 1997 lecture. The women in Jane's professional and social circles inevitably judged themselves and each other by these cultural norms. But at what cost?

Commercial illustrators Jon Whitcomb and Bradshaw Crandell made their fortunes creating images of gorgeous women. In the 1930s, their work could be found in advertisements, on magazine covers, and (especially in Whitcomb's case) in hundreds of illustrations for magazine stories by popular authors such as Jane. Both men became image mentors for and lifelong close friends of Jane. In the chapter of his 1962 book *All About Girls* entitled "You Might As Well Be Ravishing," Whitcomb described his Dream Girl: "The state of being glamorous is a solitary and unique thing, and it is produced by attitudes of independence which probably stemmed from childhood. Anybody can be attractive. But magic of any sort depends on the inner glow—this spell, if you wish—of a born witch doctor." Glamorous women exuded warmth (not incompatible with an aura of mystery) and brains ("no man can resist a woman who is intelligently interested in him"); above all, they always put their best face forward. That effort required a certain amount of distance in their relationships and often—as was certainly true of Jane—a passion for privacy.

"No one we know intimately can be glamorous for us," historian Stephen Gundle has observed. "We generally see the glamorous personality the way they want us to see them." He argues that being stylish and chic is not enough to maintain an aura of glamour; one must also "be committed to the development of a theatrical public image." The most glamorous women aviators—a profession Jane admired—knew how to exploit their exciting careers "through the adoption of a carefree attitude, fashionable dress, studied gestures, personal magnetism, and planned stunts." Louis B. Mayer was right: For a glamour girl, keeping up appearances among friends, acquaintances, and one's public was critical; it was also expensive to acquire the trappings of glamour, and very time-consuming to pull it all together. But for Jane, at least some of the time, it was fun. She liked role-playing; being an actress was the one career she'd considered but never tried. (Remember that her high school classmates had predicted Jane would be another Lynn Fontanne.) Before long, her self-esteem came from her looks as much as her talent. Jane's ambition now included becoming bewitching, mysterious, and stylish, and remaining that way for the rest of her life.

In March 1939, *Glamour* magazine had its debut as *Glamour of Hollywood*, "the way to Fashion, Beauty, and Charm." By then, Jane had become caught up in the magic of it all and put a certain amount of "stock in trade" or currency in her looks—something she'd belittled in other women as recently as nine months earlier. Surrounded by stars at work and encouraged by Jon, Brad, and her favorite photographer, Grif Griffith, Jane had been a quick study. With her face as her canvas and an abundance of artist's tools available from aggressive cosmetics manufacturers, she learned how to make the most of her natural good looks. (It was only a matter of time before she would become a blonde.) But her focus on her image was not all about Hollywood-inspired vanity.

In the thirties makeup was considered to be a necessity in many women's lives (if they could afford it); as Molly Haskell notes, using cosmetics was not yet a "political act, a crucible of self-ness, a procedure whose implications we must agonize over and decode." Among Jane's friends and colleagues there was nothing wrong with being "*seen* as trying to look good." On the contrary, it was a woman's obligation to present herself well in public. Haskell refers to her own mother's approach to the minimal amount of makeup that she wore as a "social contract" that did not imply phoniness or hypocrisy. By the 1990s, those who took too much time with their looks were accused by some of narcissism and "not having an inner self." But, Haskell observes, the ritual of women and their daughters looking into mirrors and trying to find their ideal selves goes back for generations.

As more and more articles mentioned how attractive Jane was, they fueled her need to remain being seen as young, beautiful, and chic. Each month for more than a decade in the 1930s and 1940s, Brad Crandell had produced an exquisite, sophisticated siren for the cover of *Cosmopolitan.* He—and other illustrators—became instrumental in shaping young women's perception regarding how they should look; *Time* magazine noted the way Crandell transformed "a bright eyed, blonde debutante" into a glamour girl just by featuring her on *Cosmo's* January 1940 cover. The article takes a dig at the press for covering such fluff, "while Hitler's Armies were rolling methodically through Poland, and children were being evacuated from London."

At some point in 1939, Jane found time to pose for Brad with Kate; his pastel headshots of the two "Beauties" graced the October *Cosmo* cover. Jane wears a wide-rimmed black straw hat with a yellow chiffon band over shoulder-length chestnut curls. Her complexion is flawless, the shape of her mouth perfect, but her green eyes glance upward in a wistful expression that suggests a complex psyche. Next to her is a smiling Kate, one of three dogs Crandell had placed on his covers in the arms of a woman. This one is unique: Crandell's models were usually unidentified, but Kate's dog tag reads: "Jane Hall MGM." This elegant woman would have been unrecognizable to those who had known her either as a sturdy tomboy and poet from an Arizona mining town or as a gutsy junior reporter in Manhattan Beach.

Inside the cover, in the Fashions in Fiction column, Jane and Kate can be found in a small black-and-white photo taken by Grif Griffith, "her favorite photographer." She stands on top of a rock in Central Park in a smart suit and high-fashion accessories. Underneath the picture, Lee Russell writes that "Jane Hall's secret ambition was realized when Bradshaw Crandell asked her to pose for this month's cover. She would rather be considered a glamour girl than a successful writer. She is both. She has a passion for smart clothes, hats and accessories. In New York she practically lives at '21' in her best clothes. When in California she wears slacks and gay bandanas."

This piece would be just one of several references in the press to Jane's fashionable appearance over the next two years. Even before this issue came out, Walter Winchell had announced on September 4, amidst other gossip about Elizabeth Arden, Dr. Nicholas Murray Butler, J. Edgar Hoover, and Sophie Tucker, that "Jane Hall, twenty-three-year-old author of 'These Glamour Girls,' the movie, is a glamour gal herself. So glamorous she's on the October cover of *Cosmopolitan*." Jane saw the syndicated column in Los Angeles. She pinned another tiny clipping to her copy of it: "Attractive Jane Hall, who has more on the ball than most girls twice her age has returned to the shores again. Miss Hall, at her tender years, has had 10 stories published by Cosmopolitan magazine and one in the Sat Eve Post. Currently coaxing her typewriter at Universal studio." The only thing Jane needed to complete this picture: a glamorous man.

"TOO MANY MEN SPOIL THE BROTH." The unsigned telegram to Jane arrived at the Hickses' Berkshire Hotel apartment on December 22, 1939; it may have been from a despondent Dick Clarke. Their five-year correspondence had ended that fall, but not just because Jane came east at the end of September. In August, she had met someone special who seemed to support her interest in a career. Tall, dark, and handsome, in looks a cross between Jimmy Stewart and Walter Pidgeon, Robert Frye Cutler was also a theater producer, arts patron, superb athlete, and— very important to Jane—an animal lover. She had always been drawn to older men; "Bob" was thirteen years her senior and much more reserved than Jane, but he had a wry sense of humor. His late father, philanthropist and industrialist Otis Henderson Cutler, had been active in the national Red Cross during World War I, was an important player in New York state Republican politics, and also had been instrumental in founding and running the American Brake Shoe and Foundry Company. Following Otis's premature death at fifty-two in 1922, his wife, Mary, and subsequently his four living children inherited a small fortune.

At the time of his father's death, Bob was a twenty-year-old sophomore at Williams College. He'd been raised in the shadow of a tragedy; his parents lost their five-year-old son, Otis Jr., in 1900, two years before Bob was born. Mary thereafter focused her affection on her youngest child, often being overprotective of him. In 1922, Bob's three older siblings no longer lived at Rockrest, the Cutlers' rambling Tudor mansion in Suffern, New York. Mary, alone in the house after Otis's death, insisted Bob leave Williams at the end of his sophomore year so that he could travel with her. Her suffocating presence in her son's life likely had long-term repercussions that she could not foresee.

After his mother died on Christmas Eve in 1929, Bob was bereft, though she left him Rockrest and other family property in Rockland County. Three years later, on November 29, 1932, he married a twenty-four-year-old model and aspiring actress, Nondas Metcalfe. Together they launched the [Rockland] County Theatre, one of America's most successful summer stock theaters. Forty years later, Bob Cutler would be applauded for bringing "the legitimate stage" to Rockland County in the 1930s and 1940s. A local editorial observed: "Lovers of good theater here owe him a great debt." It was a unique venture. The talent that assembled in Suffern for ten weeks each summer between 1933 and 1938 (and sporadically during the 1940s) gave him ties to Hollywood and the literary world that surely made him more interesting to Jane than her other suitors. Among the actors who played there were Estelle Winwood, Vincent Price, José Ferrer, Ruth Gordon, and Bob's close friend (and fellow Rockland County resident) Helen Hayes, who was married to playwright and MGM screenwriter Charles MacArthur.

In August 1938, at just about the time Jane moved into Sam Zimbalist's suite of offices to script *These Glamour Girls*, the *New York Times* featured Al Hirschfeld's pen-and-ink drawing of the County Theatre—Bob, Nondas, Helen Hayes, and her daughter, Mary MacArthur, are assembled around an (inaccurate) rendition of "the Cutler pool"; in the background a theater crowd flocks to see the exhibits during intermission. The following February, a revue, *One for the Money*, which had played at the County Theatre the previous September opened "by arrangement with Robert F. Cutler" at the Booth Theatre on Broadway. The intimate revue in two acts ran for 132 performances; its skits and lyrics, "having to do with life among the upper classes and café society," were by Nancy Hamilton, "one of the first women to succeed as a lyricist on Broadway."

But on the home front, Bob's world began to fall apart.

Nondas was restless. After seven years of marriage, she longed for a bigger professional career onstage than occasional appearances at the County Theatre. While Bob had helped her career along in Suffern, he "always talked her out of" trying for a role in New York, she wrote, holding forth "the lure of travel" with him. Nondas partly blamed herself for their split by saying "a woman cannot make a double success of husband and career"; because she had "loved her husband and career equally" she had failed on both counts.

When Nondas went to Hollywood for a friend's wedding, an agent "persuaded [her] to stay and look for a job." According to Nondas, "Bob, who had pretty poor health, wore himself out managing the business end of the theater the last summer we ran it." His "pretty poor health"—a euphemism for alcoholism—was an affliction people rarely alluded to in those days. As a recovering alcoholic, Bob was far more dependent on his wife than she may have realized. Once Nondas left for California, he was at loose ends. Determined to succeed in Hollywood, she remained on the West Coast. He came to California that summer, possibly to try to persuade her to return home. She refused, and they subsequently separated, but not before she introduced him to Jane Hall in August 1939 at the Garden of Allah. She "even urged him to look her up in New York when they both were back there."

At twenty-four, Jane knew full well how much her aunt hoped that she would find an appropriate husband with the kind of background and resources that Bob had. A gentleman with a generous heart and a distinguished family, he could provide well for their niece. Most of Jane's friends were married and had started families, and Rose had already urged Jane to stop encouraging serious suitors with warm friendship if she had no intention of marrying them. "You could never live in a 'wee small house in the country,' why let any man believe so?" she asked her niece. Jane, she advised, was "a prize" but should not seek the attentions of a "string of men." Now that Jane had lived and worked in Hollywood, Rose observed, it would be a mistake for her to think she could be satisfied with any of her former beaux, adding: "You have no idea what it would do to Randy and me if you made an unhappy marriage or a mess of your life." Given Jane's sense of responsibility to her guardians and her determination not to let them down, that comment must have hit home especially hard.

After nine years in the east, her aunt's strong ideas about the type of man Jane should marry had slipped into the core of her being. Her situation was a timeless one—the subject of much great literature (and many movies) including books by Jane's favorite authors, Jane Austen and Charlotte Brontë. Artist, author, and renowned screenwriter Frances Marion, Jane's far more senior colleague at MGM, had once found herself in the same quandary when, in 1911, at twenty-two, she met Robert Dixon Pike, who "represented a level of economic security and social acceptance that was very tempting," especially because Robert traveled in the same social circles as Marion's father. "Robert made it all seem so easy in place of the challenge of trying to live on her own." Once they married, Robert (as would be true of Bob Cutler) did not enjoy Marion's artist and writer friends, and Marion learned that she "would never be happy as a society wife." They divorced. Her third of four marriages, in 1919, to the love of her life—silent screen star Fred Thomson—lasted until he died suddenly in 1928.

Most glamorous, successful career women in Hollywood felt pressure to marry even if they were financially independent. MGM star Myrna Loy, who wed the first of her four husbands in 1936, noted: "I wanted marriage. Women all did, and whatever they say to show off, they apparently still do. . . . But in those days we were conditioned for marriage. Not only for propriety's sake but because even working, financially independent women were supposed to lead traditional lives." Loy admitted that she "felt a certain amount of guilt" about her great success as an actress. Although she had plenty of household help before and after her marriages, and Hollywood women were "liberated early in many ways," the desire persisted "to cater to her husband's needs, to compensate for the fact that [she] worked."

But Jane could not foresee the future or its complications. She had not dated anyone who seemed to be worth giving up her autonomy for until she met Bob. His support, she assumed, would give her more freedom to write what she wanted to write, the resources to remain a glamour girl, and the ability to help out her aunt and uncle or her brother if need be. Daysie Hall had agonized over her husband's impractical risk-taking for much of Jane and Dickie's early childhood; Jane had seen how humiliated her dying mother had been when she could not pay her own medical expenses. She had arrived in New York just as the Depression hit; the economy grew much worse during her last two years of high school, and her anxiety grew when her guardians argued continually about their finances. Bob promised long-term security, and Jane thought surely she could keep him on the wagon and his spirits high. Besides, he was so kind and thoughtful and had such an interesting background in the theater and the arts.

By December, Bob had made up his mind. Although Jane's and Bob's courtship is not well documented with letters between them, other correspondence and news items reveal the parameters of their activities in 1940. For the first eight months of 1940, Jane remained in the east and immersed herself in her new beau's life, spending part of the time at Rockrest, which had a rustic spring-fed swimming pool, clay tennis courts, and stables. Suffern became a place to entertain her New York friends as well as his. They also enjoyed evenings in New York at the theater and at smart restaurants and nightclubs. Yet that year the County Theatre had a rocky summer; reports were that Bob had sold it to Walter Armitage in the spring, but Armitage ran into financial troubles and had to close it down in the middle of August.

Bob knew enough to court Jane's guardians; at one point he even arrived at Poplar Springs with an entire carload of roses for her aunt. Rose and Randolph kept their fingers crossed. Jane began to resume the type of volunteer activities she'd engaged in during her deb years; Brad Crandell's early sketch of her—the one Dick Clarke had abhorred—appeared in the *New York Sun* to highlight her activities as a "Hostess at

Benefit Gathering" in Oyster Bay and Locust Valley late that spring. The external world Bob offered had great appeal; Jane liked the way others saw her as part of a sophisticated, chic couple.

Intellectually and emotionally, however, her diary indicates she felt less grounded. She would later reflect that once she met Bob, "it seemed, I didn't write very well anymore." Doubts about her ability as an author crept into her psyche over the next four years, imperceptibly at first. Periodically she confided to her diary that she had "tried to write" but that the work was "no good." But she had not given up yet. While Jane and Bob were dating, *Cosmopolitan* commissioned her to do a series of "Tales from the Hollywoods." "Dream Prince," which came out in September 1940, had the following tagline: "Park Avenue looks at Sunset Boulevard—and vice versa—in this mordant and amazing portrait of a Hollywood heel: the first story of a group holding the mirror up to human nature in the capital of Make Believe."

Jane's opening (again using the signature random capital letters that had been a hallmark of her father's work) sets the tone: "Hollywood has no cocktail hour . . . Lights burn late on the Lots out here, and executives Die Young. And that is why—in Hollywood—it's Noon that counts. Noon is when you find yourself Married or Fired or rewriting Shakespeare. Noon is when the legal office Exercises—and all the up-and-coming Agents stalk the Other Agents' clients—and producers' wives preview each other's $40 hats. Noon is when all the tortured Writers, with a sort of wan defiance, take two hours off for lunch."

The story zeroes in on a good-looking, narcissistic Hollywood talent agent, Curly Heroy. "Magnum" studios sends him to New York to secure an option from Lucy Gerard, the young girl expected to be the successor to the much-publicized 1938 debutante Brenda Frazier. Lucy is out for fun and wants to show off the dashing agent to her friends, but Curly is an inveterate womanizer, and he becomes infatuated with the Gerards' world of Park Avenue and East Hampton. Lucy's goal is to be a serious stage actress, not a Hollywood starlet. Besides, she's just seventeen; her parents quickly put an end to Curly's mission. The woman who really shows Curly the error of his ways is Beth Larkin, a smart, nice-looking reporter with a high-spirited personality much like Jane's. Enterprising, honest, and sincere, she intrigues Curly with wisecracks that take him down a peg. By the end of the tale, Curly regrets his misguided ways and shifts his interest to Beth.

Tale number two (*Cosmopolitan,* October 1940) bears a strong resemblance to the story of Nondas and Bob Cutler. "The Lady and the Witch," a "smart and witty story of the brand-new social order created by box office values," is set in Hollywood, where "a lady is known by the company that takes up her option." At Hollywood lunches—unlike those in New York, where women "drink daiquiris, brutalize *chefs salades* and have a Good time" —the atmosphere is "charged with Purpose." During one of these lunches at the Beverly Brown Derby, "Mrs. Pelham Temple IV was shedding Charm and Breeding like a sun lamp." Used to being in all the social columns, Eve Temple (resembling Nondas) is married to a wealthy Easterner like Bob whom she has left alone to try to launch her career as an actress. Screen tests indicate she has little talent, but Eve usually gets what she wants. One day, Pel appears unannounced at the Derby to ask his wife of eight years to come home. He appears quiet and unassuming, yet at times he is inscrutable; Eve is naïvely oblivious to how lost he feels without her. Nothing will deter her from her professional goal.

Eve introduces Pel to a lively, long-legged girl named Sherry Pearl (the witch—a stand-in for Jane) who is the talk of Hollywood. While Sherry and Pel get acquainted over the next couple of weeks, a desperate Eve fails to charm the head of Magnum into hiring her. Then she learns that an ex-boyfriend has written a book about a woman named Eve that could make a good movie; he encourages Eve to try to produce and star in it herself. Eve is sure her husband will invest the million dollars that she needs. But by then Pel has fallen for Sherry—he agrees to put up the money only if Eve will divorce him. Eve does not really want to end her marriage (any more than Nondas did), but she is positive that she can make it in Hollywood. "The Lady and the Witch" is a cautionary tale about "Ambition," which is, as one character comments, "the quality that every female is complete without!" Readers are left knowing that Eve will lose her husband, their homes in Newport and Florida, their yacht, and the lifestyle that she enjoyed in order to gamble on a not-very-promising career. They may not have realized, however, the extent to which this story reflects Jane's quandary as she tried to sort out her future.

Columnist Dorothy Kilgallen had noted in March 1940 that Bob and Nondas Cutler would split, adding that Bob's "sighs are for Jane Hall the fiction-writing post deb, and Nondas is being amused by Raphael Hakim, the French cinema mogul." His divorce in May left Bob and Jane free to become engaged in the late summer. At that point, Jane had no plans to give up her writing career or her part-time work in Hollywood. But first there would be great celebration in Virginia and New York, and in the press, about the prospective nuptials. At twenty-five, Jane was still quite seduced by the media attention. It validated her choices to the world at large.

Robert Frye Cutler

FOURTEEN

"She's Divinely Happy"

IN AUGUST 1940, MAURY PAUL ("CHOLLY KNICKERBOCKER") CAUGHT Jane on camera at the seaside resort of Montauk, Long Island, "the Mecca of prominent Mayfairites," as she strolled near the beach at the Montauk Surf Club. A light shirt jacket covers her striped bathing suit; high white open-toed heels accent her long legs. Kate tugs on her leash, eager to plunge into the ocean. About three weeks later, Paul scooped Jane's engagement the day before Rose and Randolph Hicks celebrated it on Rose's birthday, September 1. "Blond and pulchritudinous Jane Hall, who is as talented as she is pretty, has been in a romantic quandary for two months—trying to decide which of her two ardent suitors to accept. W-e-l-l-l, it's tall, personable Robert F. Cutler who won over Francis Clark." (Jane had apparently been seen quite a bit with the wealthy Francis P. Clark—in February 1940, their picture at the ultra-expensive new nightclub Fefe's Monte Carlo appeared in *Where to Go.*)

Other papers followed with the news on September 2; all mentioned that Jane would leave for Hollywood immediately after the Hickses' engagement party at Poplar Springs to work on a movie script. The *Washington Times-Herald,* which incorrectly said that Jane's first professional encounter with a typewriter "produced country gossip for the Warrenton paper," noted that her friends were "convalescing slowly from the idea that a debutante could push a pen." It had been a frenetic two weeks. At the end of August, Jane had returned to her family's Berkshire Hotel apartment after a visit to her future sister-in-law's house on Martha's Vineyard. She'd had barely a week to finish a story—possibly the third "Tale from the Hollywoods," about a veterinarian who doctors the stars' pets, though it does not appear to have made it into print.

Jane and Bob headed to Virginia for the party on Saturday, September 1. On Monday, they took off for Los Angeles on TWA's Boeing Stratoliner. Jane would live in a villa at the Garden of Allah for two months while she worked at RKO; Bob, who turned thirty-eight on September 6, probably stayed nearby for all or much of the time. The newly engaged couple must have been pleased by the letter Jane received from Rose soon after they arrived:

> Like a flame you came and left your moths crumpled and fallen: we have not yet come to. Bob's wire from Chicago delighted everyone at Poplar Springs but how we counted the hours to hear you had come down in Los Angeles! It was noon yesterday when we got our first word from California and you were working!
>
> Our party seems to have made a hit for I am still hearing very nice things about it—"the party of the Century" some are extravagant enough to call it. And such compliments for you and Bob—you really were a very handsome couple. . . . You must take time out to write me your plans. U.R. has taken a new lease on life and plans "to give you into Bob's keeping." I heard him tell Mrs. Tobin that Bob "was the only one of your Legion of Swain that he was willing to give you to" etc. . . . . Tell me which ring you selected. We were all fascinated by the little girl in you, under that great sophistication.

Rose ended by thanking her niece for "my grandest Birthday Gift" of a son-in-law. Although she maintained that Randolph had his heart set on having the wedding at Poplar Springs, Jane recognized not only that her aunt's and uncle's resources would be stretched by an elaborate wedding, but that the logistics of arranging such an affair might be highly stressful for her aunt. The solution that worked for Jane and her eager fiancé would be to elope with no fuss, or have a quiet civil ceremony in California. But first Jane had a script to write.

Between September 4 and the end of October, Jane commuted from her villa on Sunset to her RKO office at 780 Gower Street. Her assignment was to script an original comedy, "How to Meet a Man," for the Gene Towne and Graham Baker production unit; Swanie had secured the job for her in August. The studio, one of the Big Five in Hollywood, had had a rough time during the Depression, but by 1940 it was well known for *King Kong* (1933), for its screwball comedies, and for Ginger Rogers and Fred Astaire musicals. Its deal to distribute Disney features such as *Snow White and the Seven Dwarfs* (1937) had also proven highly profitable. In 1941, RKO would gain considerable notoriety for Orson Welles's controversial film, *Citizen Kane*. Welles, who was four months younger than Jane, had signed a contract with studio president George Schaefer in 1940 that gave him extraordinary creative control over his projects.

Jane's 104-page "Master Treatment with Rough Scratch Dialogue," dated October 17, 1940, outlines the fast-paced and complex story that she crafted for Towne and Baker. In a letter to Rose, after asking whether her aunt had received the one thousand strawberry plants Bob had sent her, Jane described the situation at her new office: "The work is going well but I still don't know just when I'll be finished. I'll probably be strung along from week to week, as usual, (and very grateful to be making the money, though!)—Have lost 5 pounds—Bob has gained four. Have no idea when we will be married, Aunt Rose, not till I finish this job. He would like to any time, and at first I thought it would be fun to 'elope' some weekend, but this work is too hard and the hours too long—I haven't energy enuf at the end of the day to get as far as the Airport! Every day from nine till six—including Saturday!!!"

"How to Meet a Man" provides an entertaining look at the world of radio broadcasting, popular culture, and romance in 1940. It begins as Eve Jones, an unstylish, naïve twenty-one-year-old from "Hilltown," USA, comes to New York City to find a husband. She's sure she will be lucky because she's been following the Vitamin Oats Hour on WPX radio. Its suave host, William (Bill) Gardner, is known as "the Woman's Friend" to his 33 million listeners; the show's success stems from his clever romantic advice to lonely women. Eve has written to him and,

like many others, signed her letter "Bewildered." Bill's response encourages her to come to Manhattan, "a Baghdad of opportunity," where "any
girl can get, win and marry any man she wants if she tries harder than
the next girl." Eve is furious because Bill's advice has not worked, plus
her tacky clothes lead the house detective at the Pierre Hotel to mistake
her for a floozy when she enters the bar, so he ushers her out. Eve at-
tacks the detective with her handbag and she ends up at a police station
for disorderly conduct. Still raging and now humiliated, Eve has a page
boy take a note to Bill Gardner at WPX asking him to bail her out. She
threatens to tell the newspapers that the radio show host is a fake and a
terrible guide for the lovelorn.

That does it for Bill, who is under pressure from his Vitamin Oats
sponsor to expand his audience. So he and his "Brain Trust"—Lorna Tree,
the fashion expert, Alice Brown, an author of melodramatic romances,
and Peggy Schuyler-Mason–Ten Eyck–Baker-Mills—a "fourteen-carat
mantrap," concoct a scheme to turn Eve into a savvy, attractive, and beautifully coiffed and dressed candidate who *can* capture the heart of a man.
In a move that anticipates modern reality shows, they decide to feature her
quest for true love on a segment of the Vitamin Oats Hour called "How
to Meet a Man!" Though Eve cannot afford designer clothes, Lorna shows
her how to use her funds wisely at Bonwit Teller on a beautifully made
black dress—one that she can convert from daytime to evening wear with
reasonably priced accessories. She learns how to apply makeup to look
elegant, not vulgar; to tone down the garish perfume; and to fix her hair
in a more becoming manner. Using a script, Eve relates her predicament
to Bill's WPX listeners: "I have brown hair, blue eyes and a high school
education. I come from an average American family in an average American town. I am a typist for big corporations; I get twenty-two-dollars a
week. I am looking for my Ideal Man." Bill promises his fans that if they
follow the adventures of this average American girl, to be known hence-
forth as "Diana Dunning," he will prove that there is a "Mr. Right" for
every woman no matter how modest her background.

The ploy works; the Vitamin Oats Hour experiences a huge boost
in ratings. Peggy takes Eve out to lunch at several good restaurants to
point out the pros and cons of men she might like. None of them strikes

Eve's fancy. One afternoon while she's on her own with a sandwich, Eve spots her dreamboat at an excavation site for the "Cutler Bank and Trust Company Building"—(Jane's humorous nod to her fiancé). The builder's name is Drexel A. Taylor III. He is tall, angular, and handsome; he wears tweeds, smokes a pipe, and drives a smart roadster. Eve has no idea who he really is until the team at WPX informs her that she's targeted the biggest wolf in Manhattan. Every deb in town has her eyes on Drex Taylor.

But how will "Diana" meet Drex Taylor? Bill and his brain trust concoct a charade: Eve (as "Diana") follows Drex around the course at the View Tree Golf Club, where she cheers him on. He notices her, but honest Eve puts him on the spot by refusing to pretend that a shot he missed was a practice shot so he that can earn a better score. Bill warns Eve that she can't always be totally frank; she must never puncture a man's ego. Eve ultimately wins Drex over, and they share a series of nightly comedic adventures faithfully reported to the radio show's fans. Although they are clearly an item, Drex is not willing to propose. Eve, who reports every morning to her tedious job at the City Life Insurance Company, becomes exhausted from late nights out with her new suitor. She picks up a nasty virus; Bill realizes it would be a good strategy for her to disappear for a short time for the rest she clearly needs.

Eve spends a week recuperating with Bill and his sister, Maude, in their penthouse apartment. By the end of the week, Bill and Eve have fallen for each other, though they conceal their affection behind facetious conversation. Still Bill feels he must get Eve/Diana and Drex back together for the sake of the radio show and his own future. Peggy suggests "Diana" tell Drex that she is about to leave New York as their relationship is going nowhere. The tactic succeeds, and Drex does propose. But Eve, who hates operating under a false identity, admits to him that "Diana Dunning" is a fraud. Drex is livid. Eve decides to go back to Hilltown until Bill, realizing he can't live without her, stops her on the way to the airport. His WPX listeners learn the real identity of Diana Dunning, and Eve will clearly become the future Mrs. William Gardner.

On October 29, *Daily Variety* reported that Jane had wrapped up this scripting job and "left the lot." Although she thought the radio show comedy was "going to be a swell picture," Towne and Baker never got the story into production. Jane could not have known at the time what RKO historian Richard Jewell points out—the team's ability "to produce successful films was suspect." They had been hired by George Schaefer late in 1939 as he moved RKO into "the most audacious production programming in company history." Schaefer tried them out on several literature-based productions such as *Swiss Family Robinson* and *Tom Brown's School Days,* but once these "tanked" Towne and Baker were "expelled from the RKO roster"—apparently along with Jane's project.

The news was not all bad. Jane had told Rose on October 18 that Universal "has already offered me another job—Joe Pasternak wants me to write him an original—on my own time and his money—and not even report at the studio! Just write the story. So I may turn out to have a very profitable 'honeymoon'!" Jane does not seem to have taken Pasternak up on this generous offer, though; and in 1941 he would try again.

On Thursday, November 7, Jane and Bob married quietly in Pasadena. They spent the rest of the month honeymooning in Palm Springs with Kate as a chaperone. Had Jane once dreamed of a real wedding? Was she unhappy that such an important occasion in her life became a last-minute trip to a courthouse between assignments? Maury Paul, who received a telegram from the new bride and groom, published this comment: "What 'Uncle Randy' and 'Aunt Rose' Hicks, who have been father and mother to Jane since the death of her parents, think of her unceremonious marriage, I can't guess; but knowing Jane and her dislike of any social fuss and feathers, they probably received the news with little surprise."

In September, Jane's high school pal, Muggy Gregory, now Mrs. Richard Cukor, had sent Jane a warm letter saying that she hoped that Jane would be a real bride because she "never looked lovelier" than she had in her white dress at the Nightingale-Bamford graduation. For several years, Muggy confided, she had "worried about a remark, no a statement," that Jane had made to her when they were confidantes: " 'I shall never allow myself to care a great deal for anyone—it hurts too much to lose them.' This was apropos of your [losing your] mother and father. I'm terribly glad that you've come away from that philosophy which I believe would give one more heartbreak than it would save. Do you understand what I mean?" In purple ink on pale lavender stationary, Muggy avowed that she wanted Jane's marriage to be perfect—she still felt very close to her. Jane's response, if any, was probably little more than an agreeable thank-you note, but it's telling that she kept this letter until she died.

FOR THEIR FIRST YEAR OF marriage, Jane and Bob appeared to live a magical life. December found the newlyweds back in New York just in time to attend a "Balloon Night" with prizes at the Stork Club. A silver balloon that landed in Jane's lap popped open to reveal she'd won a cocktail party at the fashionable, elitist nightclub. Stork Club chronicler Ralph Blumenthal acknowledged that Sherman Billingsley "did favor a homogenous look and type, his client of choice being young and good-looking, famous, influential, successful, rich, wellborn, and preferably WASP." Though "plenty of Jews frequented the club, to be sure," many of these were Hollywood moguls. For years, the club would be one of the Cutlers' favorite haunts. Maury Paul assured his *New York Journal and American* readers that a "gleeful" Jane and Bob would redeem their prize in a week or so—the party being "somewhat of a welcome home for them."

On December 21, at just about the time the Cutlers gave this party, the world learned of F. Scott Fitzgerald's untimely death. The forty-four-year-old author succumbed to a heart attack in Sheilah Graham's apartment in Hollywood—"while browsing through the *Princeton Alumni Weekly* and eating a Hershey bar." Marion Meade, Dorothy Parker's biographer, says that when Parker viewed his remains at Pierce Brothers Mortuaries, she "was struck by the isolation of the room, the absence of mourners or flowers, and Hollywood's complete disinterest in his death." Had Fitzgerald lived long enough to finish *The Last Tycoon*, he might not have died "believing himself a failure." (Fitzgerald's resurrection as one of America's most enduring novelists would not happen until later that decade.) It was almost Christmas when this tragedy occurred; most Americans were preoccupied with matters other than the death of an author who "seemed destined for literary obscurity."

Jane likely thought about her former colleague more than most of those who read the patronizing obituaries. Aspiration, though it was not a primary theme in her work, had also been a driving force in Jane's life. Had her burning ambition died by 1941? Clues to her state of mind can be found in a column Maury Paul wrote that winter, after he interviewed Jane and anointed her one of Cholly Knickerbocker's "Fascinating Ladies."

> Meet a fascinating lady who frankly admits she adores the life of "Café Society," thinks it a "swell" institution, the coining of the name an "inspiration" (Cholly Knickerbocker takes a bow), and [who] thoroughly enjoys making the rounds of the nightclubs until the wee sma' hours. But don't think she's frivolous. She's bright and smart and 'tis my suspicion is always on the lookout for "local color" for another of the clever fiction stories she pens for Cosmopolitan and other well-known magazines . . . She looks frivolous though—with a clinging-vine type of pulchritude that belies the wealth of grey matter behind those reddish-brown locks.

Paul continues with a synopsis of the high points of Jane's life, noting that she has "reaped in many thousands of dollars not only via magazine stories but writing movie scenarios for Hollywood consumption . . . Hollywood as a place to live in never has appealed to her much. It takes on added glamour when she's away from the town; when she gets back there, [she] always wants to come back home to New York." Paul mentions her "constant companion," Kate, and the fact that Jane, a "gay soul who adores people and parties, always adheres to the conventions of propriety and good taste." And he confirms her glamour-girl reserve— "It isn't easy to penetrate her pleasant exterior." Jane may not have been pleased to read, "I suspect there are times when she has terrific moods of depression," though Paul compensated by ending, "the bride of a few months, she's divinely happy and thrilled with just living."

Jane and Bob spent February in Sun Valley, and March and April in Hollywood and Palm Springs; by May 1, they had returned to Manhattan again. A brief article reveals her continuing interest in high fashion in May 1941. Reporter Dana Jenney noticed the "prominent young author" at the Café Pierre "equipped with all snakeskin accessories plus a snakeskin pillbox hat. The story behind the outfit adds extra color for the snake, an eight foot boa, was shot in South America by Johnny Adams, a friend of Mrs. Cutler." Jane also had two belt buckles, a handbag, and a leash for Kate made out of the hapless reptile.

During the summer of 1941, the Cutlers' guests at Rockrest included several theater luminaries such as the José Ferrers and Paul Lukases. The County Theater had been rented out to stage and screen actress Jean Muir, who tried to promote it as best she could given the "ill-will generated" by the "disastrous venture" of Walter Armitage the previous summer. Muir and her director, Sanford Meisner, had to put "cash on the line in advance for everything they need, including telephone service." Although she was eager to return the theater to the "standard set by Robert Cutler," the subscription list was only a third of what it had been in Bob's last season. The theater would not open during World War II and never fully regained its audience before it finally closed permanently in the late 1940s.

By then Jane was too caught up in the new responsibilities of her married life to focus on writing. Three notes from Henry La Cossitt, then an editor at Crowell-Collier's *The American* magazine, indicate how hard it was for Jane to concentrate on her own work. Among the luminaries who had appeared in the magazine's pages were F. Scott Fitzgerald, Upton Sinclair, Graham Greene, Sherwood Anderson, P. G. Wodehouse, and even Amelia Earhart. La Cossitt asked in June if Jane would talk over some story ideas with him. On August 5, he sent another note with droll suggestions as to how she might begin a story: "His slate blue eyes blazed with fury as. . . ," or why not "Her heart beat wildly as her lips met his in a flaming . . ." Or perhaps she could try something "like this: 'Nuts,' sighed the Duchess. She was bored—bored, that was it." The last was the most dramatic: " 'I'm pooped,' said the butcher's wife. Before her, the mutilated cadaver . . ." But no matter how she did it, La Cossitt begged Jane to "START!!" A month later, he wrote: "Dear Jane Hall: So you started. So what goes on?" What went on was that Jane had been tempted by an offer that came from her old stomping grounds.

Joe Pasternak had moved from Universal to MGM to produce the romances and light musicals that had brought him and Universal such great success. It was fun and not that taxing to work on his scripts. Scott Eyman notes that Pasternak was "a candid and happy man whose motto was 'Never make an audience think.'" He would remain at MGM for twenty-five years, turning out "consistently successful cornball product." On August 27, Swanie wired Jane at Rockrest:

METRO WANTS YOU TO START TUESDAY WITH PASTERNAK EIGHT FIFTY AND FOUR WEEK GUARANTEE. IF YOU WERE COMING OUT ANYWAY THEY DON'T SEE WHY THEY SHOULD PAY YOUR TRANSPORTATION. WIRE ME TODAY IF CAN REPORT TUESDAY AND IF SO I SHALL INSIST THEY PAY TRANSPORTA- TION WHICH IS USUAL THING. ASSIGNMENT IS A GREAT ONE AND I AM ANXIOUS TO HAVE YOU BACK HERE AND AT METRO ONCE MORE.

Pasternak's first project at Metro was "They Live by Night" (not to be confused with the later *noir* film of the same name based on the Edward Anderson novel *Thieves Like Us. Daily Variety*'s announcement of Jane's new job refers to the film as "They Love by Night.") Pasternak wanted Jane to do the script as a vehicle for Lana Turner after she finished shooting *Johnny Eager* (1941) with director Mervyn LeRoy. Bob was not tied down by a job, and the Cutlers left for the coast immediately. Jane worked on this "Torchy" through the fall and winter. Bob was enthusiastic enough about this Hollywood hiatus to buy a house for Jane in Palm Springs in October, which they planned to rent when they weren't there.

Jane enjoyed seeing her old colleagues at MGM, especially Doug Shearer and Marion Parsonnet, who by then had married a Warner Bros. starlet, Lorraine Elsie Kincherff, and fathered a baby daughter. Between September 1941 and March 1942, Jane and Bob stayed in a villa at the Garden of Allah during the week, with weekend breaks in Palm Springs. Before long, the (false) rumor in Manhattan literary circles was that they'd moved to California for good. Jon Whitcomb reported from Sundeck, his house and studio in Darien, Connecticut, that *Cosmo* editor Frances Whiting "is spreading the news that you and Bob are now permanently of the movie colony and that for her money you can now be considered as confirmed Los Angelenos. [*sic*] 'Hall fits out there', she says." Whiting would take over from longtime *Cosmopolitan* editor Harry Burton in 1942. "As for me," Jon continued, "many congratulations on your new dive in Palm Springs, and I couldn't be more pleased." Jon was at the peak of his career as an illustrator. He boasted that *Cosmo, Ladies' Home Journal, Woman's Home Companion, Collier's,* and *Good Housekeeping* had all renewed his contracts, plus he had several other irons in the fire including a commission to replace the famous pinup-girl artist George Petty as creator of the Jantzen swimsuit ads.

An account of Jane's life in Hollywood at the end of 1941, after she'd just been married a year, appears in a priceless letter that she asked her young secretary to write to her brother. Twenty-eight-year-old Dick Wick Hall, Jr. had secured teaching posts at Brown College and Pembroke College (the undergraduate men's and women's colleges, respectively, of Brown University)—though he said he did not find the male or female students very bright. He told Jane that he'd been "swimming upstream" for his entire academic life, and that university administrations were always against him "since they represent the part of the University that deals with the public directly. Even though the students worship me, the fact will always remain that I have a speech defect." Nevertheless, he continued to take speech classes and practice his exercises so that he would not lisp or stammer. Jane, who was impressed by her brother's determination and many achievements, did not want him to be a dowdy professor. She spiced up his wardrobe by sending him shirts, ties, sweaters, a jacket, a suit, and a polo coat from Bullocks Wilshire.

The unnamed secretary's letter to "Dear Professor Hall" may have amused Dickie greatly. She had gleaned through eavesdropping and the grapevine that "the general consensus of opinion here at this FAMOUS STUDIO called M.G.M. is that she's [Jane] an OK Character, a woman of talent and wit. They want to keep her on the payroll which tells the story re her work—AND if she wasn't so happily married she'd go over big and hold her own with the Village Wolves. She's also a slave-driver, in a very nice way I hear." Jane, she wrote, wears slacks for work and looks glamorous in her "girlish pompadour"; "I haven't seen a sign of 'temper' in her yet, so I guess she is either very well controlled or is feeling very fit." But she "turns out reams and reams in a day," working harder and faster than any of the more highly paid writers the secretary had ever known. "There's only one fly in the ointment, I think this Lady is homesick for New York and all it has to offer." The young secretary, who had been up late typing the letter, ends: "By the way, did you know the title of our epic is THEY LIVE BY NIGHT . . . ? *We* are realists."

This letter, dated December 4, 1941, probably reached Dickie two or three days later. In addition to his teaching responsibilities, he now had a new job analyzing information systems and encrypted messages for the navy. It was a skill that fascinated Brown's president, Henry Wriston. On December 6, Rose airmailed Jane the note that Dickie sent her about what he called his new "hobby." The letter was postmarked in New York at 12:30 a.m. on Sunday, December 7: "I have been in my office from 9 AM to midnight most of the past ten days," Dick wrote. "The Navy has invited me to take their confidential course in cryptanalysis so that I can serve the country as a civilian cryptanalyst if war is declared. They are much wiser this time than in World War I."

About twelve hours later, Rose and Randolph Hicks sat down to Sunday lunch; Dickie Hall may have been grading papers; Jane and Bob were likely enjoying morning coffee in their new home in Palm Springs. None of them realized that the Imperial Japanese Navy had just begun its surprise attack on Pearl Harbor. The particulars emerged slowly; it took time for the Associated Press and the national radio networks to pull together the facts from their local affiliates in the Pacific. As the horrifying news shattered the calm of what should have been a quiet Sunday, families across the United States switched on their radios, telegraphers tapped furiously, telephones rang incessantly, and Americans gradually absorbed the shock waves of a day that would "live in infamy." By 7:00 p.m. Pacific Time, an unnerving government-mandated darkness had descended over the entire West Coast.

FIFTEEN

"Because of the Dreams"

IN THE RAGING DEBATE BETWEEN INTERVENTIONISTS AND ISOLA-
tionists that preoccupied many Americans, Jane and her brother held
opposing views—Dickie had hoped the nation would stay out of war.
But after Pearl Harbor, there was no doubt about whether or not America would enter World War II. By the time Jane and Bob flew east for
Christmas, the conflict was a global one, with declarations of war against
the United States by both Germany and Italy.

"Hollywood was stunned," Frances Marion remembered: "a giant
foot had stepped on our anthill. Men immediately left the studios in
droves; almost two thirds of the skilled employees from the technical
crews, scores of writers, directors, cameramen and actors and even the
producer Darrell Zanuck enlisted." Historian Bruce Torrence describes
how, on the day after the attack on Pearl Harbor, the area near Culver
City immediately became a military camp: "100 studio trucks and drivers were transporting Army troops and equipment, studio arsenals were
stripped of prop rifles, machine guns, revolvers, and ammunition to for-
tify undersupplied posts along the West Coast." Though some prepara-
tions had begun before the attack, "nearby army and navy camps swelled
in size, defense plants expanded, studio buildings were camouflaged,
blackout regulations were enforced, and air raid shelters, complete with
hospital units, were built on studio lots." Hundreds of those in the entertainment industry volunteered to help out in war organizations. Stars

such as Clark Gable, Jimmy Stewart, and Robert Taylor would join the
military; others "made training films for the services." It was against
this background that Jane and Bob returned to the Garden of Allah in
January so that she could finish her work for Joe Pasternak. But, quite
possibly because of the war, the picture she worked on all that winter
was never made.

Rose begged her niece to come home again, but Jane came up with
a better, if temporary, solution: She turned her house in Palm Springs
over to her aunt and uncle for most of the month of March. They were
thrilled. Once they arrived back in New York, Rose reported that Randolph was now a "spellbound booster of Southern California."

After Jane and Bob returned east in April, they were both preoccupied by Bob's new job as codirector of stateside publicity for the Army
War Show. (He was too old to enlist.) This traveling military spectacle
of machinery, equipment, speeches, and songs had been organized by
the War Department so "that our people may see our Army and be
inspired to greater effort in supporting it, with full confidence in its
leadership and purposes." For more than four months, the Cutlers lived
out of suitcases in hotels with a pregnant Kate. At one of the stops, Kate
gave birth to five female puppies; one didn't make it. Jane named the
survivors after Lana Turner, Norma Shearer, Rita Hayworth, and Hedy
Lamarr. She gave Hedy to Brad and Micki Crandell.

During this patriotic adventure, Jane became frustrated by her loss
of momentum as an author. In response to a late-night wire that she
sent her uncle from Dallas in October, she received some strong advice.
Randolph warned that her "extensive traveling ought to be a source of
information for a writer of fiction and should beget an experience which
should develop a new line of production. You should not let the public
forget your existence by failing to go into print." Three days later he
again emphasized, "You should not lose your audience." But cooped up
in a hotel room with her husband and four newborn puppies, without a
place to work on her own, Jane could not muster the confidence to take
his advice to heart.

December 1942 found the weary couple back in Manhattan again:
"Bob and I stayed in two rooms at the Berkshire. I tried to write—

thought it was no good." That month *Cosmopolitan* rejected a story she had submitted about the continuing exploits of Fauquier County teenager Liz McKelvey. By then the "divinely happy" glow of Jane's that society columnist Maury Paul had described in the winter of 1941 had dimmed quite a bit. Her male colleagues and the friends whom she occasionally saw for lunch or dinner with Bob were away doing their part in the war effort. Cliff had flown to South America; his piloting skills would prove invaluable in both Asia and Europe. The navy had grabbed Jon Whitcomb and put his artistic talent to good use in the Pacific theater; Jane's trusted stockbroker and former beau, Andre Smolianinoff, had been commissioned as a navy lieutenant. Though they do not appear to have been in touch during these years, from 1943 until 1947 Dick Clarke served in the army.

Jane kept trying to write, but by mid-January admitted to her diary, "It is hard beyond belief; my tools are still with two years rust." She had an "excruciating time" with a story that she'd started. "Who was it said that movies are suicide for a young writer?" she asked herself. It had been tough on Jane to work under extreme time pressure; three of the screen stories she'd written were never produced, plus *These Glamour Girls* had been delayed and dissected for months by the PCA. Jane was one of many eastern writers with complaints about their dispiriting experiences in Hollywood, yet not all of them were negative.

There were obvious perks to working in Southern California among interesting colleagues. The main reason writers came west, especially in the thirties, was for the reliable and often hefty paycheck they traded for a loss of creative control. Historian Richard Fine discovered that while some writers "were treated shabbily," others—both established and struggling—benefited from their experience. Under the studio system, producers had absolute power over the script, yet Jane had been fortunate most of the time. Sam Zimbalist drove his writers hard, but after he read her treatment for *These Glamour Girls* he had asked Jane to write the script solo. Given her lack of experience, this opportunity, which she chose not to take, was a great compliment. Joe Pasternak was very supportive of her as well. Occasionally, Jane had even been allowed to work from home. Still, the range of work offered to her in Hollywood was circumscribed by the perception that the genres she knew best after 1935 were sardonic high-society romances and poignant, amusing comedy-drama.

Fine's comments that "virtually *every* writer was disquieted or unnerved" by the Hollywood experience, and almost all of them were homesick for the east, where they had more autonomy and more respect, certainly apply to Jane. He cites Raymond Chandler, who, in 1945, observed that Hollywood screenplays were written "by an employee without power or decision over the uses of his own craft, without ownership of it, and, however extravagantly paid, almost without honor for it." Working under a producer meant "both personal and artistic subordination, and no writer of quality will long accept either without surrendering that which made him a writer of quality, without dulling the fine edge of his mind, without becoming little by little a conniver rather than a creator, a supple and facile journeyman rather than a craftsman of original thought."

In spite of these challenges, Jane found the period between 1937 and 1942 the most interesting of her life. As she turned twenty-eight, at the beginning of 1943, agents urged her to continue writing; she was far too young to have permanently dulled the fine edge of her mind. Still, Jane felt stale; she found it hard to summon the psychological stamina and focus needed to become a serious author. She'd been writing about courtship since 1935, and her life no longer inspired such narratives. As a young teen, she'd had an unusually broad range; she had written across genres and about all kinds of subjects. Then, after the devastating loss of both parents, her life had gradually slipped into the years of "such mad fun." Though her skepticism about that pleasant ambience grew, during the Depression it was much easier to write about and to sell romantic satire than to mine for material in the darker resources of her heart.

After they had been married for some eighteen months, Bob slipped back into his silent, inscrutable self. He showed signs of a passive, dependent addictive personality—one that Nondas had escaped—and a side of him emerged that he had hidden quite well during his courtship of and early marriage to Jane; he became unrecognizable to her. Rose noticed the difference as well: "Indeed," she responded when Jane asked her about it, "Bob has changed to such an extent that California Robert Cutler is not our Bob." Part of the transformation may have been a recurrence of the sense of alienation that is common among heavy drinkers who are on the wagon—a quality Matthew Bruccoli describes in Fitzgerald. Though Jane was now more secure financially, her creative future and emotional well-being were both in jeopardy. Bob needed her, as Zelda had needed Scott (at least in Scott's assessment), to work too much for him and not enough for her dreams. Often he would sit stony-faced and silent when they went out with her friends from her former life.

On occasion there were compensations to being half of such an accomplished couple. On April 25, 1943, the *New York Journal-American* declared "WE TAKE OFF OUR HAT TO: Mr. and Mrs. Robert F. Cutler in their town apartment at the Berkshire Hotel. FOR: Their individual achievements in the theatre and literary world, and their combined "all-out" war effort." Accompanied by a striking photograph of the two of them, the piece praised Jane's work as a "socialite author who has won fame—and fortune—as Jane Hall, fiction writer and Hollywood scenarist," and applauded Bob's promotional efforts for the War Department. "This year he plans to turn his family estate of some 300 acres into a working farm, producing livestock, dairy products, etc., under his personal direction."

That June, Jane became pregnant for the first and only time. Though she recalled being happy, her diary reveals that she bought blouses in larger sizes and wore smocks (she hated maternity clothes) to conceal the pregnancy from her friends and even from Rose until her size made that impossible in the fall. When I was born, in February 1944, she noted that Joe Pasternak was one of many people who sent flowers to her room at New York's Doctors Hospital. My mother was furious at her brother and aunt, who raised hell because I wasn't a boy. Like almost all of her friends who had children, she found a live-in nurse to care for me. I don't recall feeling deprived by my parents' arms-length style of parenting—they lived separate lives, and my father had not expected to have children at all. My first live-in nanny, Lily Mallet, was a kindly, petite, gray-haired British woman from the island of Jersey. Thanks to

"Mallie," parenthood did not seem to distract my mother from her travels or her attempts to write. Before long, Rose and Randolph Hicks ("Mama Rose" and "Papa" to me) became my devoted surrogate grandparents.

But what had happened to Jane's literary aspirations? Through the summer of 1944, her diary entries are a mix of the mundane and the significant. August 15: "Wrote. Little by little I think I am learning how again. I wonder what the future really holds for Bob and me? I think we are terribly mismatched." On August 23, a Wednesday (and her "day to take care of the baby"), she mentioned: "Paris is being freed—the Germans supposedly on the run. I am on the Harper nine-day wonder diet. I want to weigh 118 pounds. Weigh 126 now." Carefully, she hid any depressing thoughts she had about her life at home from everyone except her diary. August 26: "Saturday worked at cottage [fixing up the caretaker's cottage near Rockrest], cooked three meals, how on earth did I ever let myself give up writing and get into this mess?"

By 1945, as her chain-smoking husband became increasingly withdrawn and his health deteriorated, Jane found herself, like Scott Fitzgerald, making the best of her situation. Like millions of her contemporaries, she reframed her priorities to fit the expectations of her husband, her aunt and uncle, and the era in which she lived. Her mother's advice to "take your troubles on the chin for the sake of those around you" defined the public face that Jane exposed to the rest of the world.

On New Year's Day, 1945, Jane promised herself, "I am going to write a story or article—at least one a month—all this year. This is my resolution, NO MATTER WHAT." She delivered the first story— noting that she wrote like a fiend to finish—to Elsie McKeogh at the end of January. "Because of the Dreams," an insightful tale about a young woman who realizes shortly after her marriage that she has picked the wrong man, was easier to write than to sell, yet very indicative of Jane's ambiguity about her own situation.

"Monica Baldwin was one of the lucky ones—Post-Depression, but Pre-War," it begins. "She had hurtled straight from Miss Bamford's Classes into one of those halcyon periods when it was possible for a well-turned-out young woman to have two or more serious suitors all at one time." Monica had had many suitors, but she was only in love with Johnny Banks and Bob McGrath. "Bob was serious and gentle the way very tall men are, and Johnny was the dashing, gay one. Bob had exciting dark eyes and his family was Old New York instead of Omaha, but Johnny had a Packard 8 and was, without a doubt, the best dancer Monnie had ever known in her life." Monica knows she must make a decision; after all, she's twenty-one and three years post-deb, after which a girl could grow stale. Once she decides on "Rabbit," which is her nickname for Bob (and Jane's for her husband, too), she explains to Johnny that while he "meant something to her that nobody else in the world ever could, Bob needed her more." They become officially engaged, as Jane and Bob had, in Cholly Knickerbocker's column. Johnny has a hard time believing that Monnie has turned him down; her last dates with him were "the happiest moments of Monica's life."

Jane describes Monica and Bob's beautiful wedding, with six bridesmaids and all the trimmings, at Manhattan's venerable St. Bartholomew's Episcopal Church; but their differences begin to surface during what should have been an idyllic honeymoon in Sun Valley. Used to lime and seltzer or an infrequent wine, Monica starts joining Bob for cocktails until she "learned to drink with a good deal of flair." One evening, toward the end of their trip, she inadvertently refers to Johnny, which makes Bob furious. He refers to her old friends as "those awful clowns you used to run around with," and that is the first sign that they are mismatched. After eighteen months of marriage, Monnie realizes that Bob has completed the "transition from Suitor to Spouse." She longs for the romance they once knew and the days when their favorite song had been "All the Things You Are." Almost every night she dreams about Johnny; Bob seems so placid, unresponsive, and uninterested in fun or seeing her friends.

After the Japanese attack Pearl Harbor, Monnie begins to worry that Johnny will be going to war. She and her husband barely speak. Once Bob enlists in the army without telling her, it's clear the marriage is over. Soon Monnie heads for Reno, Nevada, to see Johnny, and Johnny congratulates her on the divorce. To her delight, thanks to a football knee, Johnny is 4-F. Although several dates at the Stork Club, 21, and "dimmed out sidewalk cafés" confirm that they still adore each other, Johnny's Catholic church would never approve of his marriage to a divorcée, so they decide to elope. On their wedding night, Johnny reveals that he's still quite bitter about Monica's first marriage. "Didn't Bob need you as much as you thought?" he asks. Monnie answers that Johnny is so much more fun, so convivial and gay, while Bob is a "sourpuss." Instantly, she regrets the remark and adds: "Rabbit wasn't dull. He was just serious. He was sweet! And so in love with me!"

"Well, just don't let me find out I'm married to a mental polygamist, that's all!" Johnny snaps back, just before they fall into each other's arms. A small cloud has darkened this bright new marriage; Johnny, too, seems different than Monnie thought he would be. "Johnny tucked 4/5 of the covers around himself tenderly and curled up like a snail for sleep. 'Good night, darling,' he whispered. 'Happy dreams.'" Monica does have happy dreams—and this time they are about Bob.

"Because of the Dreams" is clearly semi-autobiographical. The protagonist, Monica Baldwin, mirrors Jane's own resignation as she recognizes how much compromise will be needed to remain in a difficult marriage. When I read this story for the first time, I wondered whether her description of Monica's first wedding mirrors the one that she wished had been hers.

One bright light in Jane's life—and that of her uncle and aunt—was Dickie's latest news: Brown University had not offered him a promotion, but he had accepted a position as an assistant professor of mathematics at the University of Maryland beginning in February 1943. While in Maryland, he recalled many years later, "I skipped the rank of associate professor, and was regional Governor of the Mathematical Association of America for several terms." In January 1948, one of his colleagues would introduce him to a fellow teacher, Esther Taylor, who shared his interest in music and bridge. They married almost immediately, in March of that year; their first daughter was born nine months later. It would be 1956 before Dick and Esther left College Park for Binghamton, New York, with their two daughters, Gretchen and Esther. There Dickie joined the faculty at SUNY's Harpur College, where he would remain until he retired.

On April 2, 1945, Jane had a letter from Swanie asking if she would like to work on the script for *A Date with Judy* for MGM. Joe Pasternak would produce the musical comedy that starred Wallace Beery, Jane Powell, and Elizabeth Taylor. Bob was not in favor of such a move, and Jane lacked the gumption to return to the West Coast. Ten days later, a film for which Jane shared "original story credit" with Ralph Block and Frederick Kohner, as she had on *It's a Date* (1940), opened at Loew's State in Manhattan.

Patrick the Great had been in production for just four weeks in October 1943. Jane never mentions it in her diary. The Universal Pictures comedy is a male version of *It's a Date*; Bosley Crowther's review in the *New York Times* on April 13, 1945 describes the "tale about a talented young man who is cast for the lead in a Broadway musical which first had been promised to his aging matinee-idol father" as "silly." The father-son rivalry mimics the mother-daughter situation in Pasternak's well-reviewed earlier film; apparently the story line worked much better for women.

By the time this movie was released, Jane had relinquished any thoughts of returning to her life as a screenwriter or enjoying extended stays in her beloved desert. She sold the house in Palm Springs at the end of May 1945. On an impulse, she quickly wrote an amusing story about "Eustace McCreery," a topology professor who falls under the charms of a glamorous magazine writer named Elizabeth Barnard; the story was based loosely on Dickie's summer romance with Renee Barnard, one of Jane's close friends from Cooper Union. "I finished a story, 'Acapulco Fizz.' Can't tell if it's good or not," Jane told her diary on June 28. Elsie sent it right to *Cosmopolitan*.

Jane had still not heard from the magazine on July 22 as she flipped through the pages of old *Cosmopolitans* in the attic at Rockrest, wondering why she could not write anymore. "What a fool I was to throw such a career away," she told her diary, adding that she was "depressed enuf to cut [her] throat." The following day, "in the nick of time," *Cosmopolitan* bought "Acapulco Fizz" for a thousand dollars. It came out in January 1946, illustrated by Jon Whitcomb, and with Jane's name among the authors listed on the cover. Unfortunately, this clever story did not jump-start her flagging career. After it was published, Jane made almost no further diary entries. Her aunt Rose's brother, Redondo Benjamin Sutton, who had lost everything in the Depression, committed suicide in 1946; the following year, sixty-seven-year-old Rose had a stroke that left her paralyzed on her right side and confined to a wheelchair. These were just some of the many challenges that sapped Jane's creativity and initiative. An entry in Jane's diary that she inserted in pencil some years later, on September 19, 1949, bears witness to the end of her life as an author: "I am trying so hard to write. When I look back over the things started—and never finished—I wonder what the answer is. It isn't because I stopped working. I have worked very hard. But nothing finished. It is as if I lost heart completely; no self-confidence left."

Jane was not alone in agonizing silently over her life choices. Though she was not a suburban housewife, her femininity and that of her social friends was defined by their being wives and mothers, managing well-run households, and retaining their youthful looks. Betty Friedan was only six years younger than Jane. When she interviewed her classmates who graduated from Smith in 1942, she exposed "the problem that has no name"—the "strange stirring, a sense of dissatisfaction, a yearning that women suffered in the middle of the twentieth century in the United States." She then analyzed the way educators, psychiatrists and social scientists as well as popular culture "lied to women about their need for feminine glamour." Janet Maslin posits that by using the glamorous word "mystique," Friedan put a "seductive spin on a set of dismal problems." Nor was Jane alone in finding her self-assurance shaken. Even today, highly successful women suffer a devastating lack of confidence; they underestimate their ability and often choose not to take on challenges they are not certain of overcoming. As journalists Katty Kay and Claire Shipman have pointed out, there is growing evidence that "our brains do change in response to our environment," and "the natural result of low confidence is inaction."

Jane was ahead of most of her educated, advantaged peers in that she had already achieved success in a career before she married. Still, this was not the dish that she had ordered for her thirties, to rephrase Scott Fitzgerald, who experienced his own debilitating crisis of confidence just before he returned to Hollywood for the third and last time. Fitzgerald observed that "premature success gives one an almost mystical conception of destiny as opposed to willpower. . . . The man who arrives young believes that he exercises his will because his star is shining. . . . The compensation of a very early success is a conviction that life is a romantic matter." Jane's star stopped shining far too early, for reasons that are complex though not uncommon. Although she married a man with many qualities that both she and her guardians found appealing, she had not realized—any more than Fitzgerald had of Zelda—that her kind, generous spouse grappled with demons that were too severe for a young wife to resolve.

As was expected of women in her generation, Jane became an expert at keeping up appearances. In the late 1940s, we moved to an apartment at 1100 Park Avenue, where my mother had begun her life in Manhattan almost twenty years earlier. My father's doctors had told them both that nicotine had a terrible effect on his circulation—if he didn't stop smoking, his health and perhaps his life would be in jeopardy—but even I could not persuade him to stop smoking when I asked for that as a birthday present. Over the next decade, my mother learned everything she could about real estate and investments in order to afford a life for our family in Manhattan and Virginia that was strikingly similar to the one Rose and Randolph had provided for her. She managed the Suffern property with efficiency and humor, naming our German shepherds after lawyers or taxmen (instead of movie stars). Jane's lifeline became the telephone; her greatest joy was talking with, corresponding with, and seeing old friends, especially those who had known her as D'zani—Jon Whitcomb; Brad and Micki Crandell; Grif and Debra Griffith; Marion Parsonnet and his second wife, Shirley; Cliff and Jane Zieger; and her closest friend from her Cooper Union days, Renee Barnard Wadkovsky, and her husband Alex. I remember them all with great fondness.

On July 22, 1951, thirty-six-year-old Jane penciled in one last comment in her diary: "I haven't written anything for years. I have lost so much since July 1945. I feel peaceful, quite resigned, and also, much of the time, quite dead." I was shocked and sad to read this remark a few years ago. She was so young then, even younger than my daughters are

now. But then again, Jane had suffered multiple losses. Three weeks earlier, her beloved uncle (and my "Papa") Randolph Hicks had died of lung
cancer. With Jane's help, Rose now had to manage at Poplar Springs
with round-the-clock nurses and interludes at the Washington Hospital
Sanatorium in Takoma Park, Maryland. At about this same time, my
mother also lost Kate—her faithful canine companion is buried along-
side other family pets in what was once a rose garden at Poplar Springs.

During the years when Jane had been most productive as an adult
writer, the time when she was happiest in her life, movies and magazines
portrayed love and relationships as a woman's true calling. Marriage,
then, for the vast majority of women, was incompatible with a serious
career. Jane's own stories and screenplays reflected and espoused that
universal narrative. Her guardians, several society columnists, even her
close male friends—all of them sent her subtle and not-so-subtle messages about what she "ought to need to be considered a good woman."
By the time she turned forty, in 1955, Jane's cheerful, glamorous front
masked a flagging psyche. "This was the era during which Adlai Ste-
venson, soon to make his second bid for president, told Smith College's
class of 1955: 'I think there isn't much you can do about our crisis in
the humble role of housewife. I could wish you no better vocation than
that.'" Month after month and calamity after calamity, Jane must have
wondered whether there would ever be a silver lining in her lonely
cloud. Looking back, I have often marveled at how my mother made it
through those years while retaining a cheerful disposition and a winning
sense of humor in public. Then, in the summer of 2013, I went back to
her boxes of papers and discovered the secret to her resilience hidden in
a cache of letters.

She had met a stranger who changed her life.

SIXTEEN

Goodnight Sweetheart

Love

Is nature's way of giving

A reason to be living,

The golden crown

That makes a man a king.

Excerpt from the lyrics, "Love Is a Many-Splendored Thing"
Academy Award winner, Best Music, Original Song, 1955

IT WAS A CHANCE ENCOUNTER AT A COCKTAIL PARTY DURING THE
autumn of 1955. He was a prominent Swedish businessman who preferred to be called "Johnnie"; his full name was Count Carl Johan Arthur
Bernadotte, the son of Sweden's king, Gustaf VI Adolf, and a great-
grandson of Queen Victoria. The youngest of five children, Johnnie had
been raised in the enormous Royal Palace of Stockholm. Surrounded by
the cobblestone streets and monuments of the city's medieval Gamla Stan
("Old Town") neighborhood, he developed a lifelong passion for Swedish history. Like Jane, he had suffered a great loss at a young age—his
mother, Princess Margaret of Connaught, died when he was three and a
half. Within three years, his father married Lady Louise Mountbatten.

A stubborn and romantic young man, Johnnie, to the dismay of his
family, created a scandal when he fell in love with a divorced Swedish

journalist and author, Kerstin Wijkmark, who was six years his senior. He was thirty in 1946 when they married at Riverside Church in New York City; by doing so he relinquished any claim to the Swedish throne. In 1951, Grand Duchess Charlotte of Luxembourg gave him the title of Count Carl Johan Bernadotte of Wisborg.

Jane knew nothing about this complex history when they met. Soon after being introduced to the tall, bespectacled, handsome former prince, who was fourteen months younger than she, she suggested that, royal ancestry or not, he needed a haircut. "Well, what have we here?" Johnnie asked. He decided to find out. They made a "pact" one evening over drinks—and possibly "Steak Nino," cooked tableside in sizzling butter in the elegant dining room of the Drake Hotel on Park Avenue at Fifty-Sixth Street. The exact terms of their pact remain a mystery, but they apparently agreed to respond to each other's letters within three weeks of receiving them.

In the 1950s, Johnnie occasionally came to the United States on business. At first he joined Jane and Bob for dinner with their other friends. Eventually, during his infrequent visits to Manhattan, he and Jane began having drinks in the afternoon at elegant hotel bars or at the Rainbow Room, followed by long conversations on the telephone. Their mutual respect and growing affection emerges in their correspondence; four dozen letters, more than a dozen postcards, and a handful of international wires survive from those that Johnnie sent to "Mrs. Jane Cutler" between 1955 and 1964.

Johnnie usually wrote to Jane from his Stockholm office at night or on Saturday afternoons, using tissue-thin Anglo-Nordic Traktor, A. B. or Anglo-Nordic Aviation business paper. She carefully preserved these letters in their airmail envelopes by snipping one end with scissors. Many are several pages long. When Johnnie traveled, he would send her notes from luxury hotels—the Lancaster, in Paris, or the Palace, in St. Moritz—and postcards from Rome, Florence, Monte Carlo, Copenhagen, and Baghdad. Sometimes he used personal stationery; his favorite was pale gray with a white monogram underneath a crown.

Absent, unfortunately, from this picture are the scores of warm handwritten letters that Jane wrote to Johnnie; he had asked her not to type them because longhand was "so much more personal and besides, there is a faint whiff of New York attached to the letter which gives me a very nostalgic feeling." By early 1959, Johnnie had preserved "at least fifty" of these letters in the right-hand drawer of the desk in his "pearl-grey office"; each time he opened the drawer, he told Jane, it let off a "slight distinctive whiff of her perfume" (Joy by Jean Patou, a rose and jasmine scent created after the 1929 Wall Street crash). Clues as to what Jane wrote about, and how her letters changed over the course of their relationship, can be detected in his responses. What is clear is that "D'zani," the uninhibited, fun-loving woman with a zest for life who hoped to write and to paint, managed to emerge again as the epistolary bond between her and Johnnie grew. Their friendship was no secret at all, but eventually they would need to keep the emergent spark between them hidden away in a separate pocket of their lives. Johnnie's letters never mention his wife or any problems at home.

On December 20, 1955, after Stockholm had already experienced the "severest winter in 100 years," Johnnie wrote to thank Jane for her response to his previous letter. It's unclear from this first surviving letter how long they had been in touch—his tone was already that of an old friend, comfortable enough to grumble that he wouldn't be able to ski over the holidays because of a knee injury. He was well equipped with books, though, for his family's imminent trip to a Swiss resort. He promised to toast Jane on Christmas Eve at six o'clock her time. "What about New Year's Eve? What the hell does 'indubitably' mean?" he asked at the end of the letter, obviously referring to the word she had used over her signature. Johnnie later admitted that it was "with the greatest difficulty" that he wrote in English "or for that matter" wrote at all. Still, his letters to Jane are often eloquent, despite a few misspellings and amusing errors such as "Bloody Maries."

Although they only saw each other twice in 1956, in March and November, the affection between them clearly increased. They pledged to toast each other at a certain time each day—usually at about five or six o'clock New York time. Johnnie wrote about the frigid weather, his business worries, and recent events in his life that might be of interest. In June he reported that "everybody in Stockholm is now very excited because Elizabeth and Philip of England are making a state visit here this week and there is a tremendous to do about that, and all the women here are buying new dresses and hats. I wonder for what."

He mustered far more enthusiasm for the dinners he had with Lena Horne and her husband the following month. "She certainly is attractive and also nice, but what problems they must have with her colour, and besides he is Jewish and drinks brandy like a fish." Repeatedly, he mentioned that he had gained a few pounds and wanted to lose weight; Jane had urged him to cut back on cigarettes as well. Twice Johnnie asked about Bob's health. The doctors' predictions had been right; my father's addiction to nicotine had led to a stroke in the late winter of 1956. The attack transformed the movie-star-handsome, athletic, and once witty man into a tragic figure with slurred speech, a weak right arm and right leg, and a face that drooped on one side. Despite my mother's best efforts to help him recover, like Zelda Fitzgerald, he "broke and [was] broken forever." He was lucky to be alive at all.

What intrigued me the most on reading these letters from Johnnie is how liberated he was, constantly encouraging my mother to fulfill her potential as an author and as a woman who surely no longer felt dead when she saw herself through his eyes. "Please do not let your typewriter go into a trance again," he pleaded in September 1956. Following a brief rendezvous in November, he told Jane that he missed their afternoon drinks "very much"; before long he dreamed about her at night—though he couldn't remember the details, he said, he "woke up with a smile." Without this support, it surely would have been excruciating for Jane to face the prospect of caring indefinitely for an indecipherable husband who, doctors noticed, seemed to enjoy being dependent and made little effort to recover.

As the months passed, Johnnie continued to reassure Jane that he believed in her potential: "How is your painting? Or have you started a new life and turned back to the old typewriter? Excuse me for needling you, but maybe it will do some good." Although it appears that he never made it to the United States in 1957, Johnnie's frequent letters acknowledged both the physical longing and the restraint that characterized their relationship. "I'm sitting at my desk in the office and the entire place is empty. . . . From your letter, which I have in front of me, comes a faint, but delightful whiff of your perfume. It is funny how a scent just like a tune can bring back memories. . . . Do you look as wonderful as ever? Do you miss the long and interesting telephone conversations? I do." Two weeks later, on January 29: "Why don't you try to find another studio apartment, is that so difficult? As long as you don't get one you won't be painting or writing, which seems a shame and a waste of talent. . . . Have you been buying a lot of new glamorous clothes, better for that bikini figure of yours? Do you remember how offended you were when I frankly asked you if you had a very good figure?"

By March he realized Jane was clearly "very depressed." Less than three weeks later, another calamity further tested her resilience. On April 4, while my parents and I were in Virginia, a fire destroyed Rockrest and most of the heirlooms and priceless family papers that the fifty-one-year-old mansion contained. I remember rushing to pick up the black rotary-dial phone under the staircase at Poplar Springs as it rang at the crack of dawn, hoping it wouldn't wake my parents. But then I had to run upstairs to tell them our house was on fire. Many years later, I learned from a lengthy inventory of Rockrest that a complete, signed set of F. Scott Fitzgerald's works was among the losses. Johnnie's letters never referred specifically to this crisis, so it's hard to tell what he knew about it. It must have been especially devastating for my semi-invalid father to lose his ancestral family home.

A mid-April letter from Johnnie mentioned that he had driven an hour away from Stockholm to the old university city of Uppsala, where he "saw a very light and indecent French comedy, in which everybody makes love to everybody else's wife, not too amusing." He looked forward to "going away for a long vacation to the south of France, Monte Carlo to be exact," and promised to bet on the numbers that Jane had suggested (23, 32, 34). They both loved occasional gambling and fast, glamorous cars; at the end of the year Jane purchased a black Chrysler 300 C convertible with beige leather seats. The make was the same, but its long, lean body and hefty tailfins gave it an entirely different look from her first black coupe, Hi Toots. Having her own car had always given Jane a sense of freedom and control that women lacked in so many other areas of their lives. Johnnie's reaction was predictable: "How can you resist trying it out for speed? Jake [our German Shepherd] must certainly be proud to be seen in such a beautiful piece of luxury together with his owner who looks much better than the car, either in leopard skin [prints] or not." (Years later, my mother taught me to drive in that car—it was almost impossible to navigate the narrow barn gate, and I banged up the tailfins. But I made the most of shopping expeditions into Warrenton by putting the top down, blasting the sounds of Motown on the radio as soon as I was out of earshot of the house, and—mimicking both Grace Kelly and Audrey Hepburn—donning sunglasses with a head scarf.)

On February 19, 1958, Rose Hicks died in a Manhattan nursing home after a long illness. Bedridden and fed through tubes, she yearned for release from suffering at the end. Although she left behind few liquid assets, Poplar Springs went to my mother, who began to spend more and more time in Virginia. That October, Johnnie wrote that he had been "up to my neck in business and most of it unpleasant"; but the good news was he would arrive in Manhattan on the twenty-second: "We should be able to drink martinis together on top of the world [at the Rainbow Room in Rockefeller Center] in one week's time."

Johnnie's five-week visit to New York, which lasted until the beginning of December, took his and Jane's feelings for each other to another level. Johnnie reminisced once again from a Scandinavian Airlines "flying Viking ship" as it headed home toward the North Sea. How he wished he was in our apartment at 1100 Park Avenue with Jane, watching the city lights come on over the East River, he wrote. Following another quick trip to New York at the beginning of February 1959, Johnnie was again airborne as he thought of Jane.

Sweetheart

I am following your advice and writing this before bedtime, as a matter of fact we are only about one hour out of New York. The weather outside is very good but I feel terrible because I don't feel as if all of me is here. The major part is left behind with you, obviously part of you is here. When

*turning off from Idlewild I could see the skyline of Manhattan and I could
just imagine how you were in the apartment dressed in black slacks and a
black blouse walking around now and then looking out of the window. I
am sure you were thinking of us and how the cards are stacked against us.
Darling, I am already feeling lonesome, or is it lonely, but at the same time
it is wonderful to know that you are there and that you love me. . . . Dinner
is just being served as twilight descends and I can only say that you should
be sitting next to me on our way to a destination unknown, but a destination
where all our problems are miraculously solved and we can only think of
ourselves and how we can best make a wonderful life together. Please don't
let me cease to excist [sic] ever.*

That winter, Johnnie tried to find time to write as much as possible
when he was "all by myself without interruption." Until the winter of
1959, Johnnie had never heard Jane talk "with such abandon" about herself.
"You know I am happy because I feel sure that you and I trust each other
like we do with nobody else." They never seemed to run out of things
to say. For the first time, it seems, Jane had found a true soul mate and
possibly the first romantic figure in her life who encouraged her creativity
and independence. Yet their complex responsibilities made it harder and
harder for each of them to keep up their time-consuming correspondence.

Months went by, and Johnnie worried that Jane had excised him
from her mind because he hadn't written. Finally, that December,
he was able to confirm his plans to stop in New York in January en
route to Rockford, Illinois, for a business meeting with the president
of Sundstrand Corporation. By then he was chairman of the board of
Sundstrand Hydraulic A. B. in Sweden; he was also active in promoting
the "Outer Seven," an organization devoted to lowering trade barriers
among Sweden, Great Britain, Switzerland, Austria, Portugal, Norway,
and Denmark.

It was the weekend of January 22–24, 1960. On Saturday evening,
Jane and Johnnie stayed up all night talking—he called it their "36 hour
extravaganza." Early that Sunday morning, I discovered them sitting
on the black leather stools on either side of the bar in our apartment

drinking Bloody Marys. My father was asleep in his bedroom across a narrow hallway from mine. They looked exactly as they had when they left for dinner the evening before—elegant and impeccably dressed— though I remember being amused by the delicate outline of my mother's lipstick on Johnnie's left cheek. Looking back now, I realize that this could have been a scene from one of Louis B. Mayer's 1940s movies. Sexual tension was clearly in the room, but the stars—glamorous, mysterious, reserved, yet playful—kept their self-respect.

At home in Sweden, Johnnie thought of Jane "very, very often and at the oddest times such as in the middle of a conference." She had inspired him to buy a crème-colored Jaguar with red upholstery—as "it's supposed to be very fast." During a Swiss ski vacation at the Palace Hotel in St. Moritz, Johnnie admitted that he hardly skied at all: "I do not seem to have come back from 'outer space' yet." But then months passed before he wrote again—or at least before there is another letter in Jane's papers. He became consumed by work, and each of them pursued demanding lives.

Between 1956 and 1960, Johnnie had felt enormous pressure to succeed in business, while my parents faced a series of traumas that occurred one after the other. His infrequent letters from 1960 onward indicate that he had some "very, very rough times," especially in the spring of 1961. He wanted so much to hear Jane's voice "every evening at least on the phone," but that was impossible. In April, he still felt a "very very strong and intense longing to take a cab and go up Park Avenue to meet a friend who has the most wonderful and kind understanding." He was "tired and very depressed," and pleaded with Jane to send him one of her "wonderful warm letters." There are large gaps in their surviving correspondence at this point—nothing except a wire on Christmas in 1962 and a postcard from Geneva in 1963 telling her that he had "ended up in charge of Sundstrand in London after quite a battle."

In the 1960s, while I was in boarding school followed by college, my mother spent most of her time at Poplar Springs because the country setting was much healthier for my father. On June 2, 1964, she took the Eastern Airlines shuttle to New York for just forty-eight hours. The sparse journal she kept that year indicates that while she had a several appointments scheduled for the trip, she and Johnnie had time for drinks or dinner on Wednesday, June 3. She caught the last shuttle back to Washington that night.

Once again, Johnnie sent his thoughts from somewhere over a rainbow. The postmark from Copenhagen, where his plane landed, is unmistakable: June 4, 1964.

> *Darling, It is three in the morning and the sun is up shining in the clouds over the North Sea and I feel lonely because I miss you so much. It was wonderful to see you even if it was terribly short. It is exciting to think that in spite of the long intervals it is allways [sic] as marvelous as ever to be with you and to hear you tell me that you still care for me. You looked very beautiful and as alluring as I think of you. Darling, you should be sitting next to me instead of the young unattractive girl who is on her first trip to Sweden.*

For my mother, at least, that might have been a perfect Hollywood ending.

Johnnie promised to write again soon, but if he did, the letters have not survived. There is no further correspondence in Jane's papers to guide us to the end.

BUT THERE IS ONE POSTSCRIPT: On May 7, 2012, the *New York Times* reported that "Carl Bernadotte, Prince Whose First Loyalty Was Love, Dies at 95." By then Johnnie was the last surviving great-grandchild of Queen Victoria of England. The obituary focused on his willingness to give up his title in 1946 in order to marry a woman who was not of royal lineage. His wife, Kerstin Wijkmark Bernadotte, died in 1987, five months after my mother died. Johnnie moved back to Sweden from London and found happiness again with Countess Gunilla Wachtmeister, whom he had known since they were children. Their marriage lasted for a quarter of a century until his death.

Carl Johan (Johnnie) Bernadotte
Polaroid taken by Jane Hall Cutler at
1100 Park Avenue circa 1960.

EPILOGUE

Finding D'zani

A DARK GRAY CROWN SITS ABOVE THE SCROLLED MONOGRAM ON the card that Johnnie enclosed with *A History of Sweden,* his gift to me on my sixteenth birthday. On it, he acknowledges the "special interest in history" that we shared; he hoped that Ingvar Andersson's book would give me "even better marks in school." He signed it "Affectionately, Johnnie" over his full name. Looking back now at our family situation in 1960, I am grateful that he encouraged my mother to be the author or artist she wanted to be, though with no real success. And most of all, I am glad to know now that her heart had opened and that moments of real joy (not just the scent) came into her life at what was otherwise a dismal time. Initially, I was hesitant to read Johnnie's letters to her. But as a historian, looking back today from an era in which the cultural norms are often violent, crude, and tasteless, I was charmed by the deep, intense, yet reserved and self-possessed bond these two people in their forties shared. I can see now, more than a half century later, that Jane, caught up in a challenging marriage with a silent spouse, found in Johnnie's admiration and engagement just the sort of emotional reinforcement that popular culture insisted she needed to be a true woman.

Unaware at the time of this secret romance that boosted my mother's self-esteem, I longed for a more ordinary family like that of Wally and Beaver Cleaver or David and Ricky Nelson. Popular American culture, especially sitcoms like *Leave It to Beaver* and *The Adventures of Ozzie* and *Harriet*, filled children and housewives with clear messages about what domestic life should be like. But my elegant mother and her discreet, refined Swedish companion, who were rarely if ever alone together, would never have fit into a pedestrian sitcom world. Both of them were committed to their marriages, and physical attraction was clearly only one aspect of the bond between them that lasted for at least a decade. Besides, a full-blown affair would have been uncharacteristic of my mother, for whom respectability and keeping up appearances was paramount, and whose personal code of behavior rivaled that of Production Code watchdog Joe Breen. It was a code that also explains why at least four of her former suitors, who may have been frustrated by Jane's sense of propriety, nevertheless remained her friends for life, as did their wives. Johnnie was a surprisingly progressive man of royal lineage who had become caught up in a poignant relationship that surely would have intrigued Louis B. Mayer had he known it was with one of his former scenarists. (After Britain's former King Edward VIII abdicated the British throne, Mayer suggested to a story editor that the Duke of Windsor become head of MGM's European offices.)

In the golden era of Hollywood, infidelity movies were "best loved by audiences when they are reassuring and only about a flirtation, nothing that could actually hurt anyone. Audiences liked infidelity stories that came close, but didn't deliver," Jeanine Basinger writes. "Some of the movies' most beautiful and memorable scenes involve infidelity, it was everywhere on screen"—which was surprising, she continues, "since because of censorship, technically it couldn't be anywhere at all." Jane and Johnnie may have identified with the dilemma faced by Laura (Celia Johnson) and Alec (Trevor Howard) in *Brief Encounter* (1945); or the temptations confronted by Kitty (Lucille Ball) and Larry (Bob Hope) in *The Facts of Life* (1960).

"Hollywood provides Utopian solutions to everyday desires," Richard Maltby has written, adding that in American movies the heroes and heroines are often "absolved from both guilt and responsibility for what they do." Although the studio system did produce many movies whose endings were not tied up neatly, the romances churned out by MGM (like Jane's magazine stories) had to resolve the protagonists' problems satisfactorily. Frances Marion observed in 1937 that Hollywood audiences cried out for "a substitute for actual life experience," an emotionally satisfying interlude. Above all, audiences expected to be "sent home happy"; Maltby notes that working girls and young housewives used movies as a way to take off "into a romantic fantasy or a trip." That was just the sort of escape that Johnnie wished that he and Jane could have when he wrote to her from one of his flights across the Atlantic.

Though severe economic deprivation was not part of her world, Jane's life involved its own set of compromises. She met Johnnie in the 1950s, when, according to Gail Collins, women had been "catapulted back in time to the nineteenth century." Women like Jane had been told that "truly feminine women" should not want careers; in those days many married by the time they were twenty, and three out of ten women became blondes. Betty Friedan's description of the "strange discrepancy between the reality of our lives as women and the image to which we were trying to conform"—the feminine mystique—applies not only to bored suburban housewives in the fifties and early sixties but also to urban sophisticates who delegated childcare and housework to their domestic help, but still had to adjust to living through their husbands and trying to remain youthful and attractive at all times. Those who were single, divorced, or widowed did not feel complete, and, even after fifty, embarked on a "frenzied, desperate search for a man." In 1955, the year Jane met Johnnie—the year in which her soul hit bottom—Anne Morrow Lindbergh, desperate "to be at peace" with herself and achieve an "inner harmony," mourned the many distractions that destroyed women's souls and creativity in her still-popular classic *Gift from the Sea*.

When Jane arrived in Hollywood, she had been scornful of women who put too much stake in their appearance; she'd applauded Margaret Sullavan for not being a glamour girl. But for deep-seated reasons, it had been hard for her to follow her natural instincts or the advice that she offered in her fiction and screenplays. Once artists transformed her image of herself, and society columnists' flattering remarks penetrated her ego, she felt the need to live up to their comments. The messages she received from magazines, movies, and eventually television—while at times mixed— encouraged women of her generation to hide the aging process behind an aura of mystery; many glamorous women became semi-reclusive in their later years. Aging gracefully was much easier on the telephone or through the mail in the pre-Skype era. Jane's goddaughter, psychologist Lindsay Gibson, recalls how unusual it was, especially in Virginia, that my mother wore sunglasses so often indoors as well as outside. Again, in her two-week respite by the sea, Lindbergh made an observation that could have applied directly to Jane's dilemma: "The most exhausting thing in life, I have discovered, is being insincere. That is why so much of social life is exhausting; one is wearing a mask." It was only when she found time alone that Lindbergh felt free to shed her mask.

Today, even in the West, we still live in a "gender unequal world," and, notwithstanding significant changes in the past century, news articles periodically highlight the many circumstances in which women remain marginalized. Now as much as ever, young women are encouraged to focus on their physical appearance—websites and magazines advise female teens primarily on their looks and on ways to attract a boyfriend; a glance at the cover of a current issue of *Cosmopolitan* magazine, which used to be filled with articles about important national issues and exceptional fiction, tells us how times have changed. "A woman's aspiration to be beautiful ties her to society's margins just as effectively as did her mother's mop and vacuum," and "all this polishing and strutting takes an enormous toll," Barnard College president Debora Spar acknowledges. Her concern is that women not only seek perfection in their work life, they treat "physical attributes as if they were competences."

Little girls may be urged to be whatever they want to be, but they are also "being pummeled by a bizarrely narrow set of gender stereotypes. Girls as princesses; girls as sex objects; girls as pretty things to be dressed up, jeweled up, and carried off by men." Spar's statement that women are "the ones who still equate beauty with success and thinness, in particular, with goodness," applies directly to my mother and many of her contemporaries. On the other hand, there are women who resist this obsession with their looks: As actress Kim Cattrall said recently on the PBS show *The Boomer List*, "I have wrinkles. Let it be part of the story."

In 1978, two years after my father died, Jane sold their Manhattan apartment and gave up any hope of returning to her former life. Immersed in her world at Poplar Springs with numerous pets and intermittent back pain that sabotaged her mobility, she asked me to pack up her personal things and supervise the movers. (At the time, I lived a few blocks away with my husband and two small daughters.) It was a heart-rending task that brought me face to face with the end of a life I had observed as a child. In her closets and drawers, a wardrobe fit for a movie star gathered dust: tailored suits by Mainbocher, Chanel, Dior, and her favorite designer (and friend) David Kidd; Rudi Gernreich swimsuits; sparkling cocktail and evening clothes (including the black velvet dress that appears in Crandell's portrait); felt, fur, horsehair, and taffeta hats of all sizes and shapes with veils and feathers; turbans and snoods; silk and satin caftans and lingerie; purses and kid gloves for fashion shows, glamorous lunches, and glorious evenings; soft leather and satin heels, many with peep toes from I. Miller and Sons. I wanted so much to fit into her open-toed Lucite heels with mink pom poms, but like Cinderella's sisters, my feet were much too large.

In those days my mother's style guides had been *Vogue* and *Harper's Bazaar*; much of her clothing came from Hattie Carnegie, Saks, Bergdorf Goodman, and Bonwit Teller. What a time-consuming effort it must have been to be properly turned out back then. The only part of her wardrobe the movers did not take to Virginia were her sable and silver fox stoles, muffs, and hats; her mink jacket; and her Revillon mink coat, which she kept in storage at Reiss & Fabrizio. Clothing has a transformative power; clearly this classy wardrobe (provided by the assets my father had put in her name) had made her feel good and infused her stage entrances and cocktail party appearances with considerable cachet—enough cachet, obviously, to attract a former prince.

In 1936, just as my mother began to get her glamour on, a short-lived magazine, *The New York Woman*, printed this morsel, titled "A Snare and a Delusion": "Nomination for the most misused word: glamour. According to Webster's New International Dictionary, glamour means: '(1) magic; a spell or charm, as one which deceives the sight; (2) any interest in, or association with, an object or person, through which the object or person appears delusively magnified or glorified; a deceptive or enticing charm.' In another word, phony." Certainly Brad Crandell's oil portrait is a magnified image of my mother as a movie star—it is not my mother. It reminds me of Lana Turner, who by then looked nothing like the refreshing young ingenue who played Jane Taylor in *These Glamour Girls*. In Jane's life—and in the lives of a minority of privileged women today—having the means to look and feel this glamorous makes them feel good about themselves. Often they contribute liberally of their time and money to worthwhile causes and nonprofit organizations that might not exist without their help. The world they live in may seem phony to some, but to them the combination of glamour and, hopefully, generosity is life-sustaining, and makes them the focus of flattering society or celebrity gossip.

My mother's wardrobe was shipped to Poplar Springs, where her glamour-girl clothes would rarely, if ever, be worn again. There she had been living a different kind of life in slacks and stylish blouses: Throughout the 1970s, much of her time was spent caring for aging horses, burros, numerous dogs, a handful of farm cats, various birds whose lives she had saved including a screech owl ("Sidney") and a shrike ("Speedy"), and, until about 1972, Skulnik. Skulnik, an ocelot that had bonded only with my mother in 1955, lived with us for seventeen years; he spent his golden years in a large cage on the sun porch at Poplar Springs, where, mocked by blue jays and squirrels that frolicked outside the windows, he could watch the seasons change. Once darkness fell, Skully was distracted from his natural baser instincts by the flickering lights of his favorite sitcom, *I Love Lucy*. In the cavernous stone manor house where Dick Wick Hall's desk, chair, and typewriter from Arizona stood gathering cobwebs in her one-time room on the third floor, those devoted creatures were my mother's closest companions.

Poplar Springs is now a place where sadness has been replaced by joy; it is an oasis with a spring-fed swimming pool and a spa that my mother and her aunt and uncle would have adored (http://www.poplarspringsinn.com/). Today, the great room where my mother had her first debutante party is the outstanding Manor House restaurant. Our library, where I built villages out of Rose's mah jong set, and where my mother had me arrange all the books by color, is Casanova's Bar. Poplar Springs, where so many of my mother's real and imagined courtship narratives played out, is a refuge where romances culminate in their requisite happy ending of a beautiful—yes, even glamorous—wedding; brides and grooms, movie stars for a day with dreams of happily-ever-after, occasionally leave the grounds in horse-drawn carriages.

It took me several years to turn the property into an event site while I was working at another full-time job in Washington; though we couldn't afford to keep it, I was determined not to lose access to the land that meant so much to my mother, and also to Rose and Randolph Hicks, who are buried a few hundred yards from the manor house. Perhaps I, too, wanted a way to revisit and share with others a place that had once been full of glamour and the mellow sounds of Chauncey Brown's combo wafting down from the balcony as elegant couples swirled around the great room.

Poplar Springs is also the final resting place of Kate, Skulnik, and various other pets including the dogs and cats that my own family treasured. I finally had to sell the property in 1995 to pay the mounting debt on Jane's estate taxes, but I found a buyer who shared my dream of making it a public space, as do the current owners. Visitors from far and near enjoy jazz, cocktails, alfresco dining, and mad fun on the new terrace—once Rose's formal English garden—on long, languid summer evenings. And we could do that, too, though my daughters and grandsons live in California.

My mother had written dozens of heartfelt letters to Dick Clarke from Poplar Springs when they were dating. A few days after her fatal heart attack in 1987, Dick called me from a pay phone in Seattle, Washington. At the time, I knew nothing about him except that he frequently phoned and sent Jane boxes of Super Gram III vitamins, several of which remained unopened under a table near her bed. A letter he'd sent her in 1985 was signed, appropriately, the "June in January kid."

"Your mother and I were close friends," Dick told me. "I was in love with her for a long time. Would it be all right if I call you once in a while?" I felt a twinge in my heart—*he's still in love with her,* I thought.

About six months later, I met Dick and his wife, Amy, for tea in a

hotel in Seattle. We had a congenial conversation and they both spoke
highly of Jane, but we were rarely in touch after that. Dick's optimism,
his enduring affection for my mother, and the foresight that led him to
keep every letter, postcard, and telegram that she sent him between
1934 and 1939, made it possible for me to uncover aspects of her literary
career and her life in Hollywood that would have remained a mystery.
Because Dick returned all her letters to my mother, I came to know
D'zani, the enterprising young author whose laughter echoed across
Hollywood production lots, and whose strong character and accomplishments would have made her father proud.

Appendices

APPENDIX I

"Jimmy"
Jane E. Hall, age 13
Redondo Beach *Breeze,* June 8, 1928
Headline: "Pathetic Old Man Dies in
Hermosa Redondo Hospital"

A few days ago in the Redondo-Hermosa Hospital, Jimmy died.

"Jimmy" was a gentle, peering, pathetically talkative old man, whose real name was James Globbins, whose worst fault was to abuse the floor nurses in Spanish when they threatened to confiscate his daily 'sip' of brandy. Too long he had been a slave of a merciless master, Whiskey; and in return, liquor had robbed him of his health, his friends, and nearly all of his funds; everything he had left in the world.

Chronic alcoholism was Jimmy's trouble, and every day I could see him growing weaker. Once in a while, when the flame of his fast departing strength burned brighter for an instant, he would put on his bedroom slippers and an old hat and wander aimlessly down the halls, a sorry figure in his faded blue nightshirt.

Alcohol had affected his mind to quite an extent; once when I was there, and he was sitting in bed puffing at an old pipe that had no tobacco in it, the doctor passed and Jimmy hailed him quaveringly:

"La-a-and lord . . ." he called in a thin, shrill voice, "Land lord, come here!"

The doctors were used to the incessant demands and queries of the old man and passed on.

"Why did you want the doctor, Jimmy?" I asked.

"Oh, that's not the doctor; that's the landlord!" he contradicted fretfully, "and I want to pay the rent so I can go home. What time do the cars leave tomorrow morning?"

Just to humor him, I told him (I knew Jimmy would never leave the hospital), and he asked me where I'd been. As it happened it was Sunday and we had just come from church, as I informed him.

Much to my dismay, Jimmy's eyes filled with tears, and one by one, they slid down his wrinkled cheeks.

"I wish I could go to church," he whimpered, fingering the time-blackened rosary that hung about his neck.

"Well, you can as soon as you're well enough to be out of the hospital," I tried to say soothingly, but my heart ached for the lonely old soul.

"I hope so," he said, brightening. "Will you be in tomorrow?"

"I won't be able to come tomorrow." I smiled. "But I'll see you before long. Adios!" And as I went out the door, he beamed and waved a gallant "Adios, señorita!" I like to think of that.

"Before long" never came; a few days later I learned that Jimmy had "gone home."

If every member of the human race, before he pledged himself a slave to alcohol, would think of Jimmy, who died alone and forsaken in a hospital bedroom, I wonder if he'd change his mind?

APPENDIX II

"Writer's Career Shines Bright in Future of Young Beach Girl," wrote Jim McGinnis in the Redondo Beach *Breeze* on September 10, 1929. After noting Dick Wick Hall's success in the *Saturday Evening Post,* McGinnis published a poem that had already brought Jane a silver medal from the prestigious St. Nicholas League and, according to her scrapbook, also came out in the *Manhattan News Progress* and the *Hermosa Review.*

"Midnight Seen Through an Open Window"
By Jane Hall, age 14

Deserted streets
And darkened windows.
Roads littered with the shrouds
Of yesterday's merriment.
Far off, the sound of a brush—
Ceaseless, monotonous as time.
He comes in sight at last—
And old, bent man.
Sweeping up the remains
Of someone's pleasure.
Banana peels—and empty wrappers.
Wind whips through his tattered coat.
His hands are gnarled, his thin face
Creased with care.
For him, life has been
an empty wrapper . . .
Fate is cruel.

Title page of These Glamour Girls. *Illustration by Jon Whitcomb. Hearst's* International Cosmopolitan, *December 1938. Reprinted with permission from the Hearst Corporation.*

APPENDIX III

These Glamour Girls
A Synopsis of the Novel (*Cosmopolitan,* December, 1938)

A mix of humor, satire, and pathos, the book begins: "There is nothing that can make a woman of nineteen feel quite so smooth and On-the-Town as waiting in a bar. Alone." At 5:30 on an April afternoon Carol Christy and three other young women gather near the bar at "Hymie Bernam's Birdhouse" (quite possibly a stand-in for the Stork Club) to commiserate about a crisis. The benefit they are expected to attend conflicts with "Kingston" [aka Princeton] house parties. How could they possibly miss what is clearly the most important weekend in a girl's life? Three of these post debs are glamour girls who sip hard-core cocktails, light cigarettes, and make amicable fun of their reserved, old-guard friend, Ann Van Reichton, when she orders orange juice. Petite Mary Rose Wilson glances at a headline on front page of the day's paper: "Famine Sweeps Nanking!" Her reaction: "There's never any real news in the papers. I don't see why people buy them!" Why, to look at the society columns, of course, where you can often find a picture of the leader of their group and "the season's current killer," Daphne ("Daff") Graves.

A striking brunette with exotic light gray eyes and a "piquant, aristocratic face," Daff is arrogant, always the center of attention, and often photographed. She has a "Maxfield Parrish figure," a flock of beaux, three bids for the upcoming house parties, and great pride in her membership in café society. She pays hardly any attention to her "little, faded" mother. Her minion, wide-eyed, blond Mary Rose, with "just the sort of voice that suits a wide-eyed blonde," is desolate because the boy she has her eye on, Homer Ten Eyck, has not yet sent her a bid. Mrs. Wilson, a blatant social climber joined at the hip to her Pekinese, Ming Toy, solves the problem; she invites Homer for dinner, plies him with cocktails, and coyly asks which weekend he expects her daughter for house parties. Mary Rose's parents epitomize the nouveau riche; her family moved from Bronxville to a penthouse on Park Avenue with a paneled drawing room that had been imported from an English castle. Gordon Wilson, who had gone to Michigan, cannot understand the godlike importance of the college men at Kingston until his daughter explains that "they're the glamour boys!" He's given Mary Rose all the advantages, including an ostentatious debut at the Ritz.

The third member of the group, tall, awkward Ann Van Reichton, hails from WASP roots, very old money, and an ancient brownstone mansion in Murray Hill. (In Jane's treatment, Ann's last name had been "Van Renssaeller," which her editor apparently found much too close to that of the prominent Van Rensselaer family.) "A big dark gal who had no looks, no style, and the poise of a frightened rabbit," Ann would never pass for a glamour girl. She is, however, the daughter of the former Mrs. Bailey Vleck Van Reichton, who is now the wife of Prince Nicholas Cartaroff. To Ann's domineering mother, whose bookshelf is crammed with twenty-six years of Social Registers and a copy of *Gone with the Wind,* ancestry is all that matters. The Princess scorns the "homeless waifs the papers call 'Café Society,'" and she has not allowed Ann to drink or paint her face "like a Jezebel." Yet to the astonishment of Daphne and Mary Rose, Ann has a bid for Kingston house parties from the sleek, blond smoothie, Greg Smith, who, readers later learn, is a fortune seeker. The Princess Cartaroff is not pleased—Greg is from Pittsburgh and not listed in that city's Social Register. But ultimately, with her stepfather's encouragement, Ann persuades her mother to let her accept Greg's invitation.

Chestnut-haired, brown-eyed Carol Christy is the most appealing of the Manhattan socialites; the romantic predicament faced by her character frames the novel. Because her father has lost his savings in the volatile stock market, the Christys are in a precarious situation. They no longer have household help; Mrs. Christy worries they will not be able to pay the rent on their Park Avenue apartment. But unlike Daphne and Mary Rose, Carol has a warm and loving relationship with her tall, charming, "admirably direct" mother. Carol had a romance the previous summer with a modest young man whose family had also been hard hit by the Depression; Joe Whitbeck is now a work-study student at Kingston, but he has not forgotten Carol, and she still cares deeply for him. She knows "money isn't everything"; she's fond of but not in love with her affluent, handsome, good-hearted twenty-two-year-old fiancé, the "by-product of two green-backed bluebloods." Well aware that her daughter is used to a life of privilege, Mrs. Christy warns her: " 'As Mrs. Philip Griswold your whole future is assured! Believe me, Carol, it's just as easy to make a good marriage as a bad one—and darling, so much wiser!' " So Carol is torn about what to do. How can she not be in love with a man who is the "president of his House; the richest, best looking, Biggest Shot on the whole Kingston campus"?

One evening a few days later, Phil, his suitemate Homer, and another Kingston student, Taylor Martin, stop by the "Roselane Danse Palais" to check out the merchandise. All are very tight; Phil spends the time at the bar wishing he had not come. But Taylor is fed up with debutantes who would "sell their souls" to get a bid to Kingston. He zeros in on a vivacious, blue-eyed redhead from Corn Falls, Kansas, Lana Peters, who is a refreshing change from the women he usually dates. In a moment of inebriated optimism, Tay invites Lana to house parties. Lana knows he's plastered, yet the invitation seems genuine. When he escorts her back to her West Side boardinghouse in a taxi, Tay behaves like a true gentleman. Lana is thrilled and not receptive to the skeptical cracks about Kingston men doled out by Mavis, her more world-weary roommate. She is sure this festive weekend at the beginning of May will be her chance to meet some really nice, wealthy fellows with manners.

A week later, on the train to Kingston, Lana recognizes Daphne Graves in the ladies room; she's seen her in all the newspapers. "Meeting her here now—the season's top-notch debutante—it was absolutely just as thrilling as a face-to-face with Ginger Rogers or Joan Crawford!

Daphne represented Glamour. Not the now-I'm-rich-I'll-be-a Lady kind—the *real McCoy*!" At the station, the girls pair up with their dates—Daphne is met by three young men; each is a bit flummoxed at the sight of his unexpected competition. But Taylor Martin has not shown up for Lana because he's "sleeping off a three-day drunk." Phil Griswold feels it's his responsibility to make sure everyone enjoys the weekend of mad fun, so he offers Lana a ride back to campus. "When she had squeezed in next to Carol—Carol couldn't help it—she could see her friendly manner changing since the train. (Awful—the way All-Girls-are-Enemies when any man is on the scene!)"

The rest of the novel is set amid the "blocks of academic gray-stone grandeur" with much of the action occurring at "Sanctuary," an undergraduate eating club (based on Princeton's Cloister Inn) and frequented by upperclassmen. Cots for the female guests have been set up in one of the large upstairs rooms. The boys' suites at Kingston are attractively furnished and include a full bar; partying has already started in one of them, with lots more drinking. Lana notices right away that Carol is much calmer and more genuine than Daphne. Doll-faced Mary Rose proves to be a complete flop as a siren trying to hold the interest of Homer; Daphne deviously suggests she pander to his better nature by telling him to stop drinking and smoking so much—of course, that technique backfires.

At this point, a sixth young woman joins the festivities. She has arrived with "pompous" Charley Torgler in a splendid "mile long" custom-made yellow car that—perhaps not coincidentally—evokes Jay Gatsby's iconic yellow car. Betty Ainsbridge, a "severely chic" "knockout," is now in her fifth year at Kingston house parties. She is twenty-three (Jane's age when she wrote the novel), "the last of the Glamour Girls"; most of the partygoers believe that she is too old to be there or to be single. Betty seems much too sophisticated to chase after college men and compete with debutantes. Their contempt for Betty comes out as she makes the rounds of various events and tries eagerly to attract the attention of the stags who stay focused on Daphne; even Charley shows little interest in Betty. But in a moment of boredom, Charley and Betty discover some pistols on a rack in one of the rooms and take them outside for target practice. Betty proves to be a great shot—she's a "regular Annie Oakley."

At the black-tie dinner on Friday night, Ann's date, Greg Smith, mentions a former classmate who left school in mid-semester to marry a taxi dancer, Wanda Lavereux. Daphne and Mary Rose begin sniping about Wanda the floozy, so Lana defends Wanda by admitting that she, too, is a dime-a-dance girl. Taylor is horrified—he likes Lana well enough, but thought it would be a good gag to have the others in the dark about where they met. Tay urges Lana to go back to the city; she decides to stay and have fun and ignore him. Once again, Phil Griswold steps in to help by asking Joe to look out for Lana. Phil admires the way Joe handles adversity by working hard; he hopes that being with Lana will encourage Joe to have some fun, too. Readers learn that because "of the kind of life he led, Joe showed more character than any of the rest."

Later that evening, Joe and Carol have a chance to reminisce about their summer romance. They still love each other, but Carol does not want to live life on the edge; she's known Phil for years and recognizes that she will be better off with the more comfortable standard of living that he offers. "Clothes and trips and houses" really matter to her. Although Joe argues that if you love someone, sacrifices can be fun, Carol counters: "The happy people are the ones who *get* things, not the ones who give them up!" Nevertheless, she is quite turned off by the scene around her. Well after midnight, as she heads back to Sanctuary, she passes a drunken stag as he vomits on the grass nearby. At each of the clubs, more and more people are plastered, and "prostrate bodies filled the couches. Vague-faced girls were led by boys with one track minds upstairs, down halls, or out into the tolerant darkness of the gardens."

After Carol and Joe disappear from this degenerate scene, Phil and Lana have a chance to get to know each other over burgers at a local diner. Unhappy that he's never had a chance "to have ambitions like the *average* man," Phil wants to plan his own future, but he's torn because his father wants him to take over his investment company. Phil tells Lana that what he really wants is a salary, not the predictable life of "a cruise every winter," "two sons at Groton" by the time he's forty, and "by fifty, a hankering for blondes—and that well-warmed club chair!" Lana gives him the perspective he needs—the boys back in her Kansas hometown have to fill *their* fathers' shoes behind a plow on a farm. She came to New York to be a singer or possibly a dancer, but three different jobs folded up right underneath her feet.

In the wee hours of Saturday morning, the girls flop down on their cots, only to wake a few hours later feeling hung over and worse for wear. Mary Rose and Homer had gotten drunk, and the anguished dialogue between them suggests she has slept with him and regrets it. [This is the kind of scene that caused problems for the PCA and had to be eliminated from the film version of the story.] At the tea dance that afternoon, superb dancer Greg Smith cuts in on Lana and they put on a spectacular show. Lana caps off her dance performance by singing beautifully. The other girls are envious, especially when several well-oiled young men now try to cut in on her.

Across the room, Homer bears down on lonely Betty Ainsbridge "in all his alcoholic glory"; she finds his attentions "manna from heaven." She is exhilarated as the whole gang heads for Echo Amusement Park. Homer's alcohol-induced ineptness on the roller coaster mortifies everyone except Betty. In the anonymity of the dark Tunnel of Love, Betty overhears contemptuous laughter as two girls make spiteful comments about her age. She has missed the gravy train, they snipe, and she better "take what she can get." Homer guzzles his ubiquitous flask, oblivious to these remarks, but Betty has made a decision. Homer, in a fog, agrees to go with her to Elkton, Maryland, where anyone can be married twenty-four hours a day.

The other merrymakers enjoy Echo Park until they hear newsies shouting "Extra! Extra! Getcha Saddy-night edition." Phil buys a stack of papers from one of them. To his horror, the headline reveals that his father has been indicted for embezzlement and will likely end up in prison. Phil then realizes his father has stolen money from his stockholders to keep up appearances, to pay for their three houses, their horses, and their boat. Although Carol tries to reassure Phil, he knows her concern merely reflects her good breeding; neither of them is in love with the other. They "clicked because they had the right set up"; they liked each other because they went to the same places and knew the same people. Phil's status with his peers collapses now that he is no longer wealthy. Taylor Martin, who has linked up with Mary Rose, lights a cigarette "with the studied ruthlessness so typical of cub reporters": "Well, everybody knows what a pirate old man Griswold was," Tay quips. "Here's where *he* walks the plank." And then, out of loyalty to Phil, "Joe turned and let him have it."

While this crisis unfolds, a more depressing scene plays out in the "sordid little parlor" of one of Elkton's "marriage racket ministers." Betty and Homer are not faring well. Homer has slept through most of the drive there, but suddenly, at the suggestion of marriage, Homer's head clears just enough to recoil at the whole idea. Devastated, Betty jumps into his car and takes off, leaving him to sleep it off on the preacher's couch. Matters get worse after she reaches Sanctuary, where the other girls give her a hard time for prom-trotting for so many years.

Disconsolate, Betty leaves the room; Lana follows her just in time to see the smoking gun as she crumples dead onto the ballroom floor. Although the girls are horrified by this tragedy, some think immediately of what the suicide will mean for their reputations. Perhaps they should claim Betty's death was an accident. Lana rages at all of them but aims most of her tirade at Daphne and Mary Rose.

The mad fun is clearly over, and Jane's novel moves quickly to tie up loose ends. Homer arrives back at the college in a borrowed market truck to learn the terrible news about Betty. Now that his father is at the center of a financial scandal, Phil resigns as president of Sanctuary and heads for New York to find a job. Joe decides to leave with him—he doesn't want to spend another day in "this cheap country club," earning a degree that links him to a bunch of heels. To her delight, Phil asks Lana to drive back to the city with them.

Carol is the one glamour girl who still has a critical decision to make. She longs to reunite with Joe; she asks his forgiveness and falls into his arms. But they will not all ride off into the sunset together. At the last minute, scion Charley Torgler, who had brought the tragic figure of Betty Ainsbridge to the house parties, invites Carol to go with him to a "brawl" in a nearby town. Weighing her aspirations and her mother's advice, Carol resolves to join Charley after all. Joe's heart is broken as he and Phil, "two modern cavaliers," leave the elite campus with Lana "wedged in between them." They head into the real world of the average American without looking back.

Carol watches as the three "whipped off down Clubhouse Row." She "took a deep breath, running ungloved hands across expensive leather. A tear pushed slowly underneath her amber-colored glasses. Spring day; smooth car; smooth Kingston man. She settled back in Torgler's "yellow dream sled, reached for one of Torgler's cigarettes." The novel concludes with a comment about the car, and words that echo its opening: *"There is nothing that can make a woman of nineteen feel quite so smooth . . . There is no better background for Sophisticated Women."* (Italics Jane's.) The most sympathetic of the glamour girls choses the financially secure lifestyle this "yellow dream sled" represents over a deeper, more authentic love.

AUTHOR'S NOTE

My six-year effort to reconstruct Jane's world in the 1930s has led to many surprises. I have been to or lived in all the places that shaped my mother's world view. But I owe a special debt to a terrific woman named Jane Lavers who, in 1965, stumbled upon and held on to, for almost three decades, the diary my mother kept between the time she was eighteen and twenty three. Here, briefly, is our story:

"I'm a saver—I've saved every card since my daughters were born." *Thank heavens for that*, I thought as we spoke on the phone on June 6, 2012. Her strong, pleasant voice was so hospitable I knew we had to meet in person. A month later, a petite, vivacious woman with hazel eyes and soft auburn bangs welcomed me into her home. Her orange T-shirt and slim white skirt completed the picture—she was the youngest eighty-two-year-old I'd ever seen. A retired nurse and twice widowed, Jane Lavers's glass-half-full approach to life was an inspiration. She was sure that fate brought us together, but her sharp mind and her kindness are just as responsible.

Though we didn't realize it at the time, our remarkable connection began on a sunny spring Saturday in 1965. Jane's middle school daughters, Maureen and Diane, were avid Nancy Drew fans, just as I had been a decade earlier. They had been asking their parents to let them explore an abandoned Tudor mansion in Suffern, New York, not far from their home; perhaps it held an old clock filled with secrets or even a hidden staircase. Besides, no locked gate barred the entrance, and no signs warned "Private Property." What they wanted to explore was Rockrest, the remains of my father's fire-ravaged former family home. Built by my father's father in 1906, it had been destroyed by an electrical fire set off by vandals on April 4, 1957. That's when I learned that stone houses burn up, not down, and that's why I finally met Jane Lavers and her beloved dachshund mix, Louie.

When they pushed open the charred front door and walked inside, the Lavers family knew nothing about the house. "It was like a Nancy Drew mystery coming alive," Jane recalled. "What this place must have been like!" Her girls were elated to find a hidden doorway that led from the dining room to a pantry. But in a former billiard room, mattresses and empty wine bottles were clues that vagrants had taken over a home that had once been quite grand. Jane's husband, Donald, a civil engineer, was not about to let his little girls tackle the staircase; Jane recalled that "it felt like a trampoline." As they left to return home, she picked up a brown leather-bound book in the damp grass in front of the house. Intrigued by the diary, she tried to find some record of Jane Hall, but had no luck. So she kept it on the top shelf of her basement closet for close to thirty years.

Seven years after my mother's fatal heart attack in 1987, her estate was still in the hands of a Suffern attorney, Ralph Cipriani. According to Ralph, the Lavers came to his office to discuss their will, and Mrs. Lavers noticed a large envelope on his desk labeled "Jane Hall." She mentioned that she'd found the diary of a woman with that name near Rockrest and gave it to Ralph. A few weeks later, Ralph came to Washington for a meeting and brought the diary to me. There on its fragile pages, some waterlogged, was the record of my mother's life when she was the age my daughters were in 1994. I phoned Jane Lavers to thank her for this extraordinary gift, but we did not meet in person until I had moved back to Manhattan and was well into the manuscript for this book.

A half-century has passed since Jane Lavers rescued this diary. When I gave her a farewell hug in 2012, I felt a strong bond with this grandmother of eight and great-grandmother of three. She believes the connection among the three of us is a miracle. "Your mother wanted you to know all this," she told me. "People just want to be loved." We have kept in touch, and, as of this writing, I expect to see both Jane and Louie in a few weeks.

AND THEN THERE ARE Judy and Mark Black from Thomasville, North Carolina, top sellers of photographs and other paper ephemera on eBay—their online store is "Capnhapnin." When Judy lost her job, in 2009, she began helping Mark, who started the business in 1998. Much of what they sell is unidentified photos of people—young, middle-aged, and old; alone, as couples, or in family groups. There are formal shots, but the majority are candid images both adorable and not so flattering, like a woman caught with her hair in curlers. The largest category by far is children—playing, dancing, praying, hugging their pets, climbing trees, or just looking cute. The store sells to just about every country in the world—including Muslim nations—where buyers are fascinated by bits of Americana.

Once in a while the Blacks find an interesting cache of papers that comes with a clue to its origins. Mark picked up a just such a box at a flea market in Lexington, North Carolina. It was filled with intriguing images of a glamorous young woman in the late 1930s or 1940s. There were also several pictures of a little girl and many of family pets. eBay takes a hefty cut of its store sales and, to make ends meet, the Blacks work long hours choosing keywords, providing intriguing details for each item, and creating the digital images. They began putting the photos up on eBay, but hesitated when they saw an uncashed dividend check from the Buffalo Forge Company for a "Jane Hall."

Fortunately, Judy loves to play detective. A keyword search for "Jane Hall" led her to my blog; she sent a friendly e-mail to me through the website. A few days later, we spoke on the phone for more than half an hour. She offered to take all the unsold pictures off eBay and mail the ones they still had to me. The Blacks wanted no compensation for their lost revenue. In fact, Judy began emailing me copies of the photos as well; image after image popped up on the screen of my mother—and, once in a while, my father—in the days before I was born.

I went right to eBay to visit Capnhapnin's store, which is filled with intriguing images of American life since the early twentieth century. The Blacks came up with captions such as: "Vintage 1940s Excited, Hopeful, Can We Huh? Can We??? Adorable Little Girl Kid." Mark continues his pitch: "If you're a parent you surely recognize that irresistible expression . . ." Anyone could buy this tiny black and white snapshot for just $4.99 or start a bidding war. *But wait a second,* I thought—that's me! I scrolled down further; a few more pictures jumped off the pages, including two of me at about four years old with our beloved dog, Mike: "Little Girl & her German Shepherd Protector Dog." Bidding for that started at $7.99. Thanks to Judy, within hours these images were no longer for sale.

But there was still a mystery to be solved. We never lived in North Carolina, so how in the world did this box of photos end up at auctions and flea markets there? I thought about it for a few minutes and speculated that after the fire at Rockrest in 1957, the house was vandalized. People had come in and taken whatever appealed to them. That may be where these photos came from, more than a half-century ago. Then again, my mother was robbed of several boxes after the movers took her possessions from New York to Virginia in 1978. Mark Black told me that when the original owners of photographs die, their heirs often don't recognize the old photos or don't care about them, so they end up making their way into flea markets and auction houses. That was not our situation—we wanted these photos—but let it be a instructive tale for those disposing of old photos.

Several of our family pictures had already been sold; thankfully, Judy and Mark had kept digital copies of most of those. One is part of a 1935 press release that shows Jane at twenty, a "prominent debutante," dressed as a coal miner (though the outfit is made of satin) for the "Pageant of America"—"a feature of the 1935 Birthday Ball for the President at the Waldorf-Astoria." I have no idea who purchased it. Far away, perhaps even on another continent, someone may treasure or laugh at the irony in that picture; or perhaps they bought the image of Jane on a diving board in Palm Springs or playing with Tony, her pet raccoon.

The Blacks exemplify the good side of human nature—a side that will go the extra mile for a stranger, with no ulterior motives. Judy has been exposed to extreme hardship and poverty in third world and developing countries—"a life altering experience" for her. As she put it when we first connected, "Every morning we pray that we will be a blessing to someone today. Yesterday, God chose you! This experience has been precious, not to mention how fascinating it was for us to learn about your mother and your labor of love to capture her inspiring story." Judy and Mark have inspired me as well. They are warmhearted people doing the right thing—the best America has to offer.

Employees leaving MGM in 1939 after a hard day's work.
From the Collections of the Margaret Herrick Library

ACKNOWLEDGMENTS

Providing the context for Jane Hall's literary journey through the Great Depression, and following her adventures in Manhattan and Hollywood, has been a voyage of discovery for me. Had we known each other as young children, I might have been intimidated by her exceptional talent and her sassy personality. But now I am grateful that she, like Jane Lavers and Mark and Judy Black (see Author's Note), was a saver who treasured old documents and kept a priceless record of her childhood, adolescence, and young adulthood. How fortunate, too, that Dick Clarke and Cliff Zieger, her lifelong friends, held on to and returned most or all of the letters she wrote to them during this formative period of her life.

Although the inspiration for this book came from Jane's letters and diaries, the encouragement I received in 2010 while taking an online creative nonfiction course sponsored by the *New York Times* gave me the confidence to plunge into this project for more years than I thought it would take. Thanks to the teachers, award-winning journalist Chanan Tigay (then at Stanford), who is now a professor of creative writing at San Francisco State University with a new book (*The Lost Book of Moses*) just out; and Amy Virshup, editor of the Metropolitan section at the *New York Times*; and, of course, to my fellow students.

Earlier versions of this manuscript included information about Jane's experiences in as a young prodigy in Arizona and Manhattan Beach that is now found in the "Salome to Hollywood" blog on my website, http://www.robinrcutler.com. For several years I have collected information about Jane's father, Dick Wick Hall, and his beloved town of Salome; thanks to Barbara Vaughn, Sharon Rubin, Linda Darland, and the Salome Lions Club for keeping the memory of Jane's father alive. In Manhattan Beach, California, Steve Meisenholder not only gave my daughter Carlyn and me an insightful tour of the Manhattan Beach Historical Society, but also pointed me to invaluable resources about the area in the late 1920s, when Jane lived there with her mother and brother. Therese Martinez and the archives staff for the Redondo Union High School Alumni Association and registrar Joy Scarcliff found a wealth of information about Jane's and Dickie's experiences in Redondo Beach at RUHS. Amanda Goodwin and Zoe Bullard at the Nightingale-Bamford School in New York City, as well as David Chenkin at The Cooper Union, helped me round out Jane's first years in Manhattan. Archivist Carrie Hintz is owed thanks for digging into the Columbia University archives for information about Richard Shepard Clarke; Madison White did the same at Smith College when I wanted to learn more about Elsie Finch McKeogh. I spent several weeks learning about my father's life before I was born with the help of Rockland County historian Craig H. Long. He has amassed a large collection of documents about the Cutler family and the County Theatre and shared them willingly.

One of the best experiences I had was time spent at the Academy of Motion Picture Arts and Sciences's Margaret Herrick Library in Beverly Hills. The staff could not have been more accommodating; I uncovered a treasure trove of information about Jane's work in Hollywood. Special mention should go to Jenny Romero, now head of Reference and Core Collections; Jeanie Braun, and Faye Thompson. Also supportive, though we have yet to meet, has been Martin Turnbull, who may know more than anyone else today about life at the Garden of Allah. A private tour guide and historical walking tour docent with the Los Angeles Conservancy, he has written five (so far) engaging novels set in Hollywood's Golden Age; see his two websites, his blog, and Facebook page for timelines, maps, reading lists and other information (http://www.martinturnbull.com/). Turner Classic Movies frequently airs (and sells) some of the films Jane worked on; I am grateful to Robert Osborne and, more recently, Ben Mankiewicz for keeping the enchantment of a more glamorous era alive.

Without the critical eye of conscientious readers, one can never be sure that a book makes sense. The nonfiction writers group at the New York Society Library has followed Jane's story for at least four years. Stephen Marmon deserves extra thanks for his exceptionally detailed editing; Linda Selman, Jane Simon, Starr Tomczak, Frances Vieta, Lewis Warshauer, and more recently Jim Fishman, Mary Campbell Gallagher, Karen Kiaer, and Jeffrey Scheuer are all keeping me on track. Others who have given many valuable suggestions on the evolving manuscript include Scott Eyman, David Groff, Ronald Goldfarb, Wylie O'Sullivan and, above all, my superb agent Lindsay Edgecombe. Over the past year, I've also had the privilege of being part of the Palm Beach Writers Group, where traditional and indie publishing is encouraged by founders Jim Gabler and Erik Brown, and camaraderie and valuable information is shared by monthly speakers.

For her meticulous copyediting, I am forever indebted to Molly Lindley Pisani; for proof reading and indexing to Heather Dubnick; and for both the book and cover design to Elliott Beard. Their attention to detail was outstanding; it's been a pleasure to work with them all.

Several friends have listened patiently for years to my many qualms about how far to take this story. They are a never-ending source of encouragement. Among the most forbearing: Dianne Avlon, Mary Babcock, Jacqueline Bloom, Diana Brandenburg, Ginny Butters, Heloisa DeMelo, Elspeth Furlaud, Lindsay Gibson, Mary Wiseman Goldstein, Ainslie Grannis, Rosa Herrera, Betsy Kraft, Kay Kohl, Leslie Marvin, Patti McGrath, Mikhail Parsonnet, Roberto Socas, Isabel Stuebe, Dina Harris Walker, Jayce Walker, Dave Warren, and, of course, Gretchen Hall and Esther Hall. I will always feel—as Jane did—that Poplar Springs is still home; thanks to Richard Thompson and Mike Eisele, as well as Ellen Christie, for their hospitality and enthusiasm for this project.

Above all. my immediate family—Jane's family—has accepted my years of work on *Such Mad Fun* with grace and reassurance; that has made it all worthwhile. My daughters share Jane's sense of humor, her intelligence, her resilience, and her resourcefulness, but they do not wear mink. I owe a special debt to Carlyn Maw for her patience and marvelous help with my website. Liz and Gabriel, Alex and Will, Carlyn and Tod you are my source of strength.

Robin R. Cutler

May 2016

NOTES

Abbreviations Used in the Notes

AHS   Arizona Historical Society (Tucson branch)

CZ   Clifford Zieger

Diary1   Jane Hall Diary, 1933–1937, in the author's possession

Diary2   Jane Hall Diary, 1943–1945, in the author's possession

DWH   Dick Wick Hall, Jr.

EM   Elsie McKeogh

HFP   Hall Family Papers, in the author's possession

HNS   Harold Norling ("Swanie") Swanson

JH   Jane Hall

JHC   Jane Hall Cutler (Mrs. Robert F. Cutler)

MHL   Margaret Herrick Library, Academy of Motion Picture Arts and Sciences

PCA   Production Code Administration files on *These Glamour Girls,* Margaret Herrick Library, Academy of Motion Picture Arts and Sciences

RSC   Richard S. Clarke

RRH   Robert Randolph Hicks

RSH   Rose Sutton Hicks

SAF   Swanson Agency Files, Margaret Herrick Library, Academy of Motion Picture Arts and Sciences

TC   Turner/MGM Script Collection, Margaret Herrick Library, Academy of Motion Picture Arts and Sciences

Unless otherwise noted, all of Jane Hall's diaries, letters, and telegrams are in the Hall family papers.

Prologue: All the Things You Were

2 *Arizona's favorite humorist*: Several sources compare Dick Wick Hall to Will Rogers. See Robin R. Cutler, *The Laughing Desert: Dick Wick Hall's* Salome Sun (North Charleston, SC: CreateSpace, 2012); Frances D. Nutt, ed., *An Arizona Alibi: The Desert Humor of Dick Wick Hall, Sr.* (Phoenix, AZ: Arrowhead Press,

1990); and E. W. Kutner and Sharon Rubin, *McMullen Valley*, Images of America (Charleston, SC: Arcadia Publishing, 2009). (Please note: The picture on page 29 of *McMullen Valley* is not Jane Hall.)

2 *"literary prodigy"*: "Manhattan Beach Girl, 14, Proving Literary Prodigy," *Los Angeles Examiner*, February 18, 1930; "An Arizona Girl Is on the Way," *Arizona Republican*, February 23, 1930.

3 *"belonged only to Louis B. Mayer"*: JH to CZ, 26 September 1938.

3 *"best college comedy"*: Frank S. Nugent, review of *These Glamour Girls*, MGM, *New York Times*, August 31, 1939.

3 *"culture of elegance"*: Morris Dickstein, *Dancing in the Dark: A Cultural History of the Great Depression* (New York: W.W. Norton & Company, 2009), 359.

4 *"rich in the production"*: Dickstein, *Dancing in the Dark*, 4.

4 *her first story accepted*: Jane Hall, "Bill's Greatest Victory," *Los Angeles Times*, November 8, 1925.

Chapter One: Passages

7 *In the steamy haze*: The S.S. *Virginia* set sail on her maiden voyage on December 8, 1928. A detailed history of the ship can be found at http://www.moore-mccormack.com/SS-Brazil-1938/SS-Brazil-Timeline.htm (accessed February 5, 2014). See http://www.youtube.com/watch?v=ELZ_6gtmgq8 for footage of a voyage on the *Virginia*.

7 *"seasickness on this floating hotel"*: Jane's description of the voyage, which appears in a letter to Charlie Murdock, was published in a local paper (name and date unknown) in September 1930. "Manhattan Beach Girl Writes of Boat Trip to New York," JH scrapbook, HFP.

8 *her arthritic grandmother*: Jane's funny, feisty grandmother Rosa Sutton had a strong influence on her. (She'd made sure that Jane and Dickie were baptized as Catholics when Jane was four.) Rosa Sutton is the protagonist in *A Soul on Trial*, my book about the unprecedented naval inquiry that captivated the nation in 1909 (see http://www.robinrcutler.com/press/ for more information). As a young girl, Jane loved to cook; see JH to RSH, 31 May 1930; and JH to RSH, 13 June 1930. She published a column, "Jane's Cooking Corner," in the *Los Angeles Times* in 1929.

8 *"a former member"*: "Manhattan Beach Girl Writes of Boat Trip to New York," JH scrapbook, HFP.

8 *the three of them had moved*: Steve Meisenholder, former president of the Manhattan Beach Historical Society, provided invaluable help with information about Manhattan Beach in 1928–1930.

8 *a rented home*: The Halls' house at 1148 Manhattan Avenue is now part of a building that was Talia's, an Italian restaurant, for thirty-six years. Carley Dryden, "Talia's Restaurant in Manhattan Beach to Close After 36 Years," *The Daily Breeze*, February 1, 2013, http://www.dailybreeze.com/general-news/20130201/talias-restaurant-in-manhattan-beach-to-close-after-36-years.

8 *"A terrible doubtful feeling"*: JH 1928 diary.

8 *"horribly, achingly, maddenly lonesome"*: JH to RSH, 31 May 1930.

9 *Newspapers referred to her*: "Manhattan Beach Girl, 14, Proving Literary Prodigy," *Los Angeles Examiner*, February 18, 1930; "An Arizona Girl Is on the Way" *Arizona Republican*, February 23, 1930.

9 *graduated from Redondo Union High School*: Therese Martinez and the school's archive staff located information about Jane's and Dick's years at RUHS. Especially useful were the 1930-1931 *High School Guide Book*, *The Compass*, and *High Tide*, the 1929 yearbook, plus the 1928 and 1930 yearbooks in HFP.

9 *returned to Salome, Arizona*: JH to RSH, 13 June 1930 and 22 July 1930.

10 *Dick's unexpected battle*: For details about Dick's illness and death, see *Los Angeles Times*, April 18, 1926, and April 29, 1926.

10 *Dick Wick Hall created*: See "An Arizona Alibi," reprinted in Frances Nutt, *An Arizona Alibi: The Desert Humor of Dick Wick Hall, Sr.* Phoenix: Arrowhead Press, 1990. The book also contains excerpts from the *Salome Sun*, Hall's stories from the *Saturday Evening Post*, and descriptions of his funeral from the *Arizona Republican* (May 2, 1926) and the *Mesa Journal-Tribune* (May 2, 1926). See also Cutler, *The Laughing Desert*, for a replica of the 1925–1926 *Salome Sun*, a summary of Hall's career, and a list of other references about his life.

10 *"a man who made the whole world laugh"*: A line from Jane's eulogy of her father. Handwritten copy in HFP.

11 *her "most thrilling moment"*: Jane wrote "My Most Thrilling Moment," a prize-winning Junior Times essay (*Los Angeles Times*, November 21, 1926) about the sale of her first story. JH scrapbook, HFP.

11 *she acknowledged in a poem*: "To the Arizona Desert," *Saint Nicholas Magazine*, October 1930. JH scrapbook, HFP.

12 *She had willingly paid*: Some of these bills are in HFP. Daysie was embarrassed that her sister had to cover so many of her expenses and apologized in letters to Rose.

12 *"I don't want you to be too grown up"*: RSH to JH, 11 June 1930.

12 *Jane had fantasized*: Descriptions of New York in 1930 and family letters inform this plausible but imagined scene of Jane's arrival in Manhattan. Fifth Avenue was then a two-way thoroughfare.

13 *they corresponded during World War I*: Drafts of some of Rose's letters are in HFP; she addressed Randolph as "Antoine" and signed her letters "Diana." Drafts of some of Rose's stories still exist and are in HFP. She used the pseudonym "E. F. Brooks" occasionally.

13 *"He loves me because I have a lot of character"*: RSH to JH, 10 July 1930.

13 *transferred his law practice*: "R. Randolph Hicks, Noted Attorney, 81," *New York Times*, July 2, 1951. Hicks was a prominent trial lawyer in Norfolk before he came to New York; he had also been a member of the Virginia legislature. Biographies of him appear in the *Encyclopedia of Virginia Biography*, and the *Dictionary of American Biography*.

13 *"finest training for convivial mannerly social intercourse"*: "Virginia Has the Most Beautiful Campus in the Country," *Life*, June 7, 1937, 48–49.

14 *"country children of limited means"*: "Annual Benefit for Blue Ridge Children Is to Take Place Feb.7." *New York Times*, January 23, 1927. The social activities of Mr. and Mrs. Randolph Hicks were frequently reported in the *Times*.

14 *a longtime member*: James Elliott Lindsley, *The Church Club of New York: The First Hundred Years* (New York: The Church Club of New York, 1994), 174. In this history of the Church Club, Randolph lists his home parish as Grace Church in Casanova, Virginia.

16 *"I think it's perfectly ripping"*: JH to RSH, 11 July 1930.

16 *"trips daintily along through"*: Rian James, *All About New York: An Intimate Guide* (New York: The John Day Company, 1931), 48–49.

17 *There had been 429 students*: Redondo Union High School registrar Joy Scarcliff to Robin Cutler, e-mail, 21 October 2011.

Chapter Two: "Genius Growing Cold"

19 *applauded her sense of humor*: See the Nightingale-Bamford Year Book, 1932, for these quotations. Information about Nightingale-Bamford is from the Year Books of 1931, 1932, and 1933; I also consulted 1931-1932 attendance records, honor lists, and prize lists; the 1930-1931 School Guidelines; and http://www .nightingale.org. Thanks to Zoe Bullard and Amanda Goodwin for help with information about Jane Hall's two years at the school.

20 *she'd even been the manager*: Donovan Roberts, "Desert Humorist's Daughter Writes, Too," Newspaper Enterprise Associates, undated. Clipping from un-specified newspaper in JH scrapbook, HFP.

20 *"There is no sadder story told"*: Jane's poem "Fame" was published on August 10, 1930, probably in the *Los Angeles Junior Times*, according to notations in her scrap-book.

20 *especially proud of the articles*: All have been carefully pasted into her scrapbook, HFP.

20 *The first of these*: "Eleven-year-old Salome Girl Is Writer of Fairytale with Most Impressive Moral; Shows Genius," Yuma *Morning Sun*, March 26, 1926.

20 *had enough notoriety*: When Roberts' article came out, Jane wrote Rose: "My picture and biography will be in 100 different papers all over the United States! It'll probably be in some New York papers so maybe you'll see it." The article is in her scrapbook.

21 *Jane had purchased*: The book is in the HFP.

21 *the stock market hit bottom*: Richard B. Jewell, *The Golden Age of Cinema: Hollywood, 1929–1945* (Malden, MA: Blackwell Publishing, 2007), 16.

21 *Although less than three percent*: David E. Kyvig, *Daily Life in the United States, 1920–1940: How Americans Lived Through the "Roaring Twenties" and the Great De-pression* (Chicago: Ivan R Dee, 2002), 215.

21 *Rose learned in March*: "$2115.18 lost forever": First and Final Account, Report of

Guardian and Petition for Discharge in the Matter of the Estate and Guardianship of Dick Wick Hall and Jane Elizabeth Hall, Minors, March 30, 1932. HFP.

22 *"school for respectable females"*: Geoffrey T. Hellman, "Spiritual Refuge I," *New Yorker*, August 21, 1937.

22 *an Italianate masonry brownstone*: Information about Cooper Union and the Women's Art School comes from my visit to the school library and its website, Jane's 1933 yearbook, and my correspondence with registrar David Chenkin, plus the two-part profile of Cooper Union by Geoffrey T. Hellman: "Spiritual Refuge I" (*New Yorker*, August 21, 1937: 20-26) and "Spiritual Refuge II" (*New Yorker*, August 28, 1937: 18-22).

23 *its "proletarian" atmosphere*: Hellman, "Spiritual Refuge I," 23.

23 *"Selma Cohen is one of"*: Jane's five-year diary (abbreviated in these notes as Diary1) begins in January 1933; all quotations from Jane and the information about her adventures in the city in chapters two through five come from this diary unless they are comments in letters. This entry is dated January 25, 1933.

23 *In her first year, Jane took*: David Chenkin to Robin Cutler, e-mail, 9 November 2009, includes a list of all of Jane's courses while she was at Cooper Union.

23 *at a time of transition*: Hellman, "Spiritual Refuge I," 23-24.

23 *By the winter of 1932–1933*: Details about Jane's lively social life in the following paragraphs can be found in Diary1.

Chapter Three: "I'm Coming Out"

27 *"Even during the darkest days"*: Inez Robb, "The Debutante Racket," *Cosmopolitan*, March 1940, is the source for the information in this paragraph.

28 *"When a girl comes out"*: F. Scott Fitzgerald, *This Side of Paradise* (New York: Charles Scribner's Sons, 1996.). Kindle edition.

28 *the "festive tradition continues"*: Bill Cunningham, "Evening Hours: The Debutante Cotillion," *New York Times*, January 3, 2016.

28 *"an authentic and unexpurgated record"*: The "Debutante Yearbook," HFP.

28 *One memorable weekend occurred*: The "Debutante Yearbook," HFP.

29 *"to crave being gossiped about"*: Joseph Epstein, *Gossip: The Untrivial Pursuit* (New York: Houghton Mifflin, 2011). Kindle edition.

29 *an ailing Thomas Masson*: See Thomas L. Masson, *Tom Masson's Book of Wit and Humor* (New York: J. H. Sears & Co., 1927), 35–36, for Masson's description of how he first discovered Jane's father.

29 *a wise counselor for Daysie*: Masson's two lengthy letters to Daysie after Dick died provided spiritual and professional advice. Thomas Masson to Daysie Sutton Hall, 28 May 1926; and Thomas Masson to Daysie Sutton Hall, 15 February 1927; both in HFP.

30 *As society chronicler Cleveland Amory observed*: Cleveland Amory, *Who Killed Society?* (New York: Harper and Brothers, 1960), 143–144.

31 *"the predominant American prestige symbol"*: Lyman Bryson quoted in Amory, *Who Killed Society?*, 144.

31 *the first of many articles*: Jane mentions the write-up in her diary on Monday, November 27, but it's possible the undated *Journal-American* clipping that she kept came out on the twenty-eighth. Diary1.

32 *shared Jane's penchant for wisecracks*: See "Art: Moments of Loneliness," *Time*, December 15, 1961, http://content.time.com/time/magazine/article/0,9171, 827102,00.html.

32 *sparked a weekend of festivities*: Jane describes the weekend in her debutante yearbook in great detail. "Debutante Yearbook," HFP.

33 *until his death in 1974*: Eugene Scheel, "Chauncey Brown's Dance Party Lives On," *Washington Post*, July 2, 2006.

34 *Speaking from both*: "Miss Dressler Aids Relief Campaign," *New York Times*, November 13, 1933.

36 *A unique opportunity arose*: "Miscellany: Butlers," *Time*, January 22, 1934, http://content.time.com/time/magazine/article/0,9171,746873,00.html.

37 *"All kinds of people"*: This quotation and the description of the ball that follows are sourced from "40 Parties in City Celebrate the Day." *New York Times*, January 31, 1934.

37 *"It is only in recent years"*: Franklin D. Roosevelt: "Radio Address on the President's First Birthday Ball for Crippled Children.," January 30, 1934. Online by Gerhard Peters and John T. Woolley, *The American Presidency Project*. http://www.presidency.ucsb.edu/ws/?pid=14728.

37 *"living symbols of a nation's love"*: "40 Parties in City Celebrate the Day," *New York Times*, January 31, 1934.

38 *As Jack explained to Jane*: Jack Hall to JH, 11 March 1934. The information about John "Jack" Hughes Hall in this paragraph comes from his page in the 1935 *Nassau Herald* (Princeton University's yearbook), copy sent to the author from the Princeton Alumni Archives.

39 *Richard Shepard Clarke*: Columbia University archivist Carrie Hintz to Robin Cutler, e-mail, 29 September 2011.

39 *turn-of-the century limestone town house*: The address is 417 Convent Avenue.

40 *"the big lie"*: Molly Haskell, *From Reverence to Rape: The Treatment of Women in the Movies*, 2nd ed. (Chicago: University Of Chicago Press, 1987), 1–2.

40 *"A woman's only job"*: Ibid., 125.

40 *"A woman can do anything"*: Quoted in Jeanine Basinger, *A Woman's View: How Hollywood Spoke to Women, 1930–1960* (Middletown, CT: Wesleyan University Press, 1993), 10. The original film was released in 1931.

40 *their "paramount destiny"*: Haskell, *From Reverence to Rape*, 2.

Chapter Four: "Someday You'll Get Somewhere"

41 *Curry had said one of her oils*: Information about Jane's life at Cooper Union and quotations in this chapter come from Diary1.

43 *On July 12, she heard from Mrs. McKeogh*: Diary1, July 12, 1934.

44 *Thirty-six-year-old Elsie McKeogh*: "Mrs. McKeogh, 57, Authors' Agent," *New York Times*, October 30, 1955. Further information was also obtained from Madison White at the Smith College Archives (Madison White to Robin Cutler, e-mail, 28 July 2014), who directed me to the online edition of the 1919 Class Book: https://archive.org/details/class1919smit.

44 *managing editor Arthur McKeogh*: "Arthur McKeogh, World War Hero," *New York Times*, June 16, 1937.

44 *"Eventually we predict"*: "The Phoenix Nest," *Saturday Review of Literature*, October 18, 1930, 260.

44 *"Where is this fun"*: These comments are on the year-end memoranda page for 1934, Diary1.

45 *"symbolic presentation"*: Details in this paragraph are from "Gay Pageant Here Honors President," *New York Times*, January 31, 1935.

45 *at the top of the painting*: This painting and Jane's satirical sketch of haughty patronesses at a charity dance (described in the next paragraph) are in HFP.

47 *Jane also knew Rose no longer*: Diary1, May 29, 1935.

47 *The consensus of those she spoke to*: "They all advised me to wait till summer is over," Diary1, May 3, 1935.

47 *she made it into the* New York Times: "53 at Cooper Union Win Prizes for Art," *New York Times*, May 21, 1935.

47 *Philip Francis du Pont fellowship*: Diary1, May 12, 1935.

47 *"The birds under my window"*: JH to RSC, 3 June 1935.

47 *"sheep standing on green and silver slopes"*: JH to RSC, 8 July 1935.

47 *"The feeling of impersonal power"*: JH to RSC, 8 June 1935.

48 *who organized publicity, benefits, and fashion shows*: See, for example, "Party Will Honor Stony World Group," *New York Times*, March 16, 1936.

48 *offered Jane a full-time job*: Diary1, December 9, 1935. Jane had done some volunteer work for Mrs. Hanscom while she was a debutante.

Chapter Five: "Good Luck, Little Scribble"

49 *"They want me to rewrite"*: Diary1, January 7, 1936.

49 *"Oh good luck, little scribble"*: Diary1, January 14, 1936.

49 *"I'm going to town—no detours"*: Diary1, January 17, 1936.

50 *"now belonged to commerce"*: Francis Morrone, "A Landmark Department Store," *New York Sun*, December 27, 2007, http://www.nysun.com/arts/landmark-department-store/68609/.

50 *the hard work of Dorothy Shaver*: Ann T. Keene, "Dorothy Shaver," *American National Biography Online*, February 2000, http://www.anb.org/articles/10/10-02304.html Accessed June 7, 2012.

51 *experts at selling the American dream*: Roland Marchand's *Advertising the American Dream: Making the Way for Modernity* (Berkeley: University of California Press, 1985) was my source for information about the American advertising industry in this era.

51 *a respected periodical*: See Sidney R. Bland, "Shaping the Life of the New Woman: The Crusading Years of the *Delineator*," *American Periodicals* 19, no. 2 (2012): 165–188; and Lynn O'Neal Heberling, "*The Delineator*," in *Women's Periodicals in the United States: Consumer Magazines*, ed. Kathleen L. Endres and Therese L. Lueck (Westport, CT: Greenwood Press, 1995), 58–65.

52 *1930s protagonists in women's fiction*: Nancy A. Walker, *Shaping Our Mothers' World: American Women's Magazines* (Jackson: University Press of Mississippi, 2000), 9.

52 *"A 1936 Gallup poll"*: Nancy A. Walker, ed., *Women's Magazines 1940–1960: Gender Roles and the Popular Press.* (Boston: Bedford/St. Martin's, 1998), 12.

52 *Although millions of American women*: Laura Hapke, *Daughters of the Great Depression: Women, Work, and Fiction in the American 1930s* (Athens: University of Georgia Press, 1995), xiii.

52 *Laura Hapke states*: See Hapke's excellent Afterword to the reissued edition of Faith Baldwin's *Skyscraper* (New York: The Feminist Press at CUNY, 2012). Kindle edition.

52 *"masculine bitterness"*: Ibid., Kindle edition, Loc. 4689.

52 *"husbands and lovers punish"*: Ibid., Kindle edition, Loc. 4694.

52 *"misogynistic laboring"*: Hapke, *Daughters of the Great Depression,* xix–xx.

53 *"pale short fingernails"*: JH to RSC, 10 July 1936.

53 *Elsie McKeogh's enthusiasm*: Diary1, July 22, 1936.

53 *"What little perspective"*: JH to RSC, 23 July 1936, for her lengthy reaction to the published story.

54 *"to get the best possible atmosphere"*: JH to RSC, 23 July 1936.

54 *the "best modern novel"*: JH to RSC, 16 July 1936.

54 *"thrilling and absorbing"*: JH to RSC, 24 August 1936.

54 *"to dead times"*: Quoted in JH to RSC, 16 July 1936.

54 *Scarlett, Jane argued, was "uniquely bad"*: JH to RSC, 29 August 1936.

55 *"Don't be a feminist, Jane"*: RSC to JH, 31 August 1936. She must have returned his other letters to him, and at some point he gave all of hers back to her.

55 *"the idiot wellborn"*: Molly Haskell, *Frankly, My Dear:* Gone with the Wind *Revisited* (New Haven, CT: Yale University Press, 2009), 98.

56 *"very American need"*: Ibid, 102. Haskell refers to Scarlett's "terror of sex" coupled with a "fantasy of being overpowered" that gives her "more in common with the heroines of screwball comedy than with the more overtly sexy pre–Hays Code" women.

56 *"desperately need their mothers"*: Ibid, 93.

57 *Jane had been impressed*: JH to RSC, 5 September 1936.

57 *"a deep-seated joyous feeling"*: Ibid.

57 *Elsie had sold "Older Than God"*: JH to RSC, 5 October 1936.

57 *one of the four most popular*: Walker, *Shaping Our Mothers' World,* 61. The top four in 1935, according to a Gallup poll, were *Good Housekeeping, Woman's Home Companion, McCall's,* and *Ladies' Home Journal.*

57 *"She is intelligent and clearheaded"*: See the discussion of Gertrude Lane in Walker, *Shaping Our Mothers' World,* 59–60, and Walker, ed., *Women's Magazines* 1940–1960, 6–7.

58 *" 'I'm convinced that Jane Hall is Cosmopolitan material' "*: Quoted in JH to RSC, 5 October 1936.

58 *had lived in Fauquier County's seat for two years*: Kathi A. Brown, Walter Nicklin, and John Toler, *250 Years in Fauquier County: A Virginia Story* (Fairfax, VA: George Mason University Press, 2008), 156.

58 *"I wonder if it's really to marry"*: Diary1, December 11, 1936.

58 *"the trouble is one still feels young"*: Diary1, memoranda page at the end of 1936.

59 *"One goes out without coats"*: Details in this paragraph are culled from Diary1, January 4, 1937 and January 5, 1937.

59 *Two of her favorite movies*: JH to RSC, 3 January 1937; and JH to RSC, 28 January 1937.

Chapter Six: "So Lucky at Last"

61 *had a contract for three more*: Jane made notations of when a story sold in her diary and also in a list in the back of the copy of William B. McCourtie's *Where and How to Sell Manuscripts* that she'd brought from California in 1930.

61 *that usually (but not always)*: Jane notes on February 18 that she sold a story called "Window Shopper" to *McCall's* for four hundred dollars. It does not appear to have been published.

61 *"more motion pictures are made from Cosmopolitan stories"*: "Tribute from Hollywood," *Cosmopolitan,* November 1938, 6.

61 *In 1929, William Randolph Hearst*: James Landers, *The Improbable First Century of Cosmopolitan Magazine* (Columbia: University of Missouri Press, 2010), 200–202. This book is the first exhaustive history of the magazine; Landers emphasizes the business end of its development.

62 *"on a story-by-story and serial-by-serial basis"*: Ibid., 206.

65 *By March 1937, Elsie was confident*: HNS to EM, 16 March 2013, SAF.

65 *"The years spent in running College Humor"*: H. N. Swanson, *Sprinkled with Ruby Dust: A Literary and Hollywood Memoir* (New York: Warner Books, Inc., 1989), 44, and throughout for this paragraph.

65 *He had sold Selznick*: Ibid., 54.

65 *"laced with stress"*: Ibid., 51.

65 *"writers were the main concern"*: Ibid., 51–52.

66 *"in a modest little building"*: Ibid., 65.

66 *the "ear and respect of the studio bosses"*: This quotation is from producer David Brown, as found in Peter B. Flint, "H .N. Swanson, 91, An Agent for Writers in Hollywood Deals," *New York Times,* June 3, 1991.

66 *"too slight for a picture"*: HNS to EM, 16 March 1937, SAF.

66 *"delighted with this author's work"*: HNS to EM, 3 June 1937, SAF.

66 *"We feel we have made"*: HNS to Manny Wolf et al., 5 June 1937, SAF.

66 *"The writer would be excellent"*: HNS to Warren Groat, 12 June 1937, SAF.

66 *"You know how much I like"*: HNS to EM, 27 July 1937, SAF.

66 *"and it seems to me"*: EM to HNS, 2 August 1937, SAF.

67 *"at an attractive salary"*: HNS to Edwin Knopf et al., 18 August 1937, SAF.

67 *died of pneumonia*: "Arthur McKeogh, World War Hero," *New York Times*, June 16, 1937.

67 *In its August issue*: "Over There," *Good Housekeeping*, August 1937, 5.

68 *"A deb with a difference"*: "Sidewalk Café," *Cosmopolitan*, September 1937.

70 *"What are the habits"*: Jeanine Basinger, *I Do and I Don't: A History of Marriage in the Movies* (New York: Knopf, 2013). Kindle edition.

70 *a comprehensive survey*: "Youth Problem: 1938" was the cover story of *Life*'s June 6, 1938 issue, from which the information in this paragraph was obtained. Beginning in 1935, 13,528 young people from all walks of life in the state of Maryland answered eighty questions. The magazine profiles the average American high school boy and girl, a girl with a job, a boy without a job, a farm boy, and a factory boy, as well as a wealthy girl.

74 *"hard-pressed audiences"*: Dickstein, *Dancing in the Dark*, xv.

74 *"I just discovered that one third"*: Swanson, *Sprinkled with Ruby Dust*, 68.

75 *to visit "every agency that used"*: Ibid.

75 *Randolph Hicks insisted on reviewing*: EM to HNS, telegram, 12 November 1937, SAF. Discussions related to the contract and Jane's start date continued throughout November.

75 *The Loews, Inc. contract*: EM to HNS, telegram, 23 November 1937, SAF.

75 *Swanie replied by Western Union*: HNS to EM, telegram, 23 November 1937, SAF.

75 *Daily Variety announced on October 22*: "Metro Signs Jane Hall," *Daily Variety*, October 22, 1937. The paper followed Jane's whole career, with repeated mentions of Swanson's agency. The daily paper started in 1933 and was last published in 2013.

75 *Elsie was disappointed*: EM to HNS, telegram, 27 November 1937, SAF.

75 *Jane would need to complete*: EM to HNS, letter, 3 December 1937, SAF. Elsie informed Swanie that Burton would verify Jane's contract had been fulfilled before she left for the West Coast.

75 *a "whole bunch of short stories"*: HNS to JH, letter, 2 November 1937, SAF.

76 *Elsie tried to interest Swanie*: See EM to HNS, letter, 3 December 1937, and Swanie's responses HNS to EM, 18 December 1937 and 29 December 1937, all found in SAF.

76 *getting MGM to reimburse Jane*: Swanson Agency to Floyd Hendrickson at MGM, 3 January 1938, SAF.

76 *the black Chrysler convertible*: Diary1, July 8 and 9, 1937.

76 *"I am delighted"*: EM to Edwin Knopf, 22 October 1937, SAF.

Chapter Seven: "Darned Attractive on the Surface"

77 *"the memory lingers on"*: JH to RSC, 4 December 1937.

77 *promised passengers that they would*: This ad was for sale and accessed on Amazon. com on May 20, 2013. Also see *Princeton Alumni Weekly* 33, no. 27 (April 7, 1933): 593.

77 *"nothing like the luxury"*: JH to RSC, 4 December 1937.

77 *passengers could swim*: Ibid.

77 *country-club décor*: Gordon R. Ghareeb, "A Woman's Touch: The Seagoing Interiors of Dorothy Marckwald," http://www.shawnandcolleen.com/sshsasocal/docs/touch.html. Accessed May 20, 2013.

77 *stopping along the way*: Stops on the *Santa Paula*'s route listed here are as per a Grace Lines ad for their California routes which ran in the early 1930s; see, for example, the *Princeton Alumni Weekly* 33, no. 27 (April 7, 1933): 593.

78 *"as it can't be done"*: Quoted in JH to RSC, 4 December 1937.

78 *"ghastly lost feeling"*: JH to CZ, 5 March 1938. Jane sent Cliff a long summary of her first two months in Hollywood.

78 *"The people in the acting part"*: JH to RSC, 24 December 1937.

79 *"characterized by showmanship"*: Leo Calvin Rosten, *Hollywood: The Movie Colony, the Movie Makers* (New York: Harcourt, Brace and Company, 1941), 32..

79 *"so much of Hollywood is a façade"*: Quoted in Steven Bingen, Stephen X. Sylvester, and Michael Troyan., *MGM: Hollywood's Greatest Backlot* (Solana Beach, CA: Santa Monica Press, 2011), 8.

79 *"the consumption of food and drink"*: Federal Writers Project of the Works Progress Administration, *Los Angeles in the 1930s: The WPA Guide to the City of Angels*, reissued with an introduction by David Kipen (Berkeley: University of California Press, 2011), 228.

79 *Swanie had encouraged Jane*: HNS to JH, 2 November 1937, SAF. The novels of Martin Turnbull and his website, http://www.martinturnbull.com/, showcase his extensive research about and photographs of the Garden of Allah.

79 *Years earlier, the main building*: Tom Dardis, *Some Time in the Sun: The Hollywood Years of F. Scott Fitzgerald, William Faulkner, Nathanael West, Aldous Huxley and James Agee* (New York: Limelight Editions, 1988), 31. Nazimova added the twenty-five bungalows in 1927; the complex was demolished in 1959.

79 *prompted Jane to snatch up*: JH to HNS, n.d., SAF.

79 *had been Beatrice Lillie's*: JH to RSC, 20 January 1938, SAF.

79 *she made a real effort*: JH to RSC, 26 December 1937.

80 *"They couldn't have been nicer"*: Ibid.

80 *the holiday mood at the Berkshire*: RSH to JH, 26 December 1937, for the following three paragraphs.

81 *"drive my car down the sunny roads"*: JH to RSC, 31 December 1937.

81 *"These people drive like maniacs"*: JH to RSC, 24 December 1937.

81 *"whiteness, flatness, and spread"*: FWPWPA, *Los Angeles in the 1930s*, 5.

82 *"exotic land of lofty purple mountains"*: Ibid., 4.

82 *one of several towns near Los Angeles*: Ibid., 352–353 for a description of Culver City.

82 *"complete city"*: Scott Eyman, *Lion of Hollywood: The Life and Legend of Louis B. Mayer* (New York: Simon & Schuster, 2005), 1. This superb biography is the best source for information on Mayer's personal and professional life. Figures vary, but Eyman says the studio was spread out over 167 acres.

82 *a "sense of security"*: Ibid., 285.

82 *the brand new Thalberg building*: Bingen, Sylvester, and Troyan, *MGM*, 45, describes the original building; the book is an excellent portrait of MGM, accompanied by dozens of superb photographs. Jane put "#11 new writers building" on her return address in JH to RSC, 10 January 1938.

82 *the diminutive, high-energy and volatile Mayer*: Eyman, *Lion of Hollywood*, 5 and passim.

82 *used MGM "as a pulpit"*: Quoted in Bingen, Sylvester, and Troyan, *MGM*, 44.

82 *their studio was the most successful*: "King in the hierarchy of movie prestige," according to Leo Calvin Rosten (*Hollywood*, 174).

82 *rather than the "florid spectacles"*: Ibid., 174.

82 *Mayer "fervently believed that"*: Eyman, *Lion of Hollywood*, 8.

83 *"stars, spectacle, and optimism"*: Ibid., 9.

83 *had just rolled out of bed*: Ibid,, 280.

83 *"be whatever he needed to be"*: Ibid., 11.

83 *"the system is too ridiculous"*: JH to CZ, 5 March 1938.

83 *its stable of ninety-seven writers*: Thomas Schatz, *The Genius of the System: Hollywood Filmmaking in the Studio Era* (New York: Henry Holt and Co., 1996), 255.

83 *A multipage advertisement in the* Hollywood Reporter: The ad appears across pages 20 and 21 of the June 3, 1938 issue. Many of the studios had promotional sections in various issues of both *Variety* and the *Hollywood Reporter*.

83 *"Bright and Sparkling"*: JH to CZ, 5 March 1938.

84 *liked "the picturesque side"*: JH to CZ, n.d. (early March 1938).

84 *Eddie Knopf had persuaded*: Dardis, *Some Time in the Sun*, 25–26.

84 *Determined to make it*: In addition to his published letters, my sources for Fitzgerald's Hollywood years in these paragraphs include Matthew J. Bruccoli, *Some Sort of Epic Grandeur: The Life of F. Scott Fitzgerald* (New York: Harcourt Brace Jovanovich, 1981); F. Scott Fitzgerald, *F. Scott Fitzgerald's Screenplay for Three Comrades*, edited with an afterword by Matthew J Bruccoli (Carbondale: Southern Illinois University Press, 1978); and Arthur Krystal's profile "Slow Fade: F. Scott Fitzgerald in Hollywood," *New Yorker*, November 16, 2009, 36–41.

84 *He loved the movies*: Krystal, "Slow Fade," emphasizes this point.

84 *"Scott would rather have written"*: Ibid., 37.

85 *MGM had originally hired*: Bruccoli, *Grandeur*, 428.

85 *"the greatest library of celebrated stage hits"*: So stated the ad in the *Hollywood Reporter*, June 3, 1938, 20–21.

85 *"engaged in the manufacture"*: Rosten, *Hollywood*, 306.

85 *"the unofficial oracles of society"*: Ibid., 313.

85 *"was primarily about fun"*: Neal Gabler, *Life: the Movie: How Entertainment Conquered Reality* (New York: Vintage Books, 2000), 16.

85 *"dealt with its audience as a mass"*: Ibid., 19.

86 *"sometimes [the writers] worked in teams"*: Quoted in Eyman, *Lion of Hollywood*, 156.

86 *"malleable among the collaborators"*: Fitzgerald to Dearest Pie, July 1937 "on the way to Hollywood," in *F. Scott Fitzgerald: A Life in Letters*, edited and annotated by Matthew J. Bruccoli with Judith S. Baughman (New York: Touchstone Books, 1995), 330.

86 *"a member of the palace guard"*: Bruccoli, ed., *Three Comrades*, 256.

86 *"wired that the screenplay was 'simply swell' "*: Bruccoli, *Grandeur*, 432.

86 *six more drafts of the screenplay*: Bruccoli, *Grandeur*, 433.

86 *"Jane Hall is fat and sassy"*: HNS to EM, 8 January 1938, SAF.

87 *"working like a Trojan"*: JH to RSC, 7 January 1938.

Chapter Eight: "A Luxurious, Amusing, and Stimulating Place"

89 *Often she joined her fellow writers*: Invitations to such screenings were sent to writers and readers from Eddie Knopf; Jane included one of these in JH to RSC, 13 January 1938.

89 *"from the Lion's Club"*: JH to RSC, 10 January [1938].

89 *Betting on the horses*: See Rosten, *Hollywood*, 215–220, on the significance of racing for the movie colony.

89 *Louis B. Mayer was renowned*: Eyman, *Lion of Hollywood*, 270–271.

90 *"D'zani the Gentile Girl"*: JH to CZ, 5 March 1938.

90 *her new life was "very attractive"*: JH to RSC, 14 January 1938.

90 *"Wish you could see the clothes"*: JH to RSC, 10 January 1938.

90 *One of her colleagues*: JH to RSC, 14 January 1938.

90 *he sent a copy of the tribute*: HNS to Edwin Knopf, 11 January 1938, SAF. The file includes a copy of the Salome Frog spread and Swanie's note to Jane as well.

90 *"Elsie hopes I've been looking after you"*: HNS to JH, 11 January 1938, copy in SAF.

90 *His agency had even helped*: Edgar Carter/HNS Agency to the Virginia DMV, 3 March 1938, SAF.

91 *MGM's huge chrome-and-green*: For a description of the commissary with great pictures, see Bingen, Sylvester, and Taylor, *MGM*, 60–63.

91 *Jane was introduced to Rosalind Russell*: JH to RSC, 13 January 1938.

91 *"writers (especially new ones) are so unimportant out here"*: Ibid.

91 *Jimmy Stewart had been there*: JH to RSC, 17 January 1938.

91 *"La Dietrich was just coming in"*: Ibid.

91 *"hard-boiled and appraising"*: Ibid.

91 *"that doesn't mean I approve"*: JH to RSC, 14 January 1938.

91 *"was so TIGHT she could hardly see"*: JH to RSC, 17 January 1938.

91 *a "gourmet paradise"*: Jim Heimann, *Out with the Stars: Hollywood Nightlife in the Golden Era* (New York: Abbeville Press, 1985), 75.

91 *"truly a nice person"*: JH to RSC, 17 January 1938.

92 *"I wasn't a sex symbol"*: Rosalind Russell and Chris Chase, *Life Is a Banquet* (New York: Grosset & Dunlap, 1977), 67.

92 *shared Catholic roots*: Ibid., passim.

92 *they made a great pair*: JH to RSC, 18 February 1938.

92 *she met the "charming" forty-four-year-old author*: JH to CZ, 7 March 1938. Also JH to RSC, 7 March 1938.

92 *They'd been hired*: Marion Meade, *Dorothy Parker: What Fresh Hell Is This?* (New York: Penguin Books, 2006), 287.

92 *strong communist sympathies*: discussed at length in Meade, 270.

92 *spoke in "hushed whispers"*: JH to RSC, 23 February 1938.

92 *gave the studio the right to "make anybody"*: JH to RSC, 24 February 1938.

92 *that her first assignment*: JH to CZ, 3 March 1937, summarized her first eight weeks on the job.

92 *"giving him the runaround"*: Ibid.

92 *assigned to a Luise Rainier picture*: JH to RSC, 1 March 1938.

92 *"liked what he saw"*: Ibid. and JH to RSC, 18 March 1938; JH to CZ, 3 March 1938.

92 *"threatened to isolate Culver City"*: "Storm Hits Pix Hard," *Hollywood Reporter*, March 3, 1938.

94 *California looked "clean and tired"*: JH to RSC, 5 March 1938.

94 *"I am doing flood relief"*: Ibid.; JH to CZ, 5 March 1938.

94 *"an exceptionally fine one"*: JH to RSC, 5 March 1938.

94 *integral to the good life*: Rosten, *Hollywood*, 405; and Albert Payson Terhune, "How Hollywood Treats Its Dogs," *Modern Screen* (March 1938), passim.

94 *Rosalind Russell had one*: Kirtley Baskette, "Rahs for Roz," *Photoplay*, October, 1939, 78.

95 *Jane sublet an apartment*: JH to RSC, 18 March 1938 and 3 April 1938 for the description of the apartment.

95 *"drawing room comedies"*: Rosten, *Hollywood*, 243.

95 *a simple and time-worn premise*: The quotation is from a synopsis at the top of a form filled out by reviewers for the Production Code Administration, SAF.

95 *"every afternoon we change"*: JH to RSC, 8 April 1938.

95 *Two mimeographed copies*: These are in the Turner/MGM Script Collection at MHL.

96 *"The little blue serge picture"*: JH to RSC, 22 April 1938.

96 *she wished the movie*: JH to RSC, 12 April 1938.

96 *"That great dialogue job"*: The clipping is enclosed in JH to RSC, 11 May 1938.

96 *Swanie again urged Jane*: HNS to EM, 21 May 1938, SAF for this paragraph.

96 *Jane seemed open to the idea*: JH to RSC, 28 May 1938.

96 *she could hardly report*: JH to HNS, n.d. (May 1938), SAF. Jane also mentioned that *McCall's* still had a story from her that had not been published. Six of her

magazine stories came out between December 1937 and July 1939, while she was in Hollywood.

96 *Her first opportunity*: Jane Hall, "Three Comrades—And a Girl," *Cosmopolitan*, June 1938. Unless otherwise noted, all quotations about this adventure come from Jane's article.

96 *Elsie wired Jane on March* 29: EM to JH, telegram, 29 March 1938.

97 *"the rock upon which MGM was built"*: Eyman, *Lion of Hollywood*, 220.

98 *"Women moviegoers found him"*: Victoria Wilson, *A Life of Barbara Stanwyck: Steel-True 1907–1940* (New York: Simon & Schuster, 2013), 665. (The Kindle edition of this book indicates page numbers.)

98 *he was, in fact, innately reserved*: Ibid., 489.

99 *"handsome, erudite, socially prominent"*: Ibid., 502.

100 *"the most colossal disappointment"*: Quoted in Bruccoli, *Grandeur*, 352.

100 *grossed more than $2 million*: Eyman, *Lion of Hollywood,* 277.

100 *both* Variety *and the* Hollywood Reporter*:* The critical comments are summarized in the film's American Film Institute (AFI) catalog entry, viewable at http://www.afi.com/members/catalog/DetailView.aspx?s=&Movie=8376. Accessed May 1, 2014.

100 *both "beautiful" and "memorable"*: Frank S. Nugent, review of *Three Comrades*, MGM, *New York Times*, June 3, 1938.

100 *she "wrote it as I knew Mr. Bigelow"*: JH to RSC, 13 June 1938.

100 *"Your letter amused me mightily"*: JH to CZ, 10 June 1938.

100 *"The* Three Comrades *blurb I wrote"*: JH to CZ, 17 July 1938.

101 *"There is such contrast out here"*: JH to RSC, 11 April 1938.

101 *"He's quite a riot"*: JH to RSC, 25 April 1938.

101 *"I'm going to pose"*: JH to RSC, 25 April 1938.

101 *"The mouth job is just a matter of lipstick"*: JH to RSC, 11 May 1938.

102 *"I've been riding horseback"* : Ibid.

102 *how attractive Walter Pidgeon was*: JH to RSC, n.d. (May 1938).

102 *the times she invited him to group dinners*: She would invite him again in August. JH to CZ, 5 August 1938.

102 *Jane also found him "realer"*: JH to RSC, n.d. but approximately 19 May 1938.

102 *more than a collegial interest*: From JH to CZ, 27 June 1938: "Had a dinner date with Marion (the writer—no, of course he doesn't feel Platonic. Do they ever? I am learning.)"

102 *"one of the most interesting men"*: JH to CZ, 11 July 1938.

102 *She and Marion tossed it around*: See Jane Hall and Marion Parsonnet, Original Story Summary T-741, May 23, 1938, TC 1; and JH to CZ, 8 September 1938.

103 *The setting for this comedy-drama*: See Original Story Summary T-741, May 23, 1938, TC for this and all drafts of the film's treatments and screenplays.

103 *"people are starved for entertainment"*: "That Hollywood Ego," *Hollywood Reporter*, June 21, 1938; and "New York Exhibitors," *Hollywood Reporter*, June 24, 1938.

103 *"If the writer were writing"*: Hollywood Reporter, June 14, 1938.

103 *Jane had received a telegram*: "What will protect your position as a writer?": Screen Writers Guild to Jane Hall et al., telegram, 27 June 1938, HFP.

103 *"so undignified as organized labor"*: Note written on the back of the SWG telegram and enclosed with JH to RSC, 28 June 1938.

103 *"wouldn't join because they were individuals"*: Quoted in Meade, *Dorothy Parker*, 258.

103 *he "was 'NUTS' about it"*: JH to RSC, 27 May 1938; and JH to CZ, 8 September 1938.

103 *one of a handful of producers*: Eyman, *Lion of Hollywood*, 5.

104 *Metro offered to extend*: Eddie Mannix to JH, 18 June 1938, SAF. The actual contract is not in the SAF, but the correspondence lays out the terms. Several letters in the SAF over the next eight weeks deal with this contract.

104 *quibbling over the details*: Edgar Carter to Floyd Hendrickson, 29 August 1938, SAF.

104 *"genuinely liked Hollywood"*: JH to RSC, 19 June 1938.

104 *Elsie wired the details*: EM to JH, telegram, 19 July 1938, HFP.

105 *Mrs. Delmar made it easy*: Quotations in the following three paragraphs are taken from Jane's profile, "Vina Delmar, Cosmopolite of the Month," *Cosmopolitan*, August 1939.

105 *"one of America's most successful fictioneers"*: Already noted in "Inside Stuff—Legit," *Daily Variety*, September 4, 1935.

106 *"a wonderful setting for music"*: JH to RSC, 21 July 1938.

106 *"the boy wonder of Hollywood"*: JH to RSC, 29 July 1938; JH to CZ, 29 July 1938.

106 *told her aunt Rose*: A carbon of Jane's undated letter to Rose was included in JH to CZ, 26 September 1938. I have not verified her comment about Joe Mankiewicz's compensation.

106 *"That story I did was accepted"*: JH to RSC, 29 July 1938.

106 *"Mr. Zimbalist feels"*: Undated carbon copy of letter from JH to RSH sent to CZ on 26 September 1938.

106 *"It is such a great SPIRITUAL satisfaction"*: JH to RSC, 29 July 1938.

106 *That fall,* Daily Variety *concluded*: *Daily Variety*, fifth anniversary issue, October 24, 1938, 4. The issue describes the film industry's challenges in 1938 in these terms: "The year gone by was a momentous one for the film industry—a year marked by strife between talent groups and producers, exhibitors and distributors—the Government and the industry. It was also a year of recession, a year of the survival of the fittest at the box office."

107 *"ordinary, true-to-life characters and situations"*: Catherine Jurca discusses this change in tastes in a section called "The Death of Glamour," in her book *Hollywood 1938: Motion Pictures' Greatest Year* (Berkeley: University of California Press, 2012), 101.

107 *the mainstay of Hollywood's box-office appeal*: Robert Sklar, *Movie Made America: A Cultural History of American Movies*, revised and updated (New York: Vintage Books, 1994), 240.

Chapter Nine: "Everything You Are and Do"

109 *a working girl from Corn Falls, Kansas*: All the treatments and scripts for *These Glamour Girls* [originally titled "Such Mad Fun"] are in the Turner Script Collection (TC) at the Academy of Motion Picture Arts and Sciences's Margaret Herrick Library. References identify the document by number and date.

109 *"The sign on the door of the train"*: Synopsis T-741, May 23, 1938, 1. TC.

110 *"Every successful prom-trotter"*: Synopsis T-741, May 23, 1938, 2-3. TC.

110 *into* 190 *heavily annotated pages*: Film Treatment. T-745, August 23, 1938, 40. The annotations are in Jane's handwriting. TC.

110 *she and Marion began to collaborate*: Marion had found the time. JH to CZ, 8 September 1938.

110 *"trying physically and mentally"*: JH to RSC, 8 September 1938.

110 *"at odd moments and at night"*: JH to CZ, 8 September 1938.

111 *"it kills me not to have the time to do anything"*: Ibid.; Jane also comments of the novel that "It's not written very well" in JH to RSC, 13 September 1938.

111 *On September 7, Elsie wired Jane*: EM to JH, telegram, 7 September 1938.

111 *Without telling the studio*: The debacle of the title is described in an undated September 1938 letter from JH to CZ.

111 *"an IMPORTANT picture"*: JH to CZ, 26 September 1938.

111 *But what a surprise she had*: Scott Fitzgerald stayed at the Garden of Allah while working at MGM during the spring of 1938. According to Matthew Bruccoli, and Fitzgerald's correspondence with his agent, after spending the summer in Malibu, he returned to Hollywood at the beginning of September. Harold Ober to F. Scott Fitzgerald, Esq. "How's everything going with THE WOMEN?" 2 September 1938, in *As Ever, Scott Fitz: Letters between F. Scott Fitzgerald and His Literary Agent, Harold Ober 1919–1940*, edited by Matthew J. Bruccoli. (New York: J. B. Lippincott Company, 1972), 364 and 368.

112 *the sort of "independent, determined young American woman"*: Bruccoli ed., *A Life in Letters*, xx. Jane got her start as a writer in the 1920s, when Fitzgerald was publishing stories about these fresh new characters.

112 *"permanent feeling of never quite measuring up"*: Maureen Corrigan, *So We Read On: How* The Great Gatsby *Came to Be and Why It Endures*. (New York: Little, Brown and Company, 2014). Kindle edition.

112 *"one of the greatest writers who ever lived"*: He makes this statement in a question in a letter to Edmund Wilson, as found in Corrigan, *So We Read On*, Kindle edition.

112 *"felt that he was a member"*: Bruccoli, *Grandeur*, 45.

113 *not been "the happiest time in his life"*: F. Scott Fitzgerald to John Grier Hibben, 3 June 1920, in Bruccoli, ed., *A Life in Letters*, 37–38.

113 *his first book contract*: Nancy Milford, *Zelda: A Biography*, reissue (New York: Harper Perennial, 2013). Kindle edition.

113 *"shared the responsibility"*: Bruccoli, *Grandeur*, 194.

113 *he drew on her letters*: "almost ruthlessly," according to Milford, *Zelda*, 102.

114 *reluctant to socialize*: Bruccoli, *Grandeur*, 427, describes his modesty and sense of estrangement.

114 *"a Jewish holiday, a Gentile's tragedy"*: Quoted in Bruccoli, *Grandeur*, 423.

114 *he admired Clare Boothe's work*: Sylvia Jukes Morris, *Rage for Fame: The Ascent of Clare Boothe Luce* (New York: Random House, 1997), 365.

114 *one of "the pleasantest people in the industry"*: Fitzgerald to Maxwell Perkins, 23 April 1938, in Bruccoli, ed., *A Life in Letters*, 360.

114 *" 'active, intelligent, and courageous' "*: Morris, *Rage for Fame*, 366.

114 *wanted major changes made*: Morris, *Rage for Fame*, 366.

114 *"was not regarded as bitchy enough"*: Bruccoli, *Grandeur*, 442.

114 *the perimeter of his office floor*: Bruccoli, *Grandeur*, 426. He also "carried Cokes in his briefcase"; they may also have served "to meet his need to have a glass in his hand."

114 *"a charming burned-out genius"*: JH to RSC, 13 September 1938.

114 *Writers often spent time in each other's offices*: a point noted by Fitzgerald's girl-friend, Sheilah Graham, *Hollywood Revisited: A Fiftieth Anniversary Celebration* (New York: St. Martin's Press, 1984), 87–88.

114 *"had some pretty hot talk"*: Fitzgerald to Harold Ober, 28 September 1938, in Bruccoli, ed., *As Ever*, 370.

115 *"When I was your age"*: Fitzgerald to Scottie, 7 July 1938, in Bruccoli, ed., *A Life in Letters*, 363.

115 *they belonged to "different worlds"*: This is the theme in the letter to Scottie, Ibid., 362-363.

115 *Zelda had cheated him out of his dream*: Zelda had also ruined him financially. Milford, *Zelda*, 323.

115 *He warned her not to take a drink*: Fitzgerald to "Dearest Pie," 19 September 1938, in Bruccoli, ed., *A Life in Letters*, 366.

115 *"Never boast to a soul"*: Ibid.

115 *"debutante parties in New York"*: Fitzgerald to Scottie, 18 November 1938, quoting from a letter he'd sent Ober, in Bruccoli, ed., *A Life in Letters*, 372.

116 *Fitzgerald brought Jane a copy*: The date of September 27 is confirmed in her letter to RSC, 28 September 1938.

116 *"out of his need to be needed"*: Bruccoli, *Grandeur*, 363.

116 *Fitzgerald "mercilessly exposed"*: Milford, *Zelda*, 284.

116 *a "mood of loss and waste"*: Bruccoli, *Grandeur*, 374.

116 *"primarily about money and society"*: Dickstein, *Dancing in the Dark*, 260.

116 *had a sunny, arresting cover*: The copy Fitzgerald gave to Lillian Gish, the same edition that he gave Jane, is now available in the New York Public Library's Rare Books Collection. See Jen Carlson, "F. Scott Fitzgerald Pens Letter To 'Favorite Actress' Upon Her 1st Visit To NYC," *Gothamist*, January 29, 2013, http://goth-amist.com/2013/01/29/fitzgerald_pens_letter_to_favorite.php.

116 *"Just think, Dick"*: JH to RSC, 28 September 1938.

117 *"For Lillian Gish My Favorite Actress"*: Carlson, "Fitzgerald Pens Letter," January 29, 2013.

117 *he presented* Tales of the Jazz Age: Matthew J. Bruccoli, ed., with Judith S. Baughman, *Fitzgerald in the Marketplace: The Auction and Dealer Catalogs, 1935–2006.* (Columbia: University of South Carolina Press, 2009) also has this listing, which I accessed through Google Books.

117 *his "feelings about his liaison"*: Bruccoli, *Grandeur*, 439.

117 *he'd sent her a bouquet*: Graham, *Hollywood Revisited*, 221.

117 *"very much in love" with Zelda*: Ibid., 180.

117 *"always prostrated himself"*: Corrigan, *So We Read On*. Kindle edition.

117 *Fitzgerald's theme of the subservience of men to women*: As noted by Bruccoli in *Grandeur*, 35.

118 *"back at work on a new job"*: Fitzgerald to Harold Ober, received 9 November 1938, in Bruccoli, ed., *A Life in Letters*, 367.

118 *"*METRO NOT RENEWING*"*: Fitzgerald to Harold Ober, received 29 December 1938, in Bruccoli, ed., *A Life in Letters*, 375..

118 *"Baby am I glad to get out"*: Ibid.

118 *"didn't get along with some of the big boys"*: Fitzgerald to Leland Hayward, 16 January 1940, in Bruccoli, ed., *A Life in Letters*, 429. Hayward was now Fitzgerald's Hollywood agent, although he had apparently neglected to mention that to Swanie.

118 *he had been on loan*: Bruccoli, *Grandeur*, 450.

118 *"the best novel written about the movies"*: Matthew J. Bruccoli, in the preface to F. Scott Fitzgerald, *The Love of the Last Tycoon: A Western*, edited with a preface and notes by Matthew J. Bruccoli (New York: Scribner, 1994), vii.

119 *"archetypal American hero"*: Ibid., vii.

119 *She leased another new apartment*: The move is described in detail in JH to RSC, 29 September 1938.

119 *"the only new National Science Fellow"*: As mentioned in the career summary from Dickie to Jane that he sent her shortly before she died. DWH to JHC, 2 February 1987.

119 *trying without success to boost*: JH to RSC, 22 November 1938, for this paragraph.

Chapter Ten: The Accent on Youth

121 *"The first rule of writing salable material"*: JH to RSC, 29 October 1938.

121 *"We are licking the screenplay"*: JH to RSC, 20 October 1938.

121 *"the movie of this story"*: JH to RSC, 3 November 1938.

122 *magazines played a singular role*: Walker, ed., *Women's Magazines 1940–1960*, 4 and passim.

123 *"Here is the accent on youth"*: Burton added that Jane has "just written us another entertaining story of the younger generation, 'Elizabeth, Maker of Men.' Coming soon." (When the story came out in July 1939, the title was "Elizabeth,

Femme Fatale.") This was actually the last story Jane wrote before she left for Hollywood in October 1937.

123 *In November, he'd already advised*: *Cosmopolitan*, November 1938, 4.

125 *Much of the action takes place at "Sanctuary"*: Princeton University then had no fraternities. Jane had spent at least two weekends at Cloister Inn, which is the real setting for this story. The new name "Sanctuary" seems meant to be ironic, given the tragic events in the narrative.

125 *"while closeted with two or three men"*: JH to RSC 22 November 1938.

126 *Through rewrite after rewrite*: TC has copies of all the versions of *These Glamour Girls*.

128 *"astonish the Virginia natives"*: Jane added a few notes about 1938 at the end of Diary1 that describe this trip home.

128 *"speed crazed streamliner"*: JH to RSC, 12 January 1939, also contains an report on this trip.

128 KATE IS VERY ILL: JH to RSC, telegram, 6 January 1939.

128 *"my pocket is not as full"*: JH to RSC, mailed 14 January 1939.

129 *"from the first warm yellow mists"*: JH to RSC, n.d., circa 12 January 1939

129 the*"last fifth of the picture"*: JH to RSC, mailed 14 January 1939.

129 *"THROUGH DARK AND THROUGH DAYLIGHT"*: JH to RSC, telegram, 19 January 1939.

129 *"FRONT OFFICE HAS TURNED ON THE HEAT"*: JH to RSH, telegram, 22 January 1939.

131 *Jane felt good about the new script*: The January 24, 1939 script is in the TC, T-751, 119–120. Twenty-three items that reveal the scripting process for *These Glamour Girls* are in this collection; the first (T-740) is the one-page synopsis of the original story. Several scripts contain detailed annotations by Jane; some even include a few sketches she may have done while in long story meetings. The two final items, August 12, 1939, and August 19, 1939, contain dialogue-cutting continuity by editor Harold Kress, the music report, and footage.

131 *"worn to a frazzle"*: JH to RSC, 1 February 1939.

131 *to escape to the desert*: JH to RSC, 31 January 1939.

131 *She left for the twelve-year-old*: JH to RSC, 1 February 1939, gives a detailed report on her weekend break.

131 *"caged in their offices at all times"*: JH to RSC, n.d., approximately 26 January 1939.

131 *"Everybody who has read the script"*: JH to RSC, 31 January 1939.

132 *"and those speaking with"*: Richard Maltby, "The Production Code and the Hays Office," in *Grand Design: Hollywood as a Modern Business Enterprise 1930–1939*, ed. Tino Balio (Berkeley: University of California Press, 1993), 39.

132 *"contributed significantly to Hollywood's avoidance"*: Maltby, "Production Code," 38.

132 *Mayer thought he could manage*: Eyman, *Lion of Hollywood*, 190.

132 *An anecdote told by a producer*: recounted in ibid.

132 *"The hyper-masculinity of the PCA chief"*: Thomas Doherty, *Hollywood's Censor:*

Joseph I. Breen and the Production Code Administration (New York: Columbia University Press, 2007), 83.

132 *Persuading "roughneck moguls"*: Ibid.

133 *He stayed on top of his staff*: Ibid., 84.

133 *"Again and again he told me"*: Cited in ibid., 131.

133 *"in its present form is not acceptable"*: Joseph Breen to Louis B. Mayer, 28 January 1939, PCA. Breen's comments in the following paragraphs are quoted from this letter.

133 *"the stupid letter from the censors"*: JH to RSC, 1 February 1939.

133 *"Our picture was censored"*: JH to RSC, 8 February 1939.

134 *the "impact of entertainment"*: Maltby, "Production Code," 41.

134 *So Breen insisted*: Joseph Breen to Louis B. Mayer, 28 January 1939, PCA. This letter is the source for the quotations from Breen in the next five paragraphs.

135 *elements of sophisticated comedy*: See Jane M. Greene, "Hollywood's Production Code and Thirties Romantic Comedy," *Historical Journal of Film, Radio and Television* 30, no.1 (March 2010): 61–62 and throughout for an excellent discussion of the impact of the Production Code on both sophisticated and sentimental romantic comedies in the 1930s.

136 *one of his least favorite words*: Maltby, "Production Code," 37, notes that "the British always deleted it."

136 *"in hopes of negotiating"*: Maltby, "Production Code,"65.

136 *Breen's authority was primarily advisory*: Maltby, "Production Code," 64.

136 *He'd interviewed veteran director*: JH to RSC, 12 February 1939. Vidor had replaced Victor Fleming, who was reassigned to *Gone with the Wind* in February.

136 *thought Sam might also be waiting*: JH to RSC, mailed 22 February 1939.

137 *"suspended in midair"*: Ibid.

137 *"He is a charming old man"*: JH to RSC, mailed on 22 February 1939.

137 *and bowled a 67*: JH to RSC, 28 February 1939.

137 *"This child has an imaginary friend"*: JH to RSC, 13 February 1939.

137 *the "very social" Dolly*: JH to RSC, 16 March 1939, for the rest of this paragraph.

Chapter Eleven: Off to See the Wizard

139 *Metro's publicity department*: JH to RSC, 28 February 1939.

139 *the blockbuster Technicolor production*: Aljean Harmetz, *The Making of the Wizard of Oz Movie Magic and Studio Power in the Prime of MGM and the Miracle of Production #1060* (New York: Dell Publishing, 1989) and Jay Scarfone and William Stillman, *The Wizard of Oz: The Official 75th Anniversary Companion* (New York: Harper Design, 2013), Kindle edition, provided me with extensive background information and facts about the film's production.

139 *Production on Oz had started*: Harmetz, *The Making*, 14, says production began on October 12. The AFI Catalog gives the date as October 13; recording began on September 30.

139 *"While the wind whistles"*: These notes appear in a draft of a paragraph that Jane

thought about using in the article for *Good Housekeeping*. They are written on the back of the final page of her film treatment for "Two People," which she also worked on that winter. HFP.

139 *Jane recalled the time*: Jane Hall, "The Wizard of Oz," *Good Housekeeping*, August 1939.

139 *"We're pretty much wrought up"*: Unless otherwise noted, references to Jane's experiences on the film's set come from Jane Hall, "The Wizard of Oz," *Good Housekeeping*, August 1939.

140 *"entirely responsible"*: Of course LeRoy (Jane spells it "Leroy") was one of many, but he was definitely the key person behind the production.

140 *In 1938, the average feature*: Scarfone and Stillman, *Official Companion*. Kindle edition.

142 *their 124 Munchkins*: Harmetz, *The Making*, devotes chapter 7 to the Munchkins. The terms "small performers" or "little people" are preferred to "midgets" today, but in 1939 that was not the case.

143 *But, even corseted, her character*: Rebecca Loncraine, "The Changes to Oz," in *The Wizard of Oz: An Over-the-Rainbow Celebration of the World's Favorite Movie*, ed. Ben Nussbaum, (Irvine, CA: I-5 Publishing, 2014).

143 *"a much younger, simpler girl"*: Scarfone and Stillman, *Official Companion*, Kindle edition. Judy was fifteen when her contract was signed, sixteen during the production, and seventeen during retakes.

143 *she "mortified her mother"*: Ibid.

143 *On the set Judy worked*: Ibid.

143 *was genuinely fond of Victor Fleming*: Michael Sragow, *Victor Fleming: An American Movie Master* (New York: Pantheon, 2008), 301.

145 *his "no-nonsense directing style"*: See David Denby, "The Real Rhett Butler," *New Yorker*, May 25, 2009, and Sragow, *Victor Fleming*.

145 *much preferred to work with him than with George Cukor*: Sragow, *Victor Fleming*, 317–320, for the reasons why Fleming ended up on *Gone with the Wind*. Olivia de Haviland and Vivien Leigh preferred Cukor.

145 *the "most attractive man"*: Quoted in David Denby, "The Real Rhett Butler," 74. Denby's insightful piece draws on the then new biography of Fleming by Michael Sragow and on Molly Haskell's *Frankly, My Dear*.

145 *"Six-foot-one and ruggedly handsome"*: Scarfone and Stillman, *Official Companion*, Kindle edition. Many people were surprised at the choice of Fleming, but these authors note that he had "quite competently handled juvenile actors in MGM's *Treasure Island* (1934) and *Captains Courageous* (1937)."

145 *"came in like a lion"*: Quoted in Sragow, *Victor Fleming*, 326.

145 *"like a big dog can be gruff"*: Quoted in ibid., 423.

145 *whose psychic abilities*: Rosa Sutton's alleged experiences with voices from beyond and with the ghost of her son, Jimmie, were the subject of an exhaustive study by psychical researcher James Hyslop. For a full discussion see Cutler, *A Soul on Trial* (New York: Rowman & Littlefield, 2007). Jane believed in ghosts

throughout her life. In her March 1929 journal, (in HFP) she admits that she often got in bed with her mother when she thought she saw her father's ghost.

147 *Baum believed in spirits*: Noted in Nussbaum, ed., *An Over-the-Rainbow Celebration*, Baum's interest in spiritualism is covered in greater detail in Rebecca Loncraine's book, *The Real Wizard of Oz: The Life and Times of L. Frank Baum* (New York: Gotham Books, 2009).

148 *at times chaotic production*: Harmetz, *The Making*, 264–280, gives a full description of the production's problems.

148 *"As Fleming pulled together"*: Denby, "The Real Rhett Butler." 74 and 78.

149 *Aljean Harmetz found*: See Harmetz, *The Making*, 191–204 for more about some of these challenges.

149 *"veterans of the gritty road life"*: Sragow, *Victor Fleming*, 304–307.

149 *"never raised his voice"*: Ibid., 307.

149 *"the most horrendous job"*: Harmetz, *The Making*, 264–265.

149 *"jumped from the broom straw"*: Ibid., 271–272.

150 *Even Toto (whose real name was Terry)*: Ibid., 280.

150 *"care should be taken to avoid"*: See the AFI Catalog entry for *The Wizard of Oz* for Breen's comments on this production, viewable at http://www.afi.com/members/catalog/DetailView.aspx?Movie=7892. Accessed 17 January 2013.

150 *LeRoy, a great admirer of Walt Disney*: Scarfone and Stillman, *Official Companion*, Kindle edition.

150 *screened* Snow White *at MGM*: Ibid.

150 *"early drafts of the script"*: Ibid.

150 *"dreams that you dare to dream"*: From the lyrics to "Somewhere Over the Rainbow"(1939), music by Harold Arlen, lyrics by E.Y. Harburg.

151 *"a place for all the characters"*: Sragow, *Victor Fleming*, 293.

Chapter Twelve: "Just Another Dame Who Wanted a Career"

153 *Metro's annual three-day sales convention*: Covered in "M-G-M Schedules 52 New Pictures," *New York Times*, March 21, 1939.

154 *Sam gave Jane another new project*: JH to RSC, 29 March 1939.

154 *"tear off an original"*: Ibid.

154 *"To work on such a thing"*: Ibid.

154 *Jane's forty-five page treatment*: "Two People," HFP. Found by the author for sale online at a bookseller in Virginia, this may be the only surviving copy of "Two People."

157 *"out of sync" with her times*: Susan Hertog, *Dangerous Ambition: Rebecca West and Dorothy Thompson: New Women in Search of Love and Power* (New York: Ballantine Books, 2011), 260.

158 *"I had to pay my income tax"*: JH to RSC, 29 March 1939

159 *an event duly noted*: "Mrs. R. R. Hicks Is Reopening Her Home in Virginia," *The New York Herald Tribune*, April 2, 1939.

159 *With unexpected good timing*: Jane Hall, "Elizabeth, Femme Fatale," *Cosmopolitan*, July 1939. The original title had been "Elizabeth, Maker of Men."

159 *He'd secured a contract for her*: SAF includes the contract.

159 *"was an opportunity which no one should refuse"*: RRH to RSH, 24 June 1939, HFP.

159 *In her* Voice of Broadway *column*: Dorothy Kilgallen, *New York Journal and American*, July 1, 1939, 10.

160 *Jane wired her aunt*: JH to RSH telegram, 24 June 1939. HFP.

160 *"that DEN the G of A"*: JH to RSC, n.d., circa 28 June 1939.

160 *Rose sent a long, gossipy letter*: RSH to JH, 29 June 1939.

160 *a beautiful, shy small-town girl*: Cheryl Crane with Cindy De La Hoz, *Lana: The Memories, the Myths, the Movies* (Philadelphia: Running Press, 2008), 25.

161 *had an ideal figure*: Howard Dietz and Howard Strickling. *Who's Who at Metro-Goldwyn-Mayer* (Culver City, CA: MGM Publicity Department, 1940), 85. MHL.

161 *"Lana took center stage"*: Crane, *Lana*, 200.

161 *Lew Ayres, a thirty-year-old musician*: Dietz and Strickling, *Who's Who*, 40.

161 *who had also been hand-picked by LeRoy*: Ibid., 109.

161 *"brilliant but slightly pedantic"*: Eyman, *Lion of Hollywood*, 211. A few people thought Shearer was "the weak link" in the system.

161 *"the most powerful arbiter of style"*: Ibid., 209.

162 *"Small Town Railroad Depot"*: Bingen, Sylvester, and Troyan, *MGM*, 291.

162 *"Brownstone Street"*: Ibid., 297.

162 *"Whatever you wanted"*: Harmetz, *The Making*, 7.

162 *Breen's reservations about*: Joseph Breen to Louis B. Mayer, 18 May 1939, PCA.

162 *"Please have in mind"*: Ibid.

163 *On Friday, May 26, Breen had met*: "Memorandum for the Files RE: These Glamour Girls—MGM, May 27, 1939, PCA.

163 *"good-natured, quiet and reserved"*: Eyman, *Lion of Hollywood*, 118.

163 *"at considerable length"*: Breen, "Memorandum for the Files."

163 *Writers had little clout*: Eyman, *Lion of Hollywood*, 267.

163 *Zimbalist had approved the "OK Script"*: T-756, TC.

163 *"The material is technically"*: Joseph Breen to Louis B. Mayer, 12 June 1939, PCA File.

164 *help Marion handle last-minute revisions*: T-758 and T-759, "Retakes by George Oppenheimer and Marion Parsonnet, July 27, 1939," TC.

164 *After Al Block sent Breen*: Al Block to Joseph Breen, 27 July 1939, PCA.

164 *Breen found only two scenes*: Joseph Breen to Louis B. Mayer, 28 July 1939, PCA.

164 *"our final judgment"*: Ibid.

164 *"with a desk and a secty"*: JH to RSC, date illegible, end of June 1939.

164 *the first year during the 1930s*: Jewell, *Golden Age*, 57 and 51–52 for this description of Universal.

164 *"commitment to 'clean' pictures"*: Jewell, *Golden Age*, 134.

164 *Pasternak may have encouraged*: Pasternak became a big fan of Jane's work; she continued to write for him until 1942 but turned down other opportunities after that.

164 *"the producer who has never failed"*: *Hollywood Reporter*, 28 June 1938.

165 *"In the mines"*: JH to RSC, 10 July 1939, describes her first two weeks at Universal.

165 *"I had a feud"*: Ibid.

165 *"They are letting me do"*: JH to RSC, 20 July 1939.

165 *She'd been put on the project*: HNS to JH, 31 July 1939, SAF, indicates that Jane was reassigned on July 17 "to work on the screenplay for our photoplay entitled 'IT'S A DATE,' all such assignments being made and all services rendered by you in connection with said photoplay being rendered under said contract of June 26, 1939." Treatment #8 in TC. I also consulted "It's a Date," Treatment #7, HFP.

165 *in the third week of September*: JH to RSC, 8 September 1939, and JH to Ernest Hall, 19 September 1939.

166 *The first treatments appear*: A vault copy of "It's a Date" by Jane Hall, Treatment No. 8, TC, is dated September 1, 1939.

166 *"I think we should get a feeling"*: "Pasternak #7 Treatment by Jane Hall," 40, n.d., HFP. The treatment is lightly annotated but missing pages 19–24. In this document, Georgia's love interest is named Hyatt Bogert rather than John Arlen. Possibly because of the vigilance of the PCA, the final film leaves no doubt that John Arlen was never interested in Pam romantically despite her fantasies to the contrary. Jane's treatment keeps his feelings ambiguous until the end.

167 *Beverly Hills premiere*: The premiere took place on September 27, 1939. See the AFI Catalog entry for *The Private Lives of Elizabeth and Essex*: http://www.afi. com/members/catalog/DetailView.aspx?s=&Movie=4329.

167 *"Good Queen Bette"*: Jane Hall, "Good Queen Bette," *Cosmopolitan*, January 1940.

167 *"Nunnally Johnson"*: A journalist, satirist, and prolific screenwriter, between 1935 and 1942 Johnson worked for Twentieth Century Fox and Hollywood mogul Darryl F. Zanuck. He received sole credit for the screen adaptation of Steinbeck's *The Grapes of Wrath* (1940) as well as many others.

167 *"Mark [sic] Connelly"*: Jane misspelled the name of Marc Connelly, the Pulitzer Prize–winning playwright and member of the Algonquin Round Table.

167 *she learned that Miss Davis*: Bette Davis's final films were all historical dramas; *The Private Lives of Elizabeth and Essex* is based on a Maxwell Anderson play.

167 *according to the AFI Catalog*: The film had several working titles; it became *The Private Lives of Elizabeth and Essex* to avoid copyright issues, as the late historian Lytton Strachey had published *Elizabeth and Essex: A Tragic History* in 1928.

Chapter Thirteen: Glamour Girl

169 *"They sneak previewed Glamour Girls"*: JH to RSC, 2 August 1939.

169 *"L.B. Mayer himself"*: Mayer attended almost all the previews of Metro pictures. Eyman, *Lion of Hollywood*, 298.

170 *The movie's trailer*: The trailer was put together in the second week of August. T-760, August 11, 1939, TC, MHL. Dashes indicate the individual titles; ellipses appear here as in the trailer.

170 *reviews in the trades*: The *Daily Variety* and *Hollywood Reporter* reviews are from August 15, 1939.

171 *Hedda Hopper's Hollywood column*: *Los Angeles Times*, August 15, 1939.

171 *a congratulatory telegram*: RRH and RSH et al. to JH, telegram, 22 August 1939.

172 *"The movies are a curious phenomenon"*: Nugent, review of *These Glamour Girls*. The byline is Nugent's, but the initials "B.R.C." at the end of the write-up indicate that Nugent's colleague at the *Times,* Benjamin R. Crisler, drafted the review to Nugent's satisfaction—that explains the use of the pronoun "we" throughout.

173 *two influential investors*: Marguerite and Howard Cullman to JH, telegram, 31 August 1939. The Cullmans are mentioned in several letters in the HFP. They were also close friends of Jon Whitcomb and Bradshaw Crandell. See Eric Page's obituary, "Marguerite W. Cullman, 94, an Investor in Broadway Hits," *New York Times*, July 27, 1999.

173 *The "glamor girl is today an occupation"*: "The Press: Glamor Girl," *Time*, January 1, 1940. For another perspective on this topic, and a discussion of how hard it was to define glamour in 1938, see Jurca, *Hollywood 1938*, 101–112. Among her works cited is Annette Tapert, *The Power of Glamour: The Women Who Defined the Magic of Stardom*. (New York: Crown, 1980), also a rich source on the subject.

173 *"a syntax of seeming"*: John Lahr, "Elements of Film: The Voodoo of Glamour," *New Yorker*, March 21, 1994, 113.

173 *"looking the way"*: Lahr, "Elements of Film," 120.

173 *"turned glamour into a corporate product"*: Stephen Gundle, *Glamour: A History* (New York: Oxford University Press, 2008), 176.

174 *the movies of this era "make"*: Basinger, *A Woman's View*, Kindle edition.

174 *her "natural career of love"*: Ibid.

174 *"fundamental to a woman's definition"*: Ibid.

174 *"Women's history, if they had any"*: Carolyn Heilbrun, *Women's Lives: The View from the Threshold*, The Alexander Lectures, (Toronto: University of Toronto Press, 1999), 15.

174 *"The state of being glamorous"*: Jon Whitcomb, *All About Girls* (Englewood Cliffs, NJ: Prentice Hall, 1962), 15.

174 *Glamorous women exuded*: Ibid., 218 and 17.

174 *"No one we know intimately"*: Gundle, *Glamour*, 14.

175 *"a theatrical public image"*: Ibid., 164.

175 *"the adoption of a carefree attitude"*: Ibid.

175 *"the way to Fashion, Beauty, and Charm"*: For a look at the cover of the first issue of *Glamour of Hollywood* magazine, see http://www.huffingtonpost.com/2013/03/07/glamour-magazine-first-issue-photo-_n_c2821738.html. Accessed 1/2/2014.

175 *something she'd belittled in other women*: see chapter 8 and JH to RSC, June 19, 1938.

175 *a "political act"*: Haskell, *Holding . . .*,181. The book includes this reprint of her delightful essay on makeup, "Lipstick Envy," which first appeared in *Self* magazine in February 1995.

175 "seen *as trying to look good*": Ibid., 182.

175 a "social contract": Ibid., 184.

176 "a bright eyed, blonde debutante": "The Press: Glamor Girl," *Time,* January 1, 1940.

176 *one of three dogs Crandell had placed:* Two others appear on the April 1935 and November 1937 covers. The April cover is also a wire haired Fox Terrier.

176 *photo taken by Grif Griffith:* Griffith was a photographer until the early 1960s, when he became a distinguished landscape architect in Los Angeles. His grandfather Griffith J. Griffith donated the land for Griffith Park. In the late 1940s he married former Miss Los Angeles Debra Alden (born Shirley Fedderson), who played Ruth Stockton in the 1947 film *Code of the West.* Van Griffith (Jane Hall's godson) in an interview with the author, March 17, 2014.

176 "her favorite photographer": Lee Russell, Fashions in Fiction, *Cosmopolitan,* October 1939, 6.

177 *Walter Winchell had announced:* Walter Winchell, On Broadway, *Daily Mirror,* September 4, 1939, 10.

177 "Attractive Jane Hall": The clipping is in HFP.

177 "TOO MANY MEN": Unsigned to JH, telegram, 22 December 1939.

177 *Otis's premature death at fifty-two:* Hundreds of newspaper articles followed the career of Otis H. Cutler. Among the longest obituaries is "Otis H. Cutler Dies Suddenly at Florida." *Suffern Independent,* March 11, 1922. He was beloved throughout Rockland County for his humility and generosity. See also "Otis H Cutler Dies Suddenly at Miami," *New York Times,* March 5, 1922.

178 *in the shadow of a tragedy:* On May 11, 1900, five-year-old Otis Cutler, Jr. fell off his toy express wagon as it went downhill and broke his right arm; blood poisoning set in and "little Otie suffered agony." Surgeons at Roosevelt Hospital in New York City amputated his arm, but it was too late to save his life; he died on June 12. One of several stories about this tragedy appeared in the *Nyack Star,* "Little Otis Dead," June 12, 1900.

178 "Lovers of good theater": "R. F. Cutler," editorial, Rockland County *Journal-News,* February 22, 1976. Craig H. Long, the historian for the Village of Suffern as well as Montebello and the Town of Ramapo, has collected several hundred articles about the Cutler family and the County Theatre, primarily from Rockland County newspapers; I am grateful to him for sharing these resources with me. For more on the theater, see also "Cutler's Gamble in Transforming Suffern Barn into a Theater Is Justified by Success of Season," Rockland County *Journal-News,* July 26, 1934.

178 *Al Hirschfeld's pen-and-ink drawing:* "Drama's Summer School Draws to a Fitful Close," *New York Times,* August 28, 1938, section 9, cover story. On June 12, 2008, this drawing was sold (not by me) at Swann Auction Galleries for a record $84,000.

179 *The intimate revue:* "'One for the Money' an Intimate Revue with Sketches and Lyrics by Nancy Hamilton," Brooks Atkinson, *New York Times,* February 6, 1939.

179 "having to do with": Burns Mantle, ed., *The Best Plays of 1938–39 and the Year Book*

of the Drama in America (New York: Dodd, Mead and Company, 1939), 456, lists Gertrude Macy, Stanley Gilkey, and Robert F. Cutler as producers. In a review of the season in New York, Mantle describes *One for the Money* as a "right-wing revue, staged, it was rumored, with Jock Whitney backing, and popularly produced in direct contrast to the left-wing success, 'Pins and Needles.'" (Mantle, ed., *Best Plays*, 9.

179 *"one of the first women"*: "Nancy Hamilton, Lyricist, 76, Dies," *New York Times*, February 19, 1985.

179 *Nondas was restless*: Nondas Metcalfe, "I'll Chalk It All Up to Experience," *Philadelphia Inquirer*, November 3, 1940, 3, gives her detailed explanation of the reasons for their divorce four days before Bob married Jane. All quotations from her in the following two paragraphs are from this source.

179 *"the lure of travel"*: Ibid. For example, see a personal-mention column in the Rockland County *Journal-News*, February 13, 1935: "Mr. and Mrs. Robert F. Cutler [Nondas & Bob] of Suffern returned home from Bermuda Friday. Saturday and Monday they attended the dog show of the Westminster Kennel Club at Madison Square Garden, in which they had entered their prize-winning wire-haired terrier. They sailed at noon today on the *Conte di Savoia* on a Mediterranean cruise on which they will be gone for six weeks."

179 *"a woman cannot"*: Ibid., 3. Though her acting career never took off, Nondas did secure a small part as a dinner guest in Alfred Hitchcock's *Suspicion* (RKO, 1941).

179 *Rose had already urged Jane*: RSH to JH, 1 March 1939. This long letter came after Cliff Zieger complained to Rose that he never knew where he stood with Jane.

179 *"You could never live"*: Ibid, and for the remainder of the paragraph.

180 *"represented a level of economic security"*: Cari Beauchamp, *Without Lying Down: Frances Marion and the Powerful Women of Early Hollywood* (Berkeley: University of California Press, 1997), 23.

180 *"would never be happy as a society wife"*: Ibid., 27.

180 *"I wanted marriage"*: For this paragraph, see Myrna Loy and James Kotsilibas-Davis, *Myrna Loy: Being and Becoming* (New York: Donald I. Fine, Inc. 1988), 128.

181 *Jane thought surely she could keep him*: Elspeth Banks Furlaud (Bob's niece, who knew them well as a young couple) in a conversation with the author, March 2014. Her life also bears witness to this fact.

181 *Bob had made up his mind*: He expressed his love to Jane in a poem that he gave her on Christmas Eve entitled "These Are My Thoughts." The poem is the only document in Bob's handwriting that Jane saved from their courtship. HFP.

181 *other correspondence and news items*: Such items appeared in the *Journal-News* (Rockland County, NY), March 21, 1940 and May 20, 1940; the *Ramapo Valley Independent*, May 23, 1940; and the *New York Times*, May 18, 1940. *The Eagle* (Reading, PA), March 20, 1940 also includes a picture of Nondas with her fox terrier.

181 *the County Theatre had a rocky summer*: "Armitage Barn Again Beset by Coin Head-ache," *Variety*, August 14, 1940. See also "Jean Muir, Meisner, Suffer Headaches Left by Walter Armitage at Suffern," *Variety*, June 18, 1941.

181 *"Hostess at Benefit Gathering"*: *The Sun* (New York), May 21, 1940. Jane was a host-ess "at the showings of the Long Island Gardens on the estates of Mr. and Mrs. Sidney Z. Mitchell, at Oyster Bay, and Paul D. Cravath, at Locust Valley, for the benefit of the School Nature League."

184 *Columnist Dorothy Kilgallen*: Kilgallen wrote of the pending divorce in her Voice of Broadway Column, *New York Journal and American*, March 11, 1940. (Her column was syndicated in more than 140 papers.)

184 *The divorce in May*: Nondas and Bob had agreed on a five-hundred-dollar-per-month settlement until she remarried (which she did in 1947). When he learned about Nondas's relationship with another man prior to their marriage, he stopped paying. For close to six years, Bob and Nondas engaged in a bitter court battle, which she eventually won, over the money that she claimed he owed her. It was a great strain on Jane for the first six years of her marriage.

Chapter Fourteen: "She's Divinely Happy"

185 *"the Mecca of prominent"*: "Sun Seekers," *New York Journal and American*, August 11, 1940.

185 *Paul scooped Jane's engagement*: *New York Journal and American*, August 31, 1940.

185 *Jane had apparently been seen*: *Where to Go*, February 10, 1940, 16. Also in the snapshot is Ted Straeter, who led the band at the club and worked on Kate Smith's radio show.

185 *"produced country gossip"*: *Washington Times-Herald*, September 2, 1940. The en-gagement was covered in the *New York Herald Tribune* on this same day.

185 *a frenetic two weeks*: JH to her art school pal Renee Barnard Dowling, 7 September 1940.

186 *they took off for Los Angeles*: Ibid. Also noted in *Daily Variety*, September 4 and 6, 1940.

186 *the letter Jane received from Rose*: RSH to JH, 6 September 1940.

187 *Jane commuted from her villa*: *Daily Variety* notices on September 4 and 6 establish the parameters of this assignment.

187 *Swanie had secured the job*: *Daily Variety*, August 29, 1940.

187 *104-page "Master Treatment"*: Purchased by the author in 2012 from an online bookseller. He had a small "archive of Jane Hall papers" that had once been stolen and entered the world of flea markets; this may be only copy of the treat-ment. HFP.

187 *Jane described the situation*: JH to RSH, n.d., approximately 4 October 1940.

189 *On October 29, Daily Variety reported*: "Jane Hall Ends Job," *Daily Variety*, October 29, 1940.

190 *was "going to be a swell picture"*: JH to RSH, 18 October 1940.

190 *"to produce successful films"*: Richard B. Jewell, *RKO Radio Pictures: A Titan Is Born* (Berkeley: University of California Press, 2012),179.

190 *"the most audacious"*: Ibid., 178.

190 *"expelled from the RKO roster"*: Ibid., 226.

190 *"already offered me another job"*: JH to RSH, 18 October 1940.

190 *married quietly in Pasadena*: "Jane Hall and Robert F. Cutler in Pasadena Surprise Bridal," The Smart Set, *New York Journal and American*, November 11, 1940.

190 *honeymooning in Palm Springs*: Maury Paul, Chatter Box, *Los Angeles Times*, November 20, 1940.

190 *"What 'Uncle Randy' and 'Aunt Rose' "*: Ibid.

190 *"never looked lovelier"*: Margaret Gregory to JH, 12 September 1940

191 *attend a "Balloon Night"*: "Cholly Knickerbocker Says," *New York Journal and American*, n.d. (December 1940), in HFP.

191 *"did favor a homogenous look"*: Ralph Blumenthal, *Stork Club: America's Most Famous Nightspot and the Lost World of Café Society* (Boston: Little Brown and Company, 2001),159.

191 *"while browsing through the* Princeton Alumni Weekly*"*: Marion Meade, *Dorothy Parker*, 298.

191 *"was struck by the isolation of the room"*: Ibid.

191 *"believing himself a failure"*: "A Brief Life of F. Scott Fitzgerald," in Meade, *Dorothy Parker*, 169.

191 *"destined for literary obscurity"*: Ibid.

192 *after he interviewed Jane*: These Fascinating Ladies was a regular column in the *New York Journal-American*. Paul also profiled Bob's sister, Dorothy Cutler Banks. Both clippings n.d., HFP.

192 *Jane and Bob spent February*: Jane's Career Summary, HFP.

193 *prominent young author*: Dana Jenney, "Snakeskin Trophy Yields Accessories," *New York Journal-American,* May 8, 1941.

193 *The County Theatre had been rented out*: Rockland County *Journal-News*, April, 24, 1941.

193 *"ill-will generated"*: "Jean Muir, Meisner, Suffer Headaches Left by Walter Armitage at Suffern," *Variety*, June 18, 1941, for the remainder of this paragraph.

193 *Three notes from Henry La Cossitt*: Henry La Cossitt to Mrs. Robert Cutler, June 30, August 5 and September 4, 1941. La Cossitt would become the editor of *Collier's* magazine in 1944. HFP.

194 *"a candid and happy man"*: Eyman, *Lion of Hollywood*, 332.

194 *Swanie wired Jane at Rockrest*: HNS to JHC (Mrs. Robert Cutler), August 27, 1941. HFP.

194 *Pasternak's first project at Metro*: *Daily Variety*, October 1, 1941. On Pasternak see Katz, 1096.

194 *Jane worked on this "Torchy"*: Jane saved carbon copies of two intraoffice typed notes that she sent Joe Pasternak. On December 2, 1940, she refers to their "Torchy." HFP.

194 *to buy a house for Jane in Palm Springs*: Several letters from Jane's friends and a few newspaper reports made a note of this purchase including Constance Ludwig, "Desert Resorts Herald Lively Winter Season," *Los Angeles Times*, November 9, 1941. Maury Paul also reported the purchase in Metropolitan Smart Set, *New York Journal and American*, December 17, 1941.

194 *enjoyed seeing her old colleagues*: Jane writes, "Got Marion on story" in her Career Summary, 1949, HFP.

195 *Jon Whitcomb reported from Sundeck*: Jon Whitcomb to "D'zani", 4 December 1941.

195 *had secured teaching posts*: DWH to JHC, 5 November 1941.

195 *he'd been "swimming upstream"*: DWH to JHC, n.d., early January 1942.

195 *spiced up his wardrobe*: DWH to JHC, 5 November 1941 and DWH to JHC, n.d., late December 1941.

195 *"Dear Professor Hall"*: Jane's secretary to DWH, carbon copy, 4 December 1941. The original letter includes the use of an ellipsis wherever a comma would normally be.

196 *It was a skill that fascinated Brown's president*: DWH to JHC, n.d. December 1941.

Chapter Fifteen: "Because of the Dreams"

197 *In the raging debate between interventionists*: See Lynne Olson, *Those Angry Days: Roosevelt, Lindbergh, and America's Fight over World War II, 1939–1941* (New York: Random House, 2013), Kindle edition, for a comprehensive history of these years. In her diary entry for July 7 and 8, 1943, Jane writes: "Tonight we had a big fight about helping Europe. [Dickie and his girlfriend at the time] are both such strong isolationists as to be pro-German and it makes me angry that Dick who is so bright argues with so little logic."

197 *"Hollywood was stunned"*: Beauchamp, *Without Lying Down*, 348.

197 *"100 studio trucks and drivers"*: Bruce Torrence, *Hollywood: The First 100 Years* (Hollywood, CA: The Hollywood Chamber Of Commerce, 1979), 181.

197 *"nearby army and navy camps"*: Ibid., 184.

198 *"made training films for the services"*: Ibid.

198 *Rose begged her niece*: RSH to JHC, 8 January 1942.

198 *"spellbound booster of Southern California"*: RSH to JHC, 28 March 1942.

198 *This traveling military spectacle*: *The United States Army War Show Yearbook, Provisional Task Force, 1942*. (On Bob's new job as codirector, see page 9.) Several sections of the book appear at http://www.lookingoppositely.com/army-war-show-1942. Accessed February 14, 2014.

198 *Kate gave birth to five female puppies*: JH Career Summary, HFP.

198 *"extensive traveling ought to be"*: RRH to JHC, 24 October 1942.

198 *"you should not lose your audience"*: RRH to JHC, 27 October 1942.

198 *"Bob and I stayed"*: JH Career Summary, HFP.

199 Cosmopolitan *rejected a story*: Ibid.

199 *had grabbed Jon Whitcomb*: Ibid.

199 *Jane's trusted stockbroker and former beau*: Andre Smolianinoff to "Tovarisch" [Russian for "Comrade"], 23 November 1942.

199 *Dick Clarke served in the army*: Columbia University archivist Carrie Hintz to Robin Cutler, e-mail, September 29, 2011.

199 *"were treated shabbily"*: Richard Fine, *Hollywood and the Profession of Authorship, 1928–1940*, Studies in Cinema (Ann Arbor, MI: UMI Research Press, 1979), 10–11.

200 *"virtually every writer was disquieted"*: Ibid., 13.

200 *almost all of them were homesick*: Ibid., 129.

200 *"by an employee without power"*: Ibid., 131–132, for the rest of the papargraph.

200 *the most interesting of her life*: Diary2, January 1, 1943. She felt the same way forty years later.

201 *"Bob has changed"*: RSH to JHC, 27 October 1942.

201 *the sense of alienation that is common*: Bruccoli, *Grandeur*, 427.

201 *she recalled being happy*: JH Career Summary, HFP.

202 *"Because of the Dreams," an insightful tale*: Copy in HFP.

204 *"I skipped the rank"*: DWH to "D'zani," 3 February 1987. Dickie sent her a career summary.

204 *They married almost immediately*: Gretchen Hall to Robin Cutler, e-mail, 5 February 2014, e-mail.

205 *On April 2, 1945, Jane had a letter*: Reported in Diary2 on March 27 with a note that the entry belongs on April 2, 1945.

205 Patrick the Great: The American Film Institute Catalog has a detailed entry on *Patrick the Great*, viewable at http://www.afi.com/members/catalog/Detail View.aspx?s=&Movie=24526. Accessed 20 May 2015. For the Crowther review, *New York Times*, April 13, 1945. It is paired with his scathing review of a "brainless" RKO picture called *Having Wonderful Crime*.

205 *She sold the house in Palm Springs*: [Broker] Harold Hicks to JHC, telegram, 27 May 1945.

205 *she quickly wrote an amusing story*: Jane Hall, "Acapulco Fizz," *Cosmopolitan*, January 1946.

206 *"strange stirring"*: Betty Friedan *The Feminine Mystique*, introduction by Anna Quindlen, (New York: W.W. Norton, 1997), 57.

206 *"lied to women"*: Janet Maslin, "Looking back at a Domestic Cri de Coeur." *New York Times*, February 18, 2013.

206 *Even today, highly successful women*: Katty Kay and Claire Shipman, "The Confidence Gap," *Atlantic,* May 2014, http://www.theatlantic.com/magazine/archive/2014/05/the-confidence-gap/359815/ for the rest of this paragraph. Accessed 20 February 2015.

206 *this was not the dish*: Fitzgerald referred to his forties when he made this comment in March 1936 in "Pasting It Together," one of his confessional articles for *Esquire*. The essay is reprinted in in *The Crack-Up*, ed. Edmund Wilson, reprint (New York: New Directions Books, 1993); this quotation appears on page 75.

207 *"premature success gives one"*: Fitzgerald makes this observation in his October 1937 essay "Early Success," in ibid., 89.

208 *movies and magazines portrayed*: Katie Milestone and Anneke Meyer, *Gender and Popular Culture* (Cambridge, MA: Polity Press, 2012), 86.

208 *"ought to need to be"*: Basinger, *I Do and I Don't*, Kindle edition.

208 *"This was the era"*: Maslin, "Looking back at a Domestic Cri de Coeur." *New York Times*, February 18, 2013.

Chapter Sixteen: Goodnight Sweetheart

210 *he needed a haircut*: Jane told this anecdote more than once to friends who asked how she met Johnnie.

210 *They made a "pact"*: CJB to JHC, 20 December 1955and 18 February 1956and 11 January 1957.

211 *"so much more personal"*: CJB to JHC, 21 December 1956.

211 *"at least fifty"*: CJB to JHC, 20 March 1959.

211 *the "severest winter in 100 years"*: CJB to JHC, 20 December 1955.

211 *"What about New Year's Eve?"*: Ibid.

211 *"with the greatest difficulty"*: CJB to JHC, 26 November 1956.

212 *"everybody in Stockholm"*: CJB to JHC, 7 June 1956.

212 *"She certainly is attractive"*: CJB to JHC, 9 July 1956.

212 *twice Johnnie asked about Bob's health*: CJB to JHC, 7 June 1956 and 9 July 1956.

212 *"Please do not let your typewriter"*: CJB to JHC, 15 September 1956.

212 *missed their afternoon drinks*: CJB to JHC, 26 November 1956.

212 *"woke up with a smile"*: CJB to JHC, 15 December 1956.

212 *"How is your painting?"*: CJB to JHC, 21 December 1956.

213 *"I'm sitting at my desk"*: CJB to JHC, 11 January 1957.

213 *"Why don't you try to find another studio"*: CJB to JHC, 29 January 1957.

213 *Jane was clearly "very depressed"*: CJB to JHC, 21 March 1957.

213 *a fire destroyed Rockrest*: "Cutler Place at Suffern Is Ruined by Fire, Seven Departments Fight Blaze," Rockland County *Journal-News*, April 4, 1957.

213 *"saw a very light and indecent"*: CJB to JHC, 13 April 1957.

213 *"going away for a long vacation"*: Ibid.

214 *"How can you resist trying it out"*: CJB to JHC, 12 December 1957.

214 *"up to my neck in business"*: CJB to JHC, 15 October 1958.

214 *"We should be able to drink martinis"*: Ibid.

214 *"I am following your advice"*: CJB to JHC, 1 February 1959.

215 *"all by myself without interruption"*: CJB to JHC, 21 February 1959.

215 *he was able to confirm his plans*: CJB to JHC, 15 December 1959.

215 *"36 hour extravaganza"*: CJB to JHC, 7 February 1960.

216 *thought of Jane "very, very often"*: CJB to JHC, 12 February 1960.

216 *"I do not seem to have come back"*: CJB to JHC, 19 February 1960.

216 *had some "very, very rough times"*: CJB to JHC, 15 April 1961, for this paragraph.

For many years, Johnnie and his family lived in London. In 1969, he would become the European head of Sundstrand International and its subsidiaries.

216 *"very very strong and intense"*: CJB to JHC, 15 April 1961.

Epilogue: Finding D'zani

220 *a full-blown affair would have been uncharacteristic*: My mother and I never had that conversation about the facts of life that eighteen-year-old Jane had contemplated having with her children. Instead, when I became engaged, she took me to a six-foot-tall female gynecologist with the bedside manner of a Marine Corps sergeant.

220 *Mayer suggested to a story editor*: Mayer's conversation with William Fadiman is recounted in Eyman, *Lion of Hollywood*, 247.

220 *"best loved by audiences"*: Basinger, *I Do and I Don't*, Kindle edition.

220 *"Some of the movies' most beautiful"*: Ibid.

220 *"Hollywood provides Utopian solutions"*: Richard Maltby, *Hollywood Cinema*, 2nd ed. (Malden, MA: Blackwell Publishing, 2003), 38. Maltby draws on the work of Richard Dyer and sociologists Martha Wolfenstein and Nathan Leites, who wrote in the late 1940s.

220 *"absolved from both guilt and responsibility"*: Ibid.

221 *"a substitute for actual life experience"*: Quoted in ibid., 10.

221 *"sent home happy"*: Ibid.

221 *"into a romantic fantasy or a trip"*: Ibid., 16.

221 *"catapulted back in time"*: Collins, *America's Women: 400 Years of Dolls, Drudges, Helpmates and Heroines* (New York: William Morrow, 2003), 398.

221 *"truly feminine women"*: Friedan, *The Feminine Mystique*, 58.

221 *"strange discrepancy"*: Ibid., 50. Friedan's focus is well-educated white middle- and upper-middle-class women like herself; she makes few references to African-American or working-class women.

221 *"frenzied, desperate search"*: Ibid., 63.

221 *"to be at peace" with herself*: Anne Morrow Lindbergh, *Gift from the Sea*, fiftieth anniversary edition (New York: Pantheon Books, 2005). Kindle edition.

222 *"The most exhausting thing in life"*: Ibid., 26.

222 *"gender unequal world"*: Milestone and Meyer, *Gender and Popular Culture*, 212.

222 *"A woman's aspiration"*: Debora Spar, *Wonder Women: Sex, Power, and the Quest for Perfection* (New York: Farrar, Staus and Giroux, 2013). Kindle edition.

222 *"physical attributes as if"*: Ibid.

222 *"being pummeled by"*: Ibid.

222 *"the ones who still equate"*: Ibid.

223 *"A Snare and a Delusion"*: Several issues of *The New York Woman* can be found at the New-York Historical Society; Jane noted in her diary that the magazine asked her to write an article about debutantes. Although I could not find anything by her in the surviving copies of the magazine, this note about glamour appeared in November 1936.

SOURCES

Primary Sources
HALL FAMILY PAPERS (HFP)
Dick Wick Hall Sr. (1877–1926)
Poems, stories, correspondence, albums
Jane Elizabeth Hall (1915–1987)
"First and Final Account, Report of Guardian and Petition for Discharge" in the matter of the estate and guardianship of Dick Wick Hall and Jane Elizabeth Hall minors. Rosa B Sutton, Guardian. Superior Court of the state of California, in and for the County of Los Angeles. Number 112592. (RBS, Court Petition, 1932)

Published Stories and Articles, 1936–1946
Fiction
"Tell Her Hey," *Delineator*, Aug 1936.
"Smooth as Glass," *Woman's Home Companion*, Apr 1937.
"With Moonlight on His Wings," *Good Housekeeping*, Aug 1937.
"Sidewalk Café," *Cosmopolitan*, Sep 1937.
"Sunrise Over Newark," *The Saturday Evening Post*, Oct 9, 1937.
"The Snow-Queen Type," *Cosmopolitan*, Nov 1937.
"A Lion on the Tree," *Good Housekeeping*, Dec 1937.
"Venetian Blind," *Cosmopolitan*, Mar 1938.
"Such Mad, Mad Fun," *Cosmopolitan*, May 1938.
"That Snake in Mousseline," *Cosmopolitan*, Nov 1938.
These Glamour Girls, Cosmopolitan, Dec 1938.
"Elizabeth, Femme Fatale," *Cosmopolitan*, Jul 1939.
"Tales from the Hollywoods: Dream Prince," *Cosmopolitan*, Sep 1940.
"Tales from the Hollywoods: The Lady and the Witch," *Cosmopolitan*, Oct 1940.
"Acapulco Fizz," *Cosmopolitan*, Jan 1946.

Nonfiction
"Three Comrades and a Girl," *Good Housekeeping*, Jun 1938.
"Vina Delmar: Cosmopolite of the Month," *Cosmopolitan*, Aug 1939.

"The Wizard of Oz," *Good Housekeeping*, Aug 1939.

"Good Queen Bette," *Cosmopolitan*, Jan 1940.

Scrapbook: Published Stories, Poems, Articles, Essays, and Book Reviews 1925–1932

This scrapbook includes fifty-one poems, eighteen stories and fairy tales, fourteen articles and essays, three editorials, and two book reviews written by Jane, plus seven articles about her.

Correspondence 1925–1965

Of special significance in this collection are letters from Jane to Richard S. Clarke and Clifford Zieger; to Jane from Dick Wick Hall, Jr.; and to Jane from Carl Johan Bernadotte; as well as correspondence with Rose Sutton Hicks and Randolph Hicks.

Jane's Diaries and Journals

Diary, 1926

Journal, March 1929

Journal, "Lassie—Her Record," 1929

Five-year diary, 1933–1937 (Diary1)

"A Debutante's Yearbook," 1933–1934

Five-year diary, 1943–1948 (Diary2)

"Career Summary" of Jane's life before 1949 (handwritten on stationery)

Personal Copies of Screenplays, Treatments, and Unpublished Stories

"It's a Date," "Pasternak #7 Treatment," 68 pages, 1939.

"Two People," a short story/film treatment commissioned by producer Sam Zimbalist, 45 pages, 1939.

"How to Meet a Man," "Master Treatment with Rough Scratch Dialogue," October
17, 1940, 104 pages.

"Because of the Dreams," short story, 1943.

"Dr. Burdick's Needle," short story, 1944.

Photographs and Art in HFP

Album of newspaper clippings about Jane Hall and Jane Hall Cutler since 1932.

Photograph albums and loose photographs, 1915–1960.

Various examples of artwork and sketches by Jane Hall.

Beauties, original pastel for *Cosmopolitan* cover, Bradshaw Crandell, 1939, on loan at
Poplar Springs.

Mrs. Robert F. Cutler, Bradshaw Crandell, oil on canvas c. 1952. [Now property of
Carlyn Maw.]

Jane Hall, Jon Whitcomb, pastel. c. 1945. (Recently sold.)

Warrenton Oyster Fry, oil on canvas, Jane Hall, 1934.

ACADEMY OF MOTION PICTURE ARTS AND SCIENCES
MARGARET HERRICK LIBRARY (Beverly Hills, CA)

Turner/MGM Script Collection

"Hold That Kiss," script, March 22, 1938.

"It's a Date," treatment, September 1, 1939.

"These Glamour Girls" (also known as "Such Mad Fun" and "Maiden's Prayer")

25 separate documents (May 23, 1938–August 19, 1939)

Swanson Agency Files for Jane Hall

Production Code Administration Files for "These Glamour Girls," January 28, 1939–May 1, 1940.

ARIZONA HISTORICAL SOCIETY (Tucson, AZ)

MS 321 Papers of Dick Wick Hall (includes letters from Jane as a young child)

Books

Amory, Cleveland. *Who Killed Society?* New York: Harper and Brothers, 1960.

Baldwin, Faith. *Skyscraper.* Afterword by Laura Hapke. New York: The Feminist Press CUNY, 2012. Kindle edition.

Balio, Tino. *Grand Design: Hollywood As a Modern Business Enterprise 1930–1939.* Berkeley: University of California Press, 1993.

Basinger, Jeanine. *I Do and I Don't: A History of Marriage in the Movies.* Knopf Doubleday Publishing Group. Kindle Edition. 2013.

———. *The Star Machine.* New York: Vintage Books, 2009.

———. *A Woman's View: How Hollywood Spoke to Women 1930–1960.* Middletown, CT: Wesleyan University Press, 1993.

Beauchamp, Cari, and Mary Anita Loos, eds. *Anita Loos Rediscovered.* Berkeley: University of California Press, 2003.

Beauchamp, Cari. *Without Lying Down: Frances Marion and the Powerful Women of Early Hollywood.* Berkeley: University of California Press, 1997.

Bingen, Steven, Stephen X. Sylvester, and Michael Troyan. *MGM: Hollywood's Greatest Backlot.* Solana Beach, CA: Santa Monica Press, 2011.

Blumenthal, Ralph. *Stork Club: America's Most Famous Nightspot and the Lost World of Café Society.* Boston: Little Brown and Company, 2001.

Brown, Kathi Ann, Walter Nicklin, and John Toler. *250 Years in Fauquier County: A Virginia Story.* Fairfax, VA: GMU Press, 2008.

Bruccoli, Matthew J. *Some Sort of Epic Grandeur: The Life of F. Scott Fitzgerald.* New York: Harcourt Brace Jovanovich, 1981.

Bruccoli, Matthew J., ed., with Judith S. Baughman. *Fitzgerald in the Marketplace: The Auction and Dealer Catalogs, 1935–2006.* Columbia: University of South Carolina Press, 2009.

Burton, Harry Payne. *Favorite Stories by Famous Writers.* New York: International Magazine Company, 1932.

Carnegie Hill Neighbors, *Carnegie Hill: An Architectural Guide*. New York: Carnegie Hill Neighbors, Inc., 1989.

Carr, Harry. *Los Angeles: City of Dreams*. New York: D. Appleton-Century Company, 1935.

Collins, Gail. *America's Women: 400 Years of Dolls, Drudges, Helpmates and Heroines*. New York: William Morrow, 2003.

———. *When Everything Changed: The Amazing Journey of American Women from 1960 to the Present*. New York: Little, Brown and Company, 2009. Kindle edition.

Crane, Cheryl with Cindy De La Hoz. *Lana: The Memories, the Myths, the Movies*. Philadelphia: Running Press, 2008.

Corrigan, Maureen. *So We Read On: How* The Great Gatsby *Came to Be and Why It Endures*. Little, Brown and Company, 2014. Kindle edition.

Cutler, Robin R. *The Laughing Desert: Dick Wick Hall's Salome Sun*. Charleston, SC: CreateSpace Independent Publishing, 2012. Published as part of an Arizona Centennial Legacy Project.

———. *A Soul on Trial: A Marine Corps Mystery at the Turn of the Twentieth Century*. New York: Rowman and Littlefield, 2007.

Dardis, Tom. *Some Time in the Sun: The Hollywood Years of F. Scott Fitzgerald, William Faulkner, Nathanael West, Aldous Huxley, and James Agee*. New York: Limelight Edition, 1988.

Davis, Ronald L. *The Glamour Factory: Inside Hollywood's Big Studio System*. Dallas: Southern Methodist University Press, 1993.

Deak, JoAnn, with Teresa Barker, *Girls Will Be Girls: Raising Confident and Courageous Daughters*. New York: Hyperion, 2002.

Dennis, Jan. *Manhattan Beach, California*. Images of America. San Francisco, CA: Arcadia Publishing, 2001.

———. *A Walk Beside the Sea: A History of Manhattan Beach*. Manhattan Beach, CA: JanStan Studio, 1987.

Dickstein, Morris. *Dancing in the Dark: A Cultural History of the Great Depression*. New York: W.W. Norton and Company, 2009.

Doherty, Thomas. *Hollywood's Censor: Joseph I. Breen and the Production Code Administration*. New York: Columbia University Press, 2007.

Edelman, Hope. *Motherless Daughters*. 2nd edition. Da Capo Press, 2006..

Epstein, Joseph. *Gossip: The Untrivial Pursuit*. New York: Houghton Mifflin, 2011. Kindle edition.

Eyman, Scott. *Lion of Hollywood: The Life and Legend of Louis B. Mayer*. New York: Simon & Schuster, 2005.

Federal Writers Project of the Works Progress Administration. *New York Panorama: A Comprehensive View of the Metropolis, Presented in a Series of Articles Prepared by the Federal Writers Project of the Works Progress Administration in New York City*. Reissued with a new introduction by Alfred Kazin. New York: Pantheon Books, 1984.

———. *The WPA Guide to the City of Angels: Los Angeles in the 1930s*. Reissued with an introduction by David Kippen. Berkeley: University of California Press, 2011.

————. *The WPA Guide to New York City: The Federal Writers Project Guide to 1930s New York*. Reissued with an introduction by William H Whyte. New York: The New Press, 1992.

Fine, Richard. *Hollywood and the Profession of Authorship, 1928–1940*. Studies in Cinema. Ann Arbor, MI: UMI Research Press, 1979.

Fitzgerald, F. Scott. *As Ever, Scott Fitz: Letters between F. Scott Fitzgerald and His Literary Agent, Harold Ober* 1919–1940. Edited by Matthew J. Bruccoli. New York: J. B. Lippincott Company, 1972.

————. *The Crack-Up*. Edited by Edmund Wilson. New York: New Directions Books, 1993.

————. *F. Scott Fitzgerald: A Life in Letters*. Edited and annotated by Matthew J. Bruccoli with Judith S. Baughman. New York: Touchstone Books, 1995. (Cited as *A Life In Letters*.)

————. *F. Scott Fitzgerald's Screenplay for* Three Comrades. Edited with an afterword by Matthew J Bruccoli. Carbondale: Southern Illinois University Press, 1978.

Fitzgerald, F. Scott. *The Love of the Last Tycoon: A Western*. Edited with a preface and notes by Matthew J. Bruccoli. New York: Scribner, 1994.

————. *Tender Is the Night*. New York: Scribner, 1995.

————. *This Side of Paradise*. Los Angeles: Green Light Books, 2011. Kindle edition.

Friedan, Betty. *The Feminine Mystique*. Introduction by Anna Quindlen. New York: W.W. Norton, 1997.

Gabler, Neal. *Life: the Movie: How Entertainment Conquered Reality*. New York: Vintage Books, 2000.

Graham, Sheilah. *Hollywood Revisited*. New York: St. Martin's Press, 1984.

Graham, Sheilah, and Gerold Frank. *Beloved Infidel*. New York: Quality Paperback Book Club, 1989.

Gundle, Stephen. *Glamour: A History*. New York: Oxford University Press, 2008.

Hall, Dick Wick. *An Arizona Alibi: The Desert Humor of Dick Wick Hall, Sr.* Foreword by Barry Goldwater. Compiled by Frances D. Nutt. Phoenix: Arrowhead Press Inc., 1990.

Hallett, Hillary. *Go West, Young Women!: The Rise of Early Hollywood*. Berkeley: University of California Press, 2012. Kindle edition.

Hapke, Laura. *Daughters of the Great Depression: Women, Work, and Fiction in the American 1930s*. Athens: University of Georgia Press, 1995.

Hansen, Peter and Paul Robert Herman, eds. *Tales from the Script: 50 Hollywood Screenwriters Share Their Stories*. New York: HarperCollins, 2010.

Harmetz, Aljean. *The Making of the Wizard of Oz: Movie Magic and Studio Power in the Prime of MGM and the Miracle of Production #1060*. New York: Dell Publishing, 1989.

Haskell, Molly. *Frankly, My Dear: Gone with the Wind Revisited*. New Haven, CT: Yale University Press, 2009.

————. *From Reverence to Rape: The Treatment of Women in the Movies*. 2nd Edition. Chicago: University Of Chicago Press, 1987.

————. *Holding My Own in No Man's Land: Women and Men and Film and Feminists*. New York: Oxford University Press, 1997.

Heilbrun, Carolyn G. *Women's Lives: The View from the Threshold*. The Alexander Lectures. Toronto: University of Toronto Press, 1999.

Hertog, Susan. *Dangerous Ambition: Rebecca West and Dorothy Thompson: New Women in Search of Love and Power*. New York: Ballantine Books, 2011.

Heimann, Jim. *Out with the Stars: Hollywood Nightlife in the Golden Era*. New York: Abbeville Press, 1985.

Hillis, Marjorie. *Live Alone and Like It: A Guide for the Extra Woman*. Introduction by Frank Crowninshield. New York: The Bobbs-Merrill Company, 1936.

James, Rian. *All About New York: An Intimate Guide*. Foreword by Ogden Nash. New York: The John Day Company, 1931.

Jewell, Richard B. *The Golden Age of Cinema: 1929–1945*. Malden, MA: Blackwell Publishing, 2007.

————. *RKO Radio Pictures: A Titan Is Born*. Berkeley: University of California Press, 2012.

Josephy, Helen and Mary Margaret McBride. *New York Is Everybody's Town*. New York: G. P. Putnam's Sons, 1931.

Jurca, Catherine. *Hollywood 1938: Motion Pictures' Greatest Year*. Berkeley: University of California Press, 2012.

Katz, Ephraim, *The Film Encylopedia*. 5th Edition. New York: HarperCollins, 2005.

Kitch, Carolyn. *The Girl on the Magazine Cover: The Origins of Visual Stereotypes in American Mass Media*. Chapel Hill: University of North Carolina Press, 2001.

Kyvig, David E. *Daily Life in the United States, 1920–1940. How Americans Lived Through the "Roaring Twenties" and the Great Depression*. Chicago: Ivan R Dee, 2002.

Kutner, E. W., and Sharon Rubin. *McMullen Valley*. Images of America. Charleston, SC: Arcadia Publishing, 2009. Authored with the Great Arizona Outback Rumor and Innuendo Historical Society.

Landers, James. *The Improbable First Century of Cosmopolitan Magazine*. Columbia: University of Missouri Press, 2010.

Lindbergh, Anne Morrow. *Gift from the Sea*. Fiftieth anniversary edition. New York: Pantheon Books, 2005. Kindle edition.

Lindsley, James Elliott. *The Church Club of New York: The First Hundred Years*. New York: The Church Club of New York, 1994.

Long, Craig H. *Suffern*. Images of America. Charleston, SC: Arcadia Publishing, 2011.

Loy, Myrna and James Kotsilibas-Davis, *Being and Becoming*. New York: Donald I Fine, Inc. 1988.

Maltby, Richard. *Hollywood Cinema*. 2nd ed. Malden, MA: Blackwell Publishing, 2003.

Mantle, Burns, ed. *The Best Plays of 1938–39 and the Year Book of the Drama in America*. New York: Dodd, Mead and Company, 1939.

Marchand, Roland. *Advertising the American Dream: Making the Way for Modernity*. Berkeley: University of California Press, 1985.

Marling, Karal Ann. *Debutante: Rites and Regalia of American Debdom*. Lawrence: University Press of Kansas, 2004.

Marx, Samuel. *A Gaudy Spree: The Literary Life of Hollywood in the 1930s When the West Was Fun*. New York: Franklin Watts, 1987.

Masson, Thomas L. *Tom Masson's Book of Wit and Humor*. New York: J. H. Sears & Co, 1927.

McCourtie, William B. *Where and How to Sell Manuscripts: A Directory for Writers*. Springfield, MA: Home Correspondence School, 1929.

McGilligan, Patrick, ed., *Backstory: Interviews with Screenwriters of Hollywood's Golden Age*. Berkeley: University of California Press, 1986.

————*Backstory 2: Interviews with Screenwriters of the 1940s and 1950s*. Berkeley: University of California Press, 1991.

McCreadie, Marsha. *The Women Who Write the Movies*. New York: Birch Lane Press, 1994.

Meade, Marion. *Dorothy Parker: What Fresh Hell Is This?* New York: Penguin Books, 2006.

Milestone, Katie, and Anneke Meyer. *Gender and Popular Culture*. Cambridge, MA: Polity Press, 2012.

Milford, Nancy. *Zelda: A Biography*. New York: Harper Perennial, 2013. Kindle edition. First published in 1970, this book is still the definitive biography of Zelda Sayre Fitzgerald.

Morris, Sylvia Jukes. *Rage for Fame: The Ascent of Clare Boothe Luce*. New York: Random House, 1997.

Nussbaum, Ben ed. *The Wizard of Oz: An Over-the-Rainbow Celebration of the World's Favorite Movie*. Irvine, CA: I-5 Publishing, 2014.

Olson, Lynne. *Those Angry Days: Roosevelt, Lindbergh, and America's Fight over World War II, 1939–1941*. New York: Random House, 2013. Kindle edition.

Patterson, James T. *The Dread Disease: Cancer and Modern American Culture*. Cambridge, MA: Harvard University Press, 1987.

Pennoyer, Peter, and Anne Walker. *The Architecture of Delano and Aldrich*. New York: W. W. Norton, 2003.

Peterson, Theodore. *Magazines in the Twentieth Century*. Urbana: University of Illinois Press, 1964.

Ring, Frances Kroll. *Against the Current: As I Remember F. Scott Fitzgerald*. Los Angeles: Figueroa Press, 2005.

Rosten, Leo Calvin. *Hollywood: The Movie Colony, the Movie Makers*. New York: Harcourt, Brace and Company, 1941.

Russell, Rosalind, and Chris Chase. *Life Is a Banquet*. New York: Grosset & Dunlap, 1977.

Scarfone, Jay, and William Stillman. *The Wizard of Oz: The Official 75th Anniversary Companion*. New York: HarperCollins, 2013.

Schatz, Thomas. *The Genius of the System: Hollywood Filmmaking in the Studio Era*. New York: Henry Holt and Company, 1996.

Sklar, Robert. *Movie Made America: A Cultural History of American Movies.* Revised and updated. New York: Vintage Books 1994.

Spar, Debora L. *Wonder Women: Sex, Power, and the Quest for Perfection.* Farrar, Straus and Giroux, 2013. Kindle edition.

Sragow, Michael. *Victor Fleming: An American Movie Master.* New York: Pantheon, 2008.

Swanson, H. N. *Sprinkled with Ruby Dust: A Literary and Hollywood Memoir.* New York: Warner Books, 1989.

Torrence, Bruce. *Hollywood: The First 100 Years.* Hollywood: The Hollywood Chamber Of Commerce, 1979.

Wagner, Robert J. and Scott Eyman. *You Must Remember This: Life and Style in Hollywood's Golden Age.* New York: Viking, 2014. Kindle edition.

Walker, Nancy. *Shaping Our Mother's World: American Women's Magazines.* Jackson: University Press of Mississippi, 2000.

———, ed. *Women's Magazines 1940–1960: Gender Roles and the Popular Press.* Boston: Bedford/St. Martin's, 1998.

Ware, Susan. *Holding Their Own: American Women in the 1930s.* Boston: Twayne Publishers, 1982.

Whitcomb, Jon. *All About Girls.* Englewood Cliffs, NJ: Prentice Hall, 1962.

Wilson, Victoria. *A Life of Barbara Stanwyck: Steel-True, 1907–1940.* New York: Simon & Schuster, 2013. Kindle edition.

Worden, Helen. *Here Is New York.* New York: Doubleday, Doran & Co, Inc. 1939.

Articles, Chapters, Pamphlets, and Yearbooks

Abrams, Brett. "Latitude in Mass-Produced Culture's Capital: New Women and Other Players in Hollywood, 1920–1941." *Frontiers: A Journal of Women Studies* 25, no 2: 65–95.

"Art: Moments of Loneliness." *Time*, December 15, 1961.

"Arthur McKeogh, World War Hero." *New York Times*, June 16, 1937.

Atkinson, Brooks. " 'One for the Money,' an Intimate Revue with Sketches and Lyrics by Nancy Hamilton." *New York Times*, February 6, 1939.

Baldwin, Faith. "Autobiography of America—1939: The *Cosmopolitan* Girl." *Cosmopolitan*, July 1939.

Baskette, Kirtley. "Rahs for Roz." *Photoplay*, October 1939.

Beauchamp, Cari. "The Mogul in Mr. Kennedy." *Vanity Fair*, April 2002.

Bekken, John, and Lisa Beinhoff. "Cosmopolitan," in *Women's Periodicals in the United States: Consumer Magazines.* Kathleen L. Endres and Therese L. Lueck, eds. Westport, CT: Greenwood Press, 1995, 49–57.

Bland, Sidney R. "Shaping the Life of the New Woman: The Crusading Years of the *Delineator*." *American Periodicals* 19, no. 2 (2012): 165–188.

Cacioppo, Nancy. "A Dramatic Past." Rockland County *Journal-News*, October 18, 1991.

Cardwell, Lawrence. "Salome: Where She Danced." *Arizona Highways*, April 1949.

Chaput, Donald. "'On the Ore Trail' with Dick Wick Hall." *Journal of Arizona History* 25, no. 1 (Spring 1984):1–20.

"The City of Los Angeles." *California and Western Medicine* 26, no. 4 (April 1927): 524–530.

Collins, Gail. "'The Feminine Mystique' at 50." *New York Times Magazine*, January 23, 2013.

Denby, David. "The Real Rhett Butler." *New Yorker,* May 25, 2009: 73–78.

Dietz, Howard, and Howard Strickling. *Who's Who at Metro-Goldwyn-Mayer.* Culver City, CA: MGM Publicity Department, 1940. (Available in the Margaret Herrick Library of the Academy of Motion Picture Arts and Sciences.)

Douglas, Gordon. "What is Glamour? The Production & Consumption of a Working Aesthetic." *Magazine for Urban Documentation-Opinion-Theory* (The Glamour Issue) August 26, 2009. 44–63. http://www.monu.org/mudot2/GDG_whatis.pdf.

Evans, M. Louise. "Casanova History Reveals Scotch English Background." *Fauquier Democrat,* November 23, 1950.

"53 at Cooper Union Win Prizes for Art." *New York Times,* May 21, 1935.

Flint, Peter B. "H. N. Swanson, 91, An Agent for Writers in Hollywood Deals," *New York Times,* June 3, 1991.

Ghareeb, Gordon R. "A Woman's Touch: The Seagoing Interiors of Dorothy Marckwald," http://www.shawnandcolleen.com/sshsasocal/docs/touch.html. Aaccessed May 20, 2013.

Gray, Christopher. "Streetscapes. The Architecture of Delano and Aldrich; How an Upper-Class Firm Tweaked Classical Norms." *New York Times.* April 27, 2003.

Greene, Jane M. "Hollywood's Production Code and Thirties Romantic Comedy." *Historical Journal of Film, Radio and Television* 30, no.1 (March 2010): 55–73.

Greene, Mabel. "Snooping Feared at That Ball." *The Sun* (New York), January 5, 1934.

Heberling, Lynn O'Neal. "The Delineator," in *Women's Periodicals in the United States: Consumer Magazines.* Kathleen L. Endres and Therese L. Lueck, eds. Westport, CT: Greenwood Press, 1995. 58–65.

Holiday, Wendy. "Hollywood's Modern Women: Screenwriting, Work Culture, and Feminism, 1910–1940." Doctoral dissertation. New York University (May 1995).

Jones, Mark E. "Dick Wick Hall—Arizona's Mark Twain." *Arizona Tribune,* January 14, 2002. D1.

Kay, Katty and Claire Shipman. "The Confidence Gap." *Atlantic,* May 2014..

Keene, Ann T. "Dorothy Shaver." American National Biography Online (Feb 2000). http://www.anb.org/articles/10/10-02304.html. Accessed June 7, 2012.

Koppel, Lily. "Speak, Memory." *New York Times,* July 16, 2006.

Krystal, Arthur. "Slow Fade: F. Scott Fitzgerald in Hollywood." *New Yorker,* November 16, 2009: 36–41.

Lahr, John. "Elements of Film: The Voodoo of Glamour," *New Yorker,* March 21, 1994.

La Perla, Ruth. "When Beauty Fades." *New York Times,* July 26, 2012. E1.

Maltby, Richard. "The Production Code and the Hays Office," in *Grand Design: Hollywood as a Modern Business Enterprise* 1930–1939. Tino Balio, ed. Berkeley: University of California Press, 1993. 37–72.

Maslin, Janet. "Looking back at a Domestic Cri de Coeur." *New York Times*, February 18, 2013.

McKenney, Wilson. "Dick Wick Hall of the Laughing Gas Service Station." *The Desert Magazine* 18, no. 7 (July 1955):9–12.

Metcalfe, Nondas. "I'll Chalk It All Up to Experience." *Philadelphia Inquirer,* November 3, 1940, 3.

Miller, Joseph. "The Life and Times of Dick Wick Hall." *Arizona Highways* 14, no. 7 (July 1938): 4–5, 25–27.

"Miss Gregory Is Wed to Young Hungarian." *New York Post*, January 31, 1938.

Mitten, Irma Catherine. "The Life and Literary Career of Dick Wick Hall, Arizona Humorist." Unpublished master's thesis. University of Southern California. (June 1940).

Morrone, Francis. "A Landmark Department Store." *New York Sun*, December 27, 2007.

"Mrs. McKeogh, 57, Author's Agent." *New York Times*, October 30, 1955.

Myers, Samuel I. "Dick Wick Hall, Humorist with a Serious Purpose." *Journal of Arizona History* 11, no. 4 (Winter 1970): 255–279.

"Nancy Randolph Says." *Palm Beach Daily News,* February 2, 1938.

"The Nightingale-Bamford School Bulletin 1930–1931."

The Nightingale Bamford School Yearbook. Years consulted: 1930, 1931, and 1932.

Odens, Peter. "Dick Hall of Salome: The Story of a Most Unusual Westerner." Pamphlet. Yuma, AZ: Southwest Printers, 1972.

The Pilot. The Redondo Union High School Yearbook. Years consulted: 1928, 1929, and 1930.

Porter, Amy. "Garden of Allah I Love You." *Collier's Weekly*, November 22, 1947.

Putnam, Claude George. "I Knew Dick Wick Hall." *Ghost Town News* 5, no. 32 (June 1946): 18–19.

Robb, Inez Callaway. "The Debutante Racket," *Cosmopolitan*, March 1940.

Satow, Julie. "Amanda Burden Wants to Remake New York. She Has 19 Months Left." *New York Times*, May 18, 2012.

Schallert, Edwin. "Princeton Locale of 'These Glamour Girls.'" *Los Angeles Times*, April 12, 1939.

Terhune, Albert Payson. "How Hollywood Treats Its Dogs," *Modern Screen*, March 1938.

Toler, John. "Wallis Warfield in Warrenton, and Beyond." *News and Notes from the Fauquier Historical Society* 22, no. 2 (Spring/Summer 2000).

Van Duzer, Winifred. "'Bob' Cutler Who Converted His Barn into an Art Gallery and Then Added a Theater Is Also Interested in Politics." *Rockland County Journal-News*, July 10, 1933.

"Virginia Has the Most Beautiful Campus in the Country." *Life*, (June 7, 1937): 48–49.

Movies Jane Worked On

The Toy Wife (1938) [small amount of dialogue, uncredited]

Hold That Kiss (1938)

First Love (1939)

These Glamour Girls (1939) [story and screenplay]

It's a Date (1940)

Patrick the Great (1945) [story credit because of similarity to *It's a Date*]

Nancy Goes to Rio (1950) [remake of *It's a Date*]

INDEX

Note: Page numbers in italics indicate figures; "n" indicates note. Unless noted otherwise, all references to Hall refer to Jane Elizabeth Hall who rarely used her middle name.

ABOUT THE AUTHOR

Historian Robin Cutler was the producer/writer of the award-winning PBS documentary *Indian America: A Gift from the Past*, and co-producer of ROANOAK, an Emmy-nominated dramatic series for PBS. Her first book, *A Soul on Trial*, was named a "notable naval book of 2007." She divides her time between New York, Florida, and California. For reviews, galleries, movie trailers, and her Journeys through History blog, www.RobinRCutler.com.

59482730R00197

Made in the USA
Lexington, KY
06 January 2017